Shakespeare
A Reappraisal

Volume 1

Edited by

Sunita Sinha
Carole Rozzonelli

ATLANTIC
PUBLISHERS & DISTRIBUTORS (P) LTD

Published by

ATLANTIC

PUBLISHERS & DISTRIBUTORS (P) LTD

7/22, Ansari Road, Darya Ganj,
New Delhi-110002
Phones: +91-11-23273880, 23275880, 23280451
Fax: +91-11-23285873
Web: www.atlanticbooks.com
E-mail: info@atlanticbooks.com

Branch Office
5, Nallathambi Street, Wallajah Road,
Chennai-600002
Phones: +91-44-64611085, 32413319
E-mail: chennai@atlanticbooks.com

ISBN 978-81-269-1962-8 (Vol. 1)
ISBN 978-81-269-1964-2 (Set)

Printed in India at Nice Printing Press, A-33/3A, Site-IV,
Industrial Area, Sahibabad, Ghaziabad, U.P.

Dedicated to My Grandfather

Dr. R.K. Sinha

M.A. (Pat), D. Phil. (Oxon)

Professor Emeritus, Head, Department of English
Patna University

Like a stone flung into a still lake, certain experiences in our childhood send ripples that stretch well into our futures. Perhaps, it was my grandfather's interpretation and rendition of Shakespeare that inspired me to initiate this comprehensive two-volume book.

Foreword

The latest census on Shakespeare carried out by the Federation of the World's Shakespeare Societies and other such august bodies reveals some remarkable bibliographical and cultural facts. On an average six to seven books (just in English) on the Bard are published each day in the world apart from innumerable academic papers and articles (this does not include publications on Shakespeare in regional and vernacular non-English languages across the globe).

In terms of number of productions and performances among all playwrights Shakespeare is still way up there at the number one spot. And the country leading with the number of Shakespeare productions is not England or the U.S.A. or any other Anglophone nation but, as in the last two decades, it is Germany with an average of over 2000 productions/performances of Shakespeare every year.

Whatever the detractors of Shakespeare might have to say (and there are always an eccentric fringe of odd-ball voices deriding the five century long "craze" for Shakespeare) the Bard is still the most popular and academically the most written-about and explored author across the globe today. Football World Cups and twenty20 Cricket extravaganzas come and go, Olympics and Wimbledons periodically continue to move and thrill us, but the Bard is ever and always the great entertainer on stage and screen. And he is here to stay. As far as depth and profundity are concerned, Shakespeare is up there with the epic poets—Homer and Virgil, Vyasa and Valmiki—if the avalanche of seminars, conferences, lectures, articles and books in every language is any evidence.

The "Shakespeare industry" rolls triumphantly on across the globe but it is an "industry" that leaves no "ecological waste" in its wake. In fact the conferences, the books, the films, the plays, the translations and adaptations help to keep our minds, hearts and souls "green" and raise our life-consciousness and existential awareness the way nothing else does.

Shakespeare, more than any other author, unites the warring nations of the world to constitute one global culture where all nations, groups, communities, classes, castes, sects and ideological adherents come together under the Shakespearian umbrella to sing his praise.

One such book of praise (and creative dissent) is *Shakespeare: A Reappraisal* published by Atlantic Publishers and Distributors (P) Ltd., from India's capital city. This is a two-volume edited anthology that looks at the Bard's multidimensional oeuvre from multidimensional perspectives through 33 academic papers from traditional, modern, postmodern and avant-garde positions and points of view. The editors, Dr. Sunita Sinha and Carole Rozzonelli, have brought together academics, theatre experts and scholars of high renown from across the globe. Here are the cutting-edge voices from the West and the East, the North and the South spanning the five continents (Antony Kubiak, Bryan Reynolds, Jeffery Moser, Kenneth Usongo, Joyashri Choudhury, Tapu Biswas, Suchandra Ghosh, Manju Dutta Gupta *et al.*) to provoke and thrill us through their exciting interventions.

The volumes are dedicated to the Editor's late grandfather, the internationally respected and renowned Dr. R.K. Sinha, distinguished scholar and teacher, former Professor Emeritus of Patna University who completed his Ph.D. under Lord David Cecil at Oxford. The late professor Sinha, a most extraordinary teacher and scholar acted as a wonderful bridge between India and other global cultures. The editor, Dr. Sunita Sinha ably extends that tradition in this volume of global voices across cultures commenting on Shakespeare and contemporary transformations of the Bard. Top-level scholarship, high intellect, enlightened curiosity and creative drive after all are all psychogenetic inheritances of Dr. Sunita Sinha bequeathed by her late grandfather. Dr. Sinha banks on her intellectual legacy as well as her brilliant academic career and rich professional experience (authored three books, edited twelve others, currently edits the international journal *The Atlantic Review of Feminist Studies*) to bring us a treasure-trove of re-appraisals of Shakespeare.

In bringing together this polyphony of diverse voices from diverse geographies and cultures to set up this on-going dialogue and counter-dialogue, the editor, Dr. Sunita Sinha aligns herself with what the Bard himself predicted through Cassius's words in *Julius Caesar* after Caesar's murder in Act III Sc I:

How many ages hence
Shall this our lofty scene be acted over
In states unborn and accents yet unknown

Amitava Roy

—President, Shakespeare Society of Eastern India

—Former Shakespeare Professor of English and Drama, Rabindra Bharati University, Kolkata

—Director, Shakespeare Centre for Advanced Research, RBU, Kolkata

—Joint Editor with Bryan Reynolds, Emi Hamana *et al.* of

a. *Theatre International: East-West Perspectives on Drama* (ISSN No. 2278-2036 TI)

b. *International Journal of Culture Studies and Social Sciences* (ISSN No. 2347-4777)

Preface

"That King Shakespeare", the essayist Thomas Carlyle wrote in 1840, "does not he shine, in crowned sovereignty, over us all, as the noblest, gentlest, yet strongest of rallying signs; indestructible...?" In the Preface to the First Folio, Ben Jonson anticipated Shakespeare's dazzling future when he declared, "He was not of an age, but for all time!"

A man of Renaissance England, Shakespeare still speaks to us today. Shakespeare's "divine worth" has proven to be so overpowering that, "like the sun it burns while generations pass". Shakespeare continues to speak to us, generations after generations, throughout the countries and cultures of the world. Marchette Chute, in the Introduction to her famous retelling of Shakespeare's stories, summarizes one of the reasons for Shakespeare's immeasurable fame: "William Shakespeare was the most remarkable storyteller that the world has ever known. Homer told of adventure and men at war; Sophocles and Tolstoy told of tragedies and of people in trouble. Terence and Mark Twain told comedic stories, Dickens told melodramatic ones, Plutarch told histories and Hans Christian Andersen told fairy tales. But Shakespeare told every kind of story—comedy, tragedy, history, melodrama, adventure, love stories and fairy tales—and each of them so well that they have become immortal. In all the world of storytelling he has become the greatest name." The way Shakespeare addresses several universal themes, his understanding of the unpredictable human nature, creative use of poetry and ability to create original metaphors make him relevant forever. For Prof Wells, Shakespeare's plays have stood the test of time because they are about timeless events and emotions—love, death, courage, joy, jealousy, youth and old age, laughter and grief.

Confronting the social conventions of class, genre, honour, and race, Shakespeare's plays herald a celebration of the human spirit, triumphant even when it is vanquished. They also probe, question and inquire into the intractable issues of the self and the other, the individual and the community, and the very purpose of life. In this context, the theatre director Sir Trevor Nunn's remarks seem quite pertinent: "Shakespeare has more wisdom and insight about our lives, about how to live and how not to live, how to forgive and how to understand our fellow creatures, than any religious tract. One hundred times more than the Bible."

Asimov's "immortal bard" will always be remembered for "the beauty of his poetry, as in *Romeo and Juliet*; for his wit and humour, as in *A Midsummer Night's Dream;* for his portrayal of heroism, as in *Henry V*; for his depth of human understanding, as in *Hamlet*, and for his portrayal of courage in the face of suffering, as in *King Lear*". Shakespearean renditions are still so contemporary, so very modern, posing fundamental questions that have become particularly acute in the "contemporary" era.

In an attempt to render faithfully the eclectic nature of Shakespearean Studies, the anthology, *Shakespeare: A Reappraisal,* Volume I aims at presenting new approaches to Shakespeare's plays and poetry. The sixteen well researched papers in this anthology aim at achieving a harmonious instance of academic homogeneity of themes and views in the ever larger areas of the globe and encapsulates the enormous literary dynamism and debate that characterize the field of Shakespeare studies.

In their innovative paper, "The Delusion of Critique: Subjunctive Space, Transversality, and the Conceit of Deceit in *Hamlet*", Anthony Kubiak and Bryan Reynolds discuss at length, Shakespeare's *Hamlet* from a totally new perspective. As Kubiak and Reynolds remark, "Behind all deceit, particularly in *Hamlet*, according to the Hamletic model we are proffering here, the envenomed, plotting character of thought, played out in what transversal theory refers to as "subjunctive space," the hypothetical space of both "as ifs" and "what ifs" operative in between "subjective territory" (the conceptual-emotional-physical range from which a given subject perceives and experiences) and "transversal territory" (the non subjectified, transforming space through which people journey when they defy or surpass the boundaries of their subjective territory)."

Towering over Shakespeare's romantic comedy, *The Merchant of Venice* is the tragic figure of Shylock. Viewing the play through modern eyes, Shylock can be seen as both an Elizabethan stereotype and a fully drawn human being. In his scholarly paper, "Shakespeare's Construction of the Jew", Mohit Ray makes a deft exploration of the various complex issues involved in the construction of Shylock. Some people feel that Shylock (*The Merchant of Venice*) is a static, villainous Jew, no different from the stock Jewish characters in other works of the day, such as in Marlowe's *The Jew of Malta.* Others believe that Shakespeare rises above the bigotry of his times, pleading for religious tolerance through Shylock's famous speech: "I am a Jew. Hath not a Jew eyes?" (3.1.62-73). Talking of Shakespeare's presentation of the Jew, Ray remarks poignantly, "It is, however, a profound irony of literary history that in spite of Shakespeare's perceptive criticism of the maltreatment of the Jews by the Christians for centuries, and his presentation of Shylock not as evil by nature but made evil by the treatment to which he and his race have been subjected, Shylock has become a stereotype of a Jew, an embodiment of malignity, avarice, cruelty and inhumanity. To think of a Jew is to think of Shylock whetting his knife for a pound of Christian flesh. It is a strange case where the character does not mirror history but shapes it, and wrongly."

In 1880, Roval Theatre was established in Greece, with a grant from King George I and Efstratios Rallis to give theatre a permanent home in Athens. In their scholarly paper, "Shakespeare in Greece: A Study of the Athens Royal Theatre plays", Maria Kladaki and George Papantonakis discuss the origin and development of Athens Royal Theatre and the reception of Shakespeare's plays in Greece. In the eight years of the Royal Theatre's existence, six plays by Shakespeare were staged.

"Shakespeare's plays", remarked the authors, "contributed to the formation of national and literary traditions in many European countries....Particularly in Greece, the efforts of the Royal Theatre's officials as well as of scholars of the time, were focused on the attempt to create a new national literary identity, one that would be directly linked to the country's historical past".

Chiara Biscella in her paper, "William Shakespeare on Womanhood and Motherhood", intends to explore the Shakespearean reverberations in contemporary women narrative. It focuses on the way Shakespeare's representation of women triggers in contemporary women writers, a discourse on the important issues of womanhood, motherhood and matriarchy. As Biscella states, "Through a brief analysis of the condition of women in Renaissance England and of the Shakespearean ways to depict womanhood in his historical play *Richard III*, I intend to cast a light on all these aspects, showing how Shakespeare's portrayal of women is far from being stereotypical."

Brother-and-sister writing team Charles and Mary Lamb interweave the words of Shakespeare with their oeuvre (some 200 years later in 1807) to bring his best plays to the young reader. In their paper, "Supernatural, Natural and Unnatural: From Shakespeare to the Lambs", Isabella Bruschi intends to explore how the Lambs treat the theme of the supernatural—related to the Shakespearean concepts of natural and unnatural—in their abridgement of Shakespeare's plays. How does this theme combine with their declared, however indirect, pedagogical aim? The paper tries to find an answer to these questions by outlining the cultural context in which the Lambs lived and operated and through a comparative reading of *A Midsummer Night's Dream, The Tempest, Macbeth* and their prose versions by Charles and Mary Lamb.

"Shakespeare Next: A Reappraisal" by Amitava Roy and Suchandra Ghosh, focuses on Bratya Basu's *Hemlat: Prince of Garanhata*. The authors chose to probe the new genre or sub-genres of Adaptations and Translations of Shakespeare, which was soon becoming a torrent, a flood and finally a "new Shakespeare Industry". Everyone was bitten by the Adaptation or Translation bug that germinated across cultures. "It was a creative infection", remark the authors, "that crossed all borders and seeped into the literary and cultural bloodstream of every country in the globe—Europe, the New World of the Americas, Asia, Australia, Canada, India, Africa, China, Japan."

Carole Rozzonelli and Alessandro Monti in their paper, "Shakespeare among the Cows", focus on the relocation and displacement of Shakespeare's drama in a few recent Indian films (*Omkara*, and *Maqbool*), by laying emphasis on such discursive issues as assimilation, and finally abrogation, both in the management of plots, language and sites of performance. It also deals with the colonial introduction and heritage of Shakespeare in India. This feature includes colleges' syllabi, courtly representations and the progressive decline of philological performances, in juxtaposition with the ascent of Bombay cinema (*Shakespeare Wallah*, and *The Last Lear*).

"Shakespeare examined lust in his mature works and found the magic formula to transform it into love," remarks Niranjan Goswami in his scholarly paper, "Lust for Life: Life of Lust: Shakespeare's Examination of 'A Natural Guiltiness' in *Measure for Measure* and *Antony and Cleopatra*", where he explores the representation of lust in the above-mentioned plays. In order to understand what 'lust' may have meant for Shakespeare in these two plays, Goswami begins with analysing the history of the concept since the middle ages. He further remarks, "*Measure for Measure* offers a nuanced representation of lust, which is not just one of the seven deadly sins in the medieval tradition but is an important ingredient necessary to a degree to constitute love and pleasure that finds its civil and religious sanction in matrimony. If *Measure for Measure* is about correctly judging or measuring the love/lust complexity *Antony and Cleopatra* is about Antony's "dotage" over Cleopatra that "O'erflows the measure." Antony's "dotage" in the second line corresponds to the "gipsy's lust" in the ninth line of the play. Shakespeare in this play takes up luxuria, not only in the sense of lust but in the older sense of extravagance or abundance as well. In fact, the whole play turns upon the polarities of Rome and Egypt, West and East, reason and passion, male and female and so on (Payne 266)."

Shakespeare's *King Lear* can be read as a play that interrogates sovereignty via the challenge to the rule of Lear by Goneril and Regan, as well as drama that problematizes, through the action of Edmund, the issue of inheritance in Jacobean England. Kenneth Usongo's innovative paper, "The Crises of Succession in William Shakespeare's *King Lear*", tries to demonstrate that the crises over succession (at both the state and family levels) not only bring to focus dominant traits of Shakespeare's protagonists in *King Lear,* but also engage in the questioning of the Jacobean order of succession. Put differently, the quest for political power or influence helps to externalize some of the hidden traits of the characters. Moreover, investigating the theme of succession is relevant because *King Lear* anticipates recent political upheavals such as the Arab spring.

Globalization has been defined as both "the compression of the world and the intensification of consciousness of the world as a whole" and in this light it is not surprising to state that the worldwide diffusion of William Shakespeare's works has occurred for centuries. In recent times there has been a generalized interest in placing works of literature, both Western, and non-Western, within broader cultural context. For instance, J. Johnson has compared the importance of the Mahabharata to world civilization, to that of the Bible, the works of Shakespeare, the works of Homer, Greek drama, or the Qur'an. "The Pure Trace: the Ramayana, the Mahabharata and Shakespeare" by Manju Dutta Gupta intends "to consider some characters, their situations and some devices from The Ramayana, The Mahabharata and Shakespeare in parallel and contrast". Datta remarks, "I would like to make brief comments on certain aspects of our epics which have something in common with certain features of Shakespeare's works."

Shakespeare is the most famous author in the English language and his work is still adapted more than that of any other writer, nearly four centuries after his death, the world over. Australia too is no exception. The dynamism of Shakespeare studies owes much to the sheer diversity of critical, theatrical, and historical approaches. In Australia, Shakespeare's canon and his world and a variety of his literary modes and styles are not something unexplored. In his analytical paper, "The Australian Shakespeare: The Nation in Evolvement from Bardolatory to Appropriation", Arindam Das "proposes to trace the inception-to-present-day evolvement of Shakespeare in Australia and read how the same echoes Australia's evolvement from a nation with colonial hangover to a present-day appropriated postcolonial entity".

The terms of India's encasement with Shakespeare are endlessly debated. Thomas Carlyle wrote in 1841, "Consider now, if they asked us, 'Will you give-up your Indian Empire or your Shakespeare, you English?' ... should not we be forced to answer: 'Indian Empire, or no Indian empire, we cannot do without Shakespeare!'" Outside the Western world, India has the longest and most intense engagement with Shakespeare of any country anywhere and equally intense is Shakespeare's association with Indian cinema. Ironically, though it is difficult to trace a sustained Shakespearean line through Indian cinema, yet individual directors have turned so often to the bard as to practically build up a tradition. Pratik Chowdhury's paper, "Reinventing Shakespeare Plays—A Cinematographic Approach", focuses on "the extraordinary ability of Shakespeare of rendering a scene cinematographically and attempts to reinvent Shakespeare's plays from the point of view of a contemporary art, cinema". Chowdhury concludes his innovative paper thus, "Through this short analysis, this article has demonstrated that the difference between the pictorial representation of images and scenes (through metaphors and similes, as is common in poetry), and the cinematographic representation, lies fundamentally in the momentum inherent in the images or scenes being conveyed."

"Feminist Perspectives and Post-Feminist Possibilities: A Reading of Selected Texts of Shakespeare", by Madhumita Purkayastha offers to adopt the post-colonial feminist approach towards Shakespeare's selected sonnets. In her comprehensive study, Purkayastha remarks revealingly, "The present study posits that Shakespeare possessed a rare unique bi-gender vision/consciousness, which could, by virtue of its double lens and gender fluidity, lend keen insights into human psyche and bring the verve and texture of life to his writings. The present paper attempts a study of selected sonnets of Shakespeare to validate the stated hypothesis. The paper would first examine briefly the key feminist perspectives that have lent perceptive insights into the multi-layered complexity and gendered texture of his texts."

Rasa, is an aesthetic state of mind that accompanies an audience member's experience of theatrical art and conscious reflection on his or her experience of that art. The author of the *Natya Shastra* suggests that the aesthetic experiences that theatre provides can all be sorted into eight types. The eight types of Rasa are: Shringara (Romance) Vira (Heroism), Raudra (Anger), Bibhatsa (Disgust), Hasya (Humour), Karuna (Sorrow), Adbhuta (Wonder) and Bhayanaka (Fear). In her explorative paper, "Shakespeare in The Light of Rasavada", Ratri Ray has tried to interpret *Romeo and Juliet* in the light of Rasavada. As she remarks "My first effort in this interdisciplinary direction had been an essay on *Romeo and Juliet* published in 1983. On looking it over, it seems to have been a somewhat amateurish affair, woefully in need of revision. So, that is what this present essay sets out to do all over again: interpreting *Romeo and Juliet* in the light of Rasavada."

Gautam Ghosal, in his paper, "Shakespeare Through Aurobindo's Lens", focuses on Aurobindo's perception of Shakespeare's art. Sri Aurobindo finds "life-spirit" in the Elizabethan plays, especially Shakespeare in abundance. He says, "Shakespeare's poetry for instance is that of a man with a vivid and many-sided response to life; it gives the impression of a multifarious knowledge of things but it was a knowledge picked up from life as he went." He observes that Shakespeare's characters operate on the vital consciousness, the consciousness which is the force behind all actions. "According to Sri Aurobindo, Shakespeare's themes are mundane, but his poetry draws inspiration from high spiritual planes", remarked Ghosal. As Ghosal further states, "A large part of Sri Aurobindo's prose is devoted to the basic Shakespearean substance: the human vital, the Lear and the Timon, the Hamlet and the Othello, and all its other varieties dramatically imaged by the great vital creator. Sri Aurobindo brings in Shakespeare directly in

The Future Poetry, in his letters and in his notes on *Kalidasa*. In his letters and *The Future Poetry*, he shows the evolution of poetry and the point reached in Shakespeare. In doing so, he also indicates how Shakespeare's creations or characters may be studied by examining the history of their consciousness.

The supernatural is a recurring aspect in many of Shakespeare's plays. Particularly in *Hamlet* and *Macbeth*, it is an integral part of the structure, of the plot and provides a catalyst for action, an insight into character and augments the impact of many key scenes. In her paper, "The Supernatural as a Major Determinant of Structural Form in Shakespeare's *Hamlet* and *Macbeth*", Reena Mitra states, "Shakespeare discreetly and deftly made capital out of this belief in paranormal and spectral existences but also cleverly veered away from the existent matrix of the supernatural in creating a diverse range of characters in worlds that the viewers could visualize and identify with." "Shakespeare", says Mitra, "ingeniously draws on both these applications and manoeuvres and designs his material in a manner that makes the otherworldly and spectral appear as intrinsic integrants in his plays."

Representing the combined efforts of scholars, *Shakespeare: A Reappraisal*, Volume I, is multivocal and inclusive, which would not have come to fruition without the efforts of the legion of contributors who conscientiously and patiently wrote and sometimes rewrote their articles at my request. I am beholder to them.

I also wish to thank Dr. K.R. Gupta, Honorary Advisor, Atlantic Publishers and Distributors (P) Ltd., for the confidence evinced in me and for seeing the book through the press.

Sunita Sinha

Acknowledgements 1

My kind Mr. William Shakespeare, "I can no other answer make, but, thanks, and thanks." Thanks for being ever inspiring and the reason behind this book.

Writing is not primarily a solitary pursuit but as every author knows, it is really a collaboration. And I have been fortunate to have people who have evinced faith in this book and have contributed excellent questions, challenges and ideas that have made this book, written in the most engaging style, a tour de force of brilliant insights on Shakespeare.

Firstly, I would like to thank Professor Carole Rozzonelli for accepting my invitation to co-edit this venture. For her wonderful collaboration and friendship, I am deeply indebted to her. Secondly, I want to extend my thanks to my family, colleagues and the contributors for providing support, talking things over, offering comments, assisting in the editing and seeing me through this book. I also wish to express my gratitude to Dr. K.R. Gupta, Honorary Advisor of Atlantic Publishers & Distributors (P) Ltd., for the confidence evinced in me and for seeing the book through the press.

Sunita Sinha

Acknowledgements 2

This collection of essays dealing with Shakespeare has been planned by scholars, from three different countries, India, France and Italy, who have been in touch with several other scholars from different countries and even continents. This wide range of collaborations reflects itself through the many points of views and insights concerning Shakespeare and his work, these including plays and cinema. This anthology opens fresh perspectives not only on behalf of Shakespearean scholars, but also for people working in the field of intercultural studies. The international dimension of this book puts several cultures and critical experiences in reciprocal confrontation, so as to instruct new and, we hope, seminal reflections concerning Shakespeare's heritage.

I would also like to thank warmly, Professor Sunita Sinha, for her dedication and availability. She kindly invited me to a joint collaboration in editing this anthology on Shakespeare. This collaboration stands high at the apex of a long-lasting friendship and mutual exchange in essay writing.

Thanks again, Sunita.

Carole Rozzonelli

Contents

1

The Delusion of Critique: Subjunctive Space, Transversality, and the Conceit of Deceit in *Hamlet*

Anthony Kubiak and *Bryan Reynolds*

In their recent essay, "A little touch of Harry in a night': Translucency and Projective Transversality in the Sexual and National Politics of *Henry V*," Donald Hedrick and Bryan Reynolds argue that Shakespeare's Princess Catherine potentially undermines King Henry's fantasized domination of her during sex by occupying antithetically the conceptual-emotional spacetime of Catherine's blindness by "winking" (5.2.262). In other words, Henry's fantasy of Catherine closing her eyes during sex that he shares with Burgundy ("Yet they do wink and yield, as love is blind and enforces" [5.2.259]) so that he can enter her from behind ("and so I shall catch the fly, your cousin [Catherine], in the latter end, and she must be blind too" [5.2.270-1]), inadvertently makes room for Catherine, in her imagination, to "disappear" and thereby deceive Henry. As Hedrick and Reynolds put it,

> Sex-without-seeing, from the perspective of this [Henry's] fantasy, indicates a trajectory of male and national

> domination. But a transversal reading suggests a different possibility altogether—a key to the scene, if not to the entire play: by closing one's eyes, one "disappears" the other, or even transforms the other into someone else. Instead of transversality as a becoming-other of one's own subjectivity, becoming what you are not, transversality might be now thought of in terms of transforming the other outside himself or herself, a projective transversality or "Renaissance other-fashioning." What we are suggesting is that transversality and translucency may act as mechanisms with an entirely different outcome or purpose for Catherine than for Henry in his performance of himself. (*Performing Transversally* 175)

"Disappearing" in *Hamlet*, however, is an enterprise of an entirely different character. Unlike in *Henry V*, where winking reveals irony and empowers, in *Hamlet* a wink in the face of the play's deceptions can be fatal. One cannot "disappear" what one cannot know, except for those doing the plotting successfully in what Anthony Kubiak has termed the "Hamletic guise." In fact, in the play, the retributive violence that participates in various "disappearings" is also presented in Hamletic guise; that is to say, vengeance is *plotted* like the play itself (or any play for that matter) through the machinations of fabrication and deceit, such as feigned madness, the secret taint of the swords, the hidden poisoning of drink. By *Hamlet*'s final act, deceit and vengeance meld into the same; deceit becomes the cause of violence, and violence the agency of deceit.

Behind all deceit, particularly in *Hamlet*, according to the Hamletic model we are proffering here, is the envenomed, plotting character of thought, played out in what transversal theory refers to as "subjunctive space," the hypothetical space of both "as ifs" and "what ifs" operative in between "subjective territory" (the conceptual-emotional-physical range from which a given subject perceives and experiences) and "transversal territory" (the nonsubjectified, transforming space through which people journey when they defy or surpass the boundaries of their subjective territory).[1] The profound relationship between fabrication and "subjunctive movement" implies a necessity in the organic patterns of thinking that gives rise to emplottedness, deceit, and violence—a kind of murderous Kantian *a priori*. It is as if in some overarching trajectory of natural history, beyond the pale of mere species evolution or accountable spacetime, the primal/primate mind has framed and indeed authored itself as tragedy. To contextualize this idea, we follow Reynolds's understanding of tragedy:

> Several factors determine the extent to which an action or event [such as thinking or a thought] is a tragedy. First of all, as with any performance (defined here as a self-consciously presented expression for an intended audience,[2] how the event is framed needs be taken into consideration. Framing refers to the aesthetic, social, cultural, political, ideological, and historical context established for the performance, whether it takes place in a stage-play or during a sports game or at a particular venue, like in a courtroom, university classroom, chapel, theatre, or a pub. The sociopolitical conductors that work to instill our biases and predilections shape our relationship to that context and thus to what is expected to happen there. In most cases, when the framing is less apparent and less understood, the potential for a tragedy-producing performance is greater. In other words, the more sudden and unexpected the injuring action, the more tragic potential it has. But framing also has to do with investment. The degree to which the audience invests itself in the damaging event and its victims emotionally, conceptually, physically, financially—in terms of spacetime, energy, and emotion—directly affects the potential for tragedy; the greater the investment, the greater the potential for loss, the greater the potential for tragedy. (*Performing Transversally* 13)

Hence, framed within this rather tragic view of humanity's investiture in itself as a high-risk endeavour combined with the idea of a "deceitful imperative" is what could be construed as a "natural" emergence, a conception of tragedy that moves outside of the realm of literary form, convention, or genre, and comes to represent the structure of thought "comings-to-be" through the biosocial necessity of deceit. This "comings-to-be" of thought is, moreover, "framed" in/by mind—the thinking that "makes it so." Yet this "frame of mind" must always remain unseen, unknowable. The "frame of mind" that turns something into theater is precisely the "language game" (following Wittgenstein), or the Unconscious (following Freud) that can never be seen in mind—the unseen and unseeable proscenium.

In this formulation, deceit best precipitates success when least expected, especially if misleading or injuring people—physically and psychically—is, in part, the measure of efficacy (we must, of course, remember that the other measure of its efficacy is how much harmony and stability is retained in the social unit through the uses of deceit). When the subject, in this case human thought, loses control during processes of "becomings-other" and becomes more of/or something else than anticipated and/or desired, comings-to-be are occurring. According to transversal theory, becomings-other are active engagements, usually self-inaugurated and pursued intentionally, whereas comings-to-be, however spurred by becomings, are generated by the energies, ideas, people, societies, and so on to which the subject aspires, is lured toward, or encounters accidentally. Empathy and assimilation are no longer self-consciously accomplished. Instead, they happen unwittingly and unconsciously through ideological, emotional, and/or physiological adaptation and change. Transversal theory refers to the dynamics that cause and are caused by the linked processes of comings-to-be and becomings as "pressurized belongings."[3] For a subject to become a member of an alternative group, to incorporate the qualities of a different subjective territory and/or to operate within a foreign official territory, assimilation and expulsion must occur at the expense of aspects of these destinations. The transformed subject causes overflow, expansion, or reconfiguration such that not all of the extant elements can remain or remain the same if the system is to maintain equilibrium.

The point here, however, relates to the selection by human beings, however inadvertently, of the specific play, *Hamlet*, as the bellwether play of lies, subjunctivity, and pressurized belongings. Although over-critiqued and palimpsested throughout literary history, *Hamlet* remains framed as The Play in the Euro-American history of performance. It is the play of the world's most celebrated poet, Shakespeare, that is most invested in by dominant sociopolitical conductors (familial, educational, juridical, and governmental structures) of the state machinery (the amalgamation of the conductors that work to foster a cohesive society) of all Western societies because, we would argue, it deceives deceit itself. In effect, *Hamlet* creates a window through which people can become and come-to-be, among other things, Hamletic. *Hamlet* thus exemplifies what transversal theory calls "deceit conceits," which are clever schemes involving artifice and fiction performed in order to fracture, transform, and/or expand the conceptual and/or emotional range of an individual or individuals, which is to say, a targeted subjective territory or subjective territories, such as those occupied by many of *Hamlet*'s audiences throughout history (see chapter 4). These are audiences who have engaged, to some degree, in the particular "articulatory space"—a discursive, multidimensional conceptual-emotional interface—that Donald Hedrick and Bryan Reynolds have termed "Shakespace,"[4] and the sometimes subset, sometimes superset, but nevertheless always related, "Hamletspace." Simply put, Shakespeare's play, *Hamlet*, is brilliantly, strategically transversal.

Else and Or? Spaces of Subjunctivity

Indeed, in Shakespeare's Elsinore, the setting for the action of *Hamlet*, the manipulations, deceits, ironies, and performances —the subjunctive and transversal movements—are multifarious. The character Hamlet pretends madness so that he might uncover the secret of his father's murder (recalling Henry's pretending in *1 Henry IV* to be genuine member of Falstaff's gang only to become the secret of his own success). But the madness is no mere pretense, or rather, the pretense is itself pretended: "I am but mad north-north-west: when the wind is southerly I know a hawk from a handsaw" (2.2.374-5). His social performance, in other words, is an amalgam of remembering (to act mad) and forgetting (that he is acting), then remembering again (that he is forgetting), *ad infinitum*. Here remembering (to act), and forgetting (that one is acting) are both equally indispensable functions of consciousness, that is, regardless of the subject's subjective territory, certain performances must occur for the subject to be aware of anything, much less itself, operating anywhere in spacetime. Remembering and forgetting are not successes or failures of consciousness, but consciousness in action, performed, sustained.

This is why, in our view, theater is appropriate as a model for understanding consciousness; consciousness depends on theatricality, the continual framing, unframing, and reframing of performances, such as of remembering and of forgetting that one is acting in a particular spacetime; and theater, structurally, reflects consciousness, with its multiple framings and vistas of experience. Theater, then, the communal product of human beings, and not the "Cartesian theater" often imagined as central to the organization of an individual's brain, is phenomena of interactive liveness, sentience, and awareness more apt to understanding consciousness than, say, computer models, such as Stephen Blaha's "classical probabilistic account,"[5] or Daniel Dennett's "multiple drafts model," neither of which consider phenomena of reactive and communicative reciprocity among the brain and entities beyond its own material limits.

Getting back to *Hamlet*, Claudius the killer, remembering and forgetting, reveals himself concealing his crime: "My words fly up, my thoughts remain below:/ Words without thoughts never to heaven go" (3.3.98-9). Aware of, if nothing else, the inappropriateness of Hamlet's performance, Gertrude conceals her complicity (or seeming complicity, if any) by castigating Hamlet in his grief, "Why seems it so particular with thee?" (1.2.74). She launches her query as if death, indeed regicide and fratricide, had not come to Elsinore, and she thus enjoys still untainted the office of queen, or at least must appear so, having forgotten the loss of her husband, and remembering that she has a new one, while all along she remembers to act the role of queen, and forgets any grief that might distract her from this performance. The Machiavellian tricksters Rosencrantz and

Guildenstern, subjected to Hamlet's counter machinations, are themselves tricked to death, while Ophelia is humiliated and confounded by Hamlet's seeming and seamy accusations of infidelity; she is thereby pushed into an all-consuming transversality.[6] Hamlet sets up the play within the play by which he will "catch the conscience of the king," and the play within *that* play, a dumb show, that doubly inscribes the murderous deed (presumably) done. Theater frames consciousness by which the theatrical world of the play is exposed, made cognizant. A fun house of mirrors that can be outlined, as Herbert Blau has shown, like this: Hamlet sets into motion—precipitating movements among the audience that are recollective, subjunctive, and/or transversal—by means of the play (both large and small) a theatrical panopticon of universal surveillance—Claudius watching the play, Gertrude watching Claudius watch the play, Hamlet watching Gertrude watching Claudius watch the play, Ophelia watching Hamlet, *ad infinitum*, *ad nauseum*: all speculations and meanings drowned in the concentric wash of the watching.[7] All the while, we, the audience, watch, and are watched, and so on (by the theater's security, our peers, other audience members, the state machinery...).

Yet these are the more obvious manifestations or symptoms of deceit, the possibility of deceit (the performative deceit) being the immediate cause for the compulsion for surveillance, for the insecurity, uncertainty, and mistrust that deceit breeds. *Hamlet*'s theater is woven of lies given over to our scrutiny, and lies concealed (as we will see later in one of Hamlet's more famous soliloquies). In seducing us with the obvious lie, Shakespeare slips the deeper deceit in the backdoor, so to speak. Thus, while we congratulate ourselves for our perspicacity, we are blindsided by Hamlet who lies to our faces. Finally, there are those lies that exist in a kind of liminal space: Hamlet feigns madness, but then sees ghosts no one else can see, or Hamlet leads Polonius to see whales and weasels where there are none, then leads Horatio to imagine the king/no-king illusively "frighted with false fire" (3.2.260). We come to suspect that deceit, employed here with purpose as deceit conceit, is more than a human instrumentality; it is an agent of action in the play (personified in Claudius,

Hamlet, Rosencrantz, etc.), more than a social or political strategy: *it is an initial state of mind that needs resistance.* Yet whatever honesty does appear is merely honesty grafted onto lies, lies becoming the bedrock of perception (causing another king, Oedipus, to rake out his eyes), and truth nothing but a hallucinatory touchstone grounding the inevitability of deceit. Hence, the play's deceit conceits are, in salvo, a *tour de force* in projective transversality, which is to say that they powerfully promote transversal movements in all subjective territories exposed to the play, even those of the characters within it. Deceit, as the play's ethos, is, in other words, not a perversion of human conduct, but its first principle. We are born to deceit, *Hamlet* suggests, and we must learn the strategies of truth-telling, or rather, we must *unlearn* the Darwinian impulse to lie. Here, we would suggest, transversality would also appear in the extraordinary perversity of truth-telling, resisting the genetic predisposition for deceit.

To be sure, an effect of the many forms and degrees of deceit conceits perpetrated within and by *Hamlet* is to make us—as we are made to move transversally—suspect that there is something radically amiss "in this distracted globe" (1.5.97), in the The Globe itself, within and beyond the worlds of the play, and in that special space of phantoms that gives the stage its birth: the brain. Brain and stage become one not through the manifestation of the true, the beautiful, the tragic, the imaginary, the artistic, but through the very architectures of deceit, and perhaps no demonstration of deceit in the play is as calculating and nefarious as this:

> Now I am alone.
> O, what a rogue and peasant slave am I!
> Is it not monstrous that this player here
> But in a fiction, in a dream of passion,
> Could force his soul so to his own conceit
> That from her working all his visage wann'd,
> Tears in his eyes, distraction in's aspect,
> A broken voice, and his whole function suiting
> With forms to his conceit? and all for nothing!
> (2.2.543-51)

In this aside, the most direct invocation to a Coleridgean "willing suspension of disbelief," there seems to be a contract or trust between actor and audience that runs against the grain of the obvious: it operates in violation of "ocular proof"—so elusive in *Othello* (3.3.366). The actor is, after all, standing on stage, his fellow actors waiting in the wings, cueing on his words, in a theater filled with spectators, all eyes on him. And what is presumed to be an introspective recitative expression must be heard in the back rows: the aside, in other words, like the fourth wall or proscenium in modern theater, is a convention, a lie universally recognized and accepted, and so necessarily invisible and forgotten.

But in this case, the convention is complicated beyond its normal "confessional" mode. The Beckettian "all for nothing," an emotional Black Monday in the collapse of psychic economy, gives us pause, thinking back through the speech in memory: "Is it not monstrous that this player here...". But wait. Which player where? Is Hamlet indicating the recently departed First Player (who is certainly not *here*, but rather *there*, in memory), or himself—and a player twice removed, an equity actor (Derek Jacobi in the canniest of performances, staring with barely concealed mirth at the camera), an actor playing an actor playing the prince of Elsinore feigning madness? Here, in a very real sense, the issue of performativity reaches a kind of conceptual and perceptual crisis: Which is the fiction, who is dreaming the dream of passion, or better, who most obviously telling the lie? The First player, Shakespeare, Hamlet, or Jacobi? Who, and for what purpose? "For Hecuba!" of course (echoes of Hecate, that devil, patron saint of actors), but then, "What's Hecuba to him, or he to Hecuba, / That he should weep for her?" (2.2.552-55). Where is the psychic investment? What are the expectations? Where the risk? Who, exactly, is in danger of being found out? Where is the surprise? How, exactly, is Judith Butler's idea of interpellation, the performative, running here? And then the *coup du théâtre*, the lying double bind:

> What would he do,
> Had he the motive and the cue for passion
> That I have? He would drown the stage with tears

> And cleave the general ear with horrid speech,
> Make mad the guilty and appal the free,
> Confound the ignorant, and amaze indeed
> The very faculties of eyes and ears.
> Yet I,
> A dull and muddy-mettled rascal, peak,
> Like John-a-dreams, unpregnant of my cause,
> And can say nothing. (2.2.559-64)

"What would he do... say nothing." Why, he would do what he (who?) is doing—act. For there is no Hamlet, and never has been—that is certainly one point of the play over time—only "this player here," the very knot and configuration of performative deceit, a deceit conceit plainly revealed, but hidden. The deceit conceit exploits the audience's desire for a "willing suspension of disbelief" and the seeming impossibility of it (both characteristics of Western theater), revealing an audience "taken" by the con: the grifter gets the mark to willfully give up his money (like the prospect of Catherine being taken from behind), and then the mark's consciousness, upon recognition, is momentarily paused—the surprise: "I've been taken"—the world has changed. But for whom? For the mark, perhaps, but certainly for the con-man/contra-man, who remains largely unconcerned with the mark's recognition of being-conned. It is of no consequence to the con-man whether the mark ever finds out. It is the game that gives pleasure—the play. And so the traditional anthem—a Hamlet "unable to act," a "John-a-dreams, unpregnant of my cause"—is itself a bald lie: that is all Hamlet can do—he acts. He is most himself, or rather most what he is, when designating himself at the outset, "this player here . . ." (as Macbeth would have us believe, "That struts and frets his hour upon the stage . . . Signifying nothing" [*Macbeth*, 5.5.25-28]). Hamlet tells us to our faces that he, like the first actor, *is* merely acting his passions, just "pretending," and we still do not get it because we trust him at his word, believe in his world. We are, Hamlet (or Shakespeare, or Jacobi, or someone...) tells us to our faces, fools.

"What a rogue and peasant slave am I" (*Hamlet* 2.2.544), certainly, but also in the canny way the play surreptitiously begins over and over again, creating a *mise en abîme* of suspicion, skewed perception, and self-delusion: the opening line, "Who's there?"; Hamlet speaking to the ghost; the play within the play; the final scene, in which Horatio (echoing oration, "Flights of angels ..." [5.2.366]) gives the order:

> that these bodies
> High on a stage be placed to the view,
> And let me speak to th'yet unknowing world
> How these things came about. So shall you hear
> Of carnal, bloody, and unnatural acts,
> Of accidental judgements, casual slaughter,
> Of deaths put on by cunning and forc'd cause.
> (5.2.382-88)

He becomes the freak show barker, the porn show pimp, the stage manager ready to mount the whole bloody business one more time, right from the beginning, creating a new frame, fusing deceit and its strange attractor, repetition ("What, has this thing appeared again tonight?" [1.1.24]), into something like a genome project for theater's yet unformed history—the playing of roles whose scripts lie concealed within the fury of concealment itself, a performativity that is in reality a theater whose promptbooks and castings have been archived in the cultural unconscious, engendered in an interpellative moment that both expands and recedes hopelessly around us: "Who's there?", but also the turning back, "Nay, answer me, stand and unfold yourself" (1.1.1-2). And finally, the seeming end to it all in the invocation of the interpellation itself, "Long live the king!" (1.1.3). But which king is being hailed: the living king or the king dead?

The Pith and Marrow of Our Attribute

What is the nature of this maddening interpellative moment? In her book, *Bodies That Matter*, Butler claims that "in Althusser's notion of interpellation, it is the police who initiate the call" that establishes subjectivity (121). However, it is not only the police in Althusser's essay that initiate the interpellation, but also God, a stranger on the street, and a friend knocking at the door. It is in fact the latter that the old con-man Althusser mentions first, giving a much less authoritarian face to the process of individuation that Butler invokes, encouraging doubt about, say, one's friends, implying that our world is not as it appears, or, rather, that interpellation is not simply the result of cultural authoritarianism, but of something cellular, genetic, primal. This is no mere quibble. Butler's misreading of Althusserian misreadings is indicative of a series of misapprehensions both large and small that are in the end suggestive of critical theory's general misapprehension of apprehension itself, characterized by Butler's failure to understand the theater of her own discourse.

When Althusser introduces his critical notion of interpellation or "hailing," he gives the example of a knock on the door, followed by our question, "Who's there?" (Again, the Hamletic impasse). The friend, still unseen and unknown answers, "It's me." We open the door, and discover, indeed, that it is "her." Both she and we are constituted through reciprocal acknowledgement of presence. Similarly, out on the street someone yells, "Hey, you!" and "nine times out of ten," according to Althusser, the "correct person" responds and turns around (173-75). Putting aside the problematic question of where Althusser's "nine times out of ten" statistic comes from, his claim that this hailing or interpellation works not out of a sense of guilt—such that one says, "I turn because I know I have done something for which I might be apprehended"—but rather because the turning toward the voice, or the response, "It's me!," constitute "me" as a subject, and so in some way one comes to recognize that interpellative constitution as the means, the only means, by which one comes to exist within a society governed by "Ideological and Repressive State apparatuses"—what transversal theory refers to as state machinery.[8] The uses in either case of the universal/personal pronouns you/me underscores Althusser's recognition, out of Jacques Lacan, that it is in the pronomial that one is constituted, not as a self with a particular name, but as a subject (of a sentence), therefore constituted in a sentence. Yet one is not necessarily sentenced to subjectivity in this process. One can resist, or even turn the interpellation into aggression: "Nay, answer me. Stand and unfold yourself" (*Hamlet* 1.1.2).

But apart from the possibility of resistance, there is also in the Althusserian interpellative moment, actually central to it, a misapprehension (*méconnaissance*)—an "otherness" to recognition that enforces its power. One might say: "When I am called, I turn because it really is me; I have not been misrecognized. At the same time, I turn to assure myself—hence the common response of pointing to oneself and asking the silently mouthed, 'Me? Really?'" Misrecognition, the surprise, the transversal movement, or its possibility, thus informs the allure of recognition and one's responses to it. Or so Althusser suggests, and Butler reiterates. Butler's contribution to the schema is to suggest that interpellation is not (as Althusser suggests, she claims) unilateral. When one is constituted as an "I," there immediately arises the possibility, as we have mentioned, that one will resist the interpellation (as Catherine may "disappear" Henry).[9]

While both Althusser and Butler are careful to point out that this process of interpellation does not work in the simple, linear, sequential way described, that the interpellative process is an "always-already," to quote Althusser, a construction or "performative" (to use Butler's misappropriation of Austin) that begins literally before we are born (the giving of a name in utero), both Althusser and Butler miss a crucial point: this process of interpellation cannot exist but for theater. Indeed, even though Butler, in her later work, has grudgingly admitted to theatrical resonances in her theory, she is adamant that the interpellative moment, the moment of performativity, is largely beyond our control, and so not, as she supposes theater to be, subject to rehearsal, but is rather reiterative, merely repetition. However, this is impossible, given that events can never be exactly repeated. She is not aware that her subjective territory, like all subjective territories, although scripted and revised in response to changes in sociopolitical conductors, state machinery, official territory, and other forces, needs to be rehearsed, adapted, and produced over and over again to be convincingly affirmed. This requires preparation, practice, interaction, and amendment in negotiation with audiences, and not just reiteration and exclusion, as Butler would have us believe, even if this were possible. To be sure, Butler does not know the secret: that transversal power can be mutually channeled through theater to endow the subject with agency to rehearse, adapt, and produce, and thereby dismiss Butler's own misuse of Austin's term "performative," to show it to be an untruth that Butler espouses. Austin's point is that language most often does something (it acts) rather than signifies something and therefore its efficacy can be seen, experienced, and measured.

Butler is not aware that consciousness occupies "theaterspace," works like theater, and vice versa. And even Althusser, for all of his invocation to theatrical metaphor in his discussion of the state apparatus, declines the theatrical consciousness suggested in the interpellated moment: "Hey, you!," re-echoing of course the Hamletic preamble, spoken by Barnardo, that sets into motion a veritable torrent of interpellation that *fails* again and again throughout the play, exposing a theater at the heart of the interpellative moment, at the moment of performativity that is predicated on the necessary failure of interpellation, a theater at the heart of performativity that has been performance, to be sure, theater, all along.

When Butler misreads this theater as the societal stage—and the stage in its most perverse form, as deceit, robotics, and evacuation—that ensures the failure of all constitutive acts, the outcome of such failure is, ultimately, not liberation (even the restricted liberation of mimicry she imagines), but rather alienation, insanity, poverty, abjection, death. The *absence* of the constituting authoritative interpellation—of framing—does not usher in possibilities for resistance, empowerment, and transformation, but rather the dissolution of identity, selves, and agency—both personal and political. Such attempts in critical theory to reduce authoritative conductors to repressive apparatuses or to negate them, not only fail, but also unproductively oversimplify what are usually complex situations: for all of their repressive tactics and modalities, authorities are often positively experienced across history as organizing mechanisms in the interest of identity formations, state power, and society, and so operate out of necessity—absolutely neither "good" nor "evil"—and thus simultaneously supply us with worlds and refuse us entry to other worlds. It is, in fact, the doubleness of authority—in the sense of its Janus-faced ability to deceive and affirm—that constitutes subjects and preconditions tragedy. It is for this reason that theater as a reconfiguring mechanism (a framed, rehearsed, developed, interactive performance praxis) can be a powerful sociopolitical conductor of transversal power self-consciously deployed in order to change the parameters that oblige us to certain authorities, and allow us to change the authorities themselves.

Earth, Yield me Roots

> For each true word, a blister; and each false
> Be as cauterizing to the root o' th' tongue,
> Consuming it with speaking!
> (Shakespeare, *Timon of Athens* 5.1.131-3)

In line with a research methodology of transversal poetics commonly referred to as the "investigative-expansive mode," we would like our discussion to follow a lead. The investigative-expansive mode requires that the subject matter under investigation be divided up into variables that are then partitioned and examined in relation to other influences, both abstract and empirical, beyond the immediate vicinity. A chief objective of this expansive approach is to contextualize historically, ideologically, and critically both the subject matter and the analysis itself within local and greater milieu. Mobile and vine-like, the investigative-expansive mode resists anything resembling predetermination or circumscription. Instead, it calls for continuous analytical maneuverings and reparameterizations in response to unexpected, even sudden, emergences of glitches, quagmires, and new information as it deduces, trail blazes, follows off-beat leads, and takes tangential excursions. The present analysis encourages us to take just such a tangential foray into a related area of inquiry, primatology, as a means by which to achieve a more expansive perspective on how we are coming to understand deceit and its relationships to theater, consciousness, and transversal power.

Among other things, so far we have seen that the multifarious (or nefarious) nature of deceit is perhaps its most salient and maddening quality. The forms of deceit are so many and so varied, so seamlessly graded from one type to another, that it is difficult to determine just what the lie is, what constitutes it; and a deceit conceit is typically only recognizable in its revealed achievements, floundering, or failings vis-à-vis a designated subjective territory. Still, it may be safe to say that among the many activities that have been seen as consummately human, lying has remained within the realm of the purely social, the performed, and thus the purely human. But do other animals deceive? Of course some animals engage in mimicry (the false coral snake). Some feign injury to protect young (the killdeer). Some play dead to escape harm (the opposum). But do other, non-human animals lie on purpose; or more precisely, do animals know that they deceive; *do animals have a theory of mind*?

This remains an important question because lying has for most of our philosophical history been seen as quintessentially social, quintessentially problematic, and quintessentially a constructed, human activity. The epistemology of lying (philosophy), the ethics of lying (philosophy and theology), the analysis of lying (criminology), the uses of lying (psychology), and, finally, the hermeneutics of lying (psychoanalysis), have all been studied as primarily human behaviour. Indeed, Lacan himself asked the question, "Can animals lie?" and answered "No."[10] And if animals cannot lie, they certainly cannot create illusions, delude others, employ fictions, or construct *mise en scenes*. Animals cannot, in effect, translate behaviours from one domain to another through the operations of an unconscious to produce fictive scenes, illusions, theaters. They cannot, that is, *unless they are primates* and primates of a certain level of intelligence. Primates lie, and, moreover, primates do not merely deceive using a theatricalized intelligence, intelligence in primates (and thus in humans) *is* deception. Put differently, intelligence is the combined awareness of deception's possibility and the capacity to imagine and generate creative representations.

This, then, is a true story,[11] a dumb show, not particularly subtle or ingenious, but one accompanied by, as Artaud says of the Theater of Cruelty, "cries, groans, apparitions, surprises, theatrical tricks... a kind of unique language halfway between gesture and thought" (245; 242). A baboon, known as ML in the literary account, digs in the earth, trying to discover "one poor root."[12] A young member of the baboon troupe approaches and watches. He is known in the literature as PA. For PA time passes, but PA keeps watch, always keeps watch, yet no one else is there, no one else sees them. ML digs roots, PA watches, and watches to make certain others are not watching. When the root is nearly uncovered, young PA begins to scream. Hair-raising, inconsolable terror. This is what really happened, but here the story is at the same time not true—there is no danger near. No one is attacking him. It is just PA and the other baboon, ML. The troupe's alpha male, JG, hears the cry and appears over the crest of the hill. He shows raw fury, running and striking the digging baboon, who runs a short distance away, and waits for him to disappear over the crest of the hill again. When he is gone, ML resumes digging. PA, the child baboon, watches.

Now here the true story continues, that is also not true: when the root is fully unearthed, the child, PA, again begins to scream. Again, hair-raising terror. But again there is no danger. Again, no one is attacking him. Again, the protective male, JG, appears over the crest of the hill showing bared teeth. This time he runs at the digging ML and chases her away, over the crest of a different hill, and then leaves. The child-baboon, PA, now alone, picks up the cherished and much-planned-for root and begins to eat. He is, perhaps, amused, even delighted at the sensation that tickles the back of his mind. A faint sensation. Deception? Perversity? The perversity of subversion, perhaps. Or perhaps the more disturbing (for us) perversity of the non-perverse: that in the lie (though the story is true) the young baboon is following the very stage directions of a theatricalized, Darwinian mind that simply does not understand its own strangeness.

PA has over time used similar subterfuge. Screaming, crying, calling for help, a guardian running to help him, driving others away from food they have discovered—a scheme enabling him to eat it in their stead. Once, twice, five times—a simian conman.

And there are countless other scenarios, other actors in the troupe: different deceptions and subterfuges, some so intricate and multilayered that it is at first hard to believe they have been planned and played-out by mere juveniles and primate juveniles at that. In fact, the observations have so intrigued and puzzled primatologists, that, beginning in the late 1980s, a new theory of intelligence (and by extension, we would argue, consciousness) arose; this theory is called "Machiavellian Intelligence." Contrary to earlier assumptions—that intelligence developed in primates and subsequently in humans as a result of technical need; that being slower, weaker, lacking claws and individual killing power, primates and humans were selected for an intelligence that allowed for planning, communication, and social cooperation, and thus survival as a group—this new approach argues that intelligence was in fact selected because it allowed for the use of deception within the social sphere, and consequently enabled survival and prosperity of the individual within the group.

According to observations in the field, primatologists began to realize that primate groups, especially the more intelligent and social species (chimpanzees, bonobos, baboons), rarely utilized the sophisticated intelligence with which they were endowed for solving the logistical and "technological" problems of hunting, group-defense, or food-gathering that supposedly gave rise to higher and higher levels of intelligence. In a follow-up volume to their first book, *Machiavellian Intelligence*, Andrew Whiten and Richard Byrne explain the issue in a succinct preface:

> How can the intelligence of monkeys and apes, and the huge brain expansion that marked human evolution, be explained? In 1988, *Machiavellian Intelligence* was the first book to assemble the early evidence suggesting a new answer: that the evolution of intellect was primarily driven by selection for manipulative, social expertise within groups where the most challenging problem faced by individuals was dealing with their companions.[13]

If Whiten and Byrne are correct (and the issues are controversial), the potential ramifications of this re-definition are enormous and cut across a huge range of post-humanist disciplines: primatology, of course, but studies of human development as well. These include psychology and philosophy, but also the history of consciousness, as well as studies of social behaviour, ethnic and gender theory, performance theory, more precisely, and theater theory, primarily. If Whiten and Byrne's ideas hold merit, we might need to re-think central issues in psychoanalysis, Marxism, and critical theory in general: is deception, for example, and thus performance/theater, merely a constructed behavior—is it, in other words, something "grafted on," even unconsciously, to operational intelligence, or is intelligence "always already" deception? Might the perception of deception, an understanding of its etiology, be the highest, most sophisticated form of deception? Are the patterns, plans, outcomes of deception—self or otherwise—ideological? If so, is intelligence possible without ideology? Can, in other words, Marxist analysis claim the ideological high-ground if all analysis itself is predicated upon deception—strategic deceptions from the illusory "as ifs" of subjunctive space, to the densely argued discourses of propaganda?

While present modes of critical theory might presuppose a certain cynicism permeating the hegemonic forces of late capitalism, while they might, indeed, agree that deception is the rule in capital and not the exception, critical theory would almost to the person claim dispensation from the desperation of the Machiavellian double-bind, a double-bind that goes back at least as far as David Hume: that is, how can we know the truth of what we think? If deceptions, or the more creative "as ifs" and "what ifs" of subjunctivity, are the very *substance* and substrate of thought, if "the problem of representation" is not merely that it slips, or misses its object, but purposely leads us astray in a kind of perpetual gaming that is the very mechanism of our survival, then is not the rational, even in its guise as poststructural skepticism, which is to say, critical theory, nothing more than "always already" self-parody? As a discipline, critical theory, we think, would, predominantly, say no. Conveniently, this is because the gaming and illusions of thought and culture can be re-apprehended, re-deconstructed, the fantasy can be recast, "consciousness raised" again, ideological misperceptions corrected, if only partially, or "contingently." For example, in her book, *Simians, Cyborgs, and Women*, and again in *Primate Visions*, Donna Haraway describes, in the work of primatologists, something like the humanization of primate groups, or more precisely, the projection of ideologies of gender onto those groups. As she puts it, "Scientific debate about monkeys, apes, and human beings, that is, about primates, is a social process of producing stories, important stories that constitute public meanings" (81). She continues:

> We find the themes of modern America reflected in detail in the bodies and lives of animals. We polish an animal mirror to look for ourselves.... The science of non-human primates, primatology, may be a source of insight or a source of illusion. The issue rests on our skill in the construction of mirrors. (21)

While following the now unquestioned Foucaultian assertion that knowledge is constructed not discovered, even empirical, scientific knowledge, Haraway forages blindly before the subterfuge of her own intellect, an intellect that, in the terms of Machiavellian Intelligence, is born neither through a need to construct or discover, nor through a need to master an environment through technique, but rather, through the need for deceit, machination (cybernetic or otherwise), and self-delusion. Both primate and human intelligence came into being—underwent comings-to-be—because it was naturally selected for its ability to produce deceptive behavior. By extension, we are referring to the lies and subterfuges, that, along with cooperative behavior, constitute social and cultural life (subterfuge cannot work, after all, unless there is trust and cooperation seemingly ahead of it). This predicament, as evidenced in Haraway's conclusions, suggests a rather profound and disturbing possibility that even the primatologists often miss: human intellect is not merely prone to dissembling, dissembling is no mere weakness within human character and mind, no aberration or "subversive" activity, dissembling and deceit are, again, what constitute mind—a mind constructed, as we have said, in the subjunctive modes of "as if" and "what if," in the interstices between subjective and transversal territories.

Against the accusation that such a view is overly cynical, we should remind ourselves that what is remarkable are not the sins of a species so determined, but the apparent altruism that seems to outweigh the self-interest (we have, after all, survived this long). To be sure, Machiavellian theorists would argue that self-interest, in the final analysis, is necessary to social survival at both the individual and group level: this aspect of intelligence is what allows the physically weaker (though perhaps smarter and more creative) members of the group to survive and thrive. In fact, this Machiavellian aspect of intelligence, contra Machiavelli himself, serves the purposes of the weaker individual far more than it serves the interests of the prince, or president, who everyone, in the political scheme of things, suspects is lying. And if, as Haraway might argue, the primatologists are merely seeing their own nefarious scientific practices in the actions of primates, although this is doubtful given the secretly filmed, non-edited simian sequences demonstrating deceit the primatologists provide as evidence, the idea of this projection merely begs the question all over again: Why would critical intelligence fail so easily and obviously unless in some sense consciousness wanted to be deceived—wanted to be lied to even when it knows it is being lied to (picture Derek Jacobi delivering Hamlet's "what a rogue and peasant slave am I" speech). In other words, if primatologists are projecting their own deceit onto innocent apes, what does that say about the deep structure of mind, the unconscious itself?

Critical theory, especially in its more political modalities, still seems to believe itself capable of discovering the secret ideologies of capitalism, the substrate of sexism, or the representational malaise of gender itself, while believing its own agendas to be relatively transparent. Theater, we would submit, or at least the theater that is the very embodiment of the Machiavellian mind, is not so sure. Theater, the very subjunctive location of deception, subterfuge, and creativity at polymorphous and multifarious levels, because of its ability to willfully move transversally, has always known the lying truth of the Machiavellian mind, while critical theory, in its affirmation of the possibilities of intellectual liberation, however slight, gained through endless analyses (often in bad faith) of "dominant culture," has for the most part willingly suspended disbelief in its own secret agendas and self-delusional scams. It is through the transversal power of theater, perhaps in collaboration with the critical theory that—while playing its own games—elucidates theater's opportunities, that worlds can be changed. This can happen through the transposition of deceit in theater, through deceit conceits that work simultaneously to project transversally deceit-as-other outside of subjective and official territories and to reconfigure subjunctively deceit-as-becomings. As both the mind it reflects and the praxis it performs, theater can expand our understanding and experience of deceit to include unlimited, positive potentialities in the worlds it ingeniously creates. But this, perhaps, may be impossible, if consciousness' first impulse is indeed to deceive: whereas we might believe we are working for enlightenment and liberation, we may be, unbeknownst to us, seeking our own desecrations and death. What do you tell yourself?

NOTES

1. For more on "subjunctive space" beyond coverage in this book, see Bryan Reynolds, "Transversal Performance: Shakespace, the September 11 Attacks, and the Critical Future" in his *Performing Transversally: Reimagining Shakespeare and the Critical Future* (New York: Palgrave Macmillan, 2003): 1-28. For detailed discussion on "subjective territory" and "transversal territory" beyond coverage in this book, see Bryan Reynolds: "The Devil's House, 'or worse': Transversal Power and Antitheatrical Discourse in Early Modern England" (*Theatre Journal* 49.2 [1997]: 143-67); *Becoming Criminal: Transversal Performance and Cultural Dissidence in Early Modern England* (Baltimore: John Hopkins University Press, 2002), 1-22; and *Performing Transversally: Reimagining Shakespeare and the Critical Future* (New York: Palgrave Macmillan, 2003), 1-28.
2. But we need to ask, of course, if this is in fact how "performance" or the performative is currently understood. Rather, out of Butler et al., performance seems precisely that mode of "doing" that *lacks* self-consciousness. "Performance," as the term is currently employed, seems to mean little more than "doing." See in this regard Jon McKenzie, *Perform or Else: From Discipline to Performance* (New York: Routledge Press, 2001).

3. The term "pressurized belongings" was coined by Glenn Odom and Bryan Reynolds in their essay, "Becomings Roman/Comings-to-be Villain: Pressurized Belongings and the Coding of Ethnicity, Religion, and Nationality in Peele & Shakespeare's *Titus Andronicus*," which is Chapter 8 of this book.
4. On Shakespace, see Donald Hedrick and Bryan Reynolds, "Shakespace and Transversal Power," in Hedrick and Reynolds Ed., *Shakespeare Without Class*: 3-50; and for more on articulatory spaces, see Reynolds, *Performing Transversally*: 1-28.
5. See Stephen Blaha, *Cosmos and Consciousness: Quantum Computers, Super* strings, *Programming, Egypt, Quarks, Mind Body Problem, and Turing Machines* (Auburn, New Hampshire: Pingree-Hill Publishing, 2002) and Daniel Dennett, *Consciousness Explained* (Boston: Little, Brown and Company, 1991).
6. See Jacques Lacan, "Desire and the Interpretation of Desire in *Hamlet*," *Literature and Psychoanalysis: The Question of Reading: Otherwise*, Ed. Shoshana Felman (Baltimore: Johns Hopkins University Press, 1982).
7. Herbert Blau, *The Dubious Spectacle: Extremities of Theater, 1976-2000* (Minneapolis: University of Minnesota Press, 2002): 107.
8. Reynolds coined the term state machinery for a society's governmental assembly of conductors as a corrective to the political philosophy of Althusser. With state machinery, a term that simultaneously connotes singularity and plurality, he adapted Althusser's conception of what he calls the "Repressive State Apparatus," which includes the governmental mechanisms, such as the military and the police, that strive to control our bodies, and fused it with his subsidiary "Ideological State Apparatuses," the inculcating mechanisms that strive to control our thoughts and emotions. Reynolds emphasizes that a society's drive for governmental coherence is always motivated by assorted conductors of state-oriented organizational power that are at different times and to varying degrees always both repressive and ideological. This is a sociopower dynamic in which various conductors work, sometimes individually and sometimes in conjunction with other conductors, to substantiate their own positions of power within the sociopolitical field. Hence, use of the term state machinery should make explicit the multifarious and discursive nature of state power, and thus prevent the misperception of the sociopower dynamic as the result of a conspiracy led by a monolithic state. This is not to say, however, that conspiracies do not occur and take the form of state factions. On the contrary, this must be the case for the more complex machinery to run. See Reynolds, *Becoming Criminal*, 1-22.

9. The very process that constitutes a "me," therefore, is the means through which an "I" can challenge that constitution. Dick Hebdige perhaps says it best when discussing the punk movements of the seventies: the reason for the piercing, provocatively torn clothing and scarification of punk teenagers living within the surveillances of the British police and social service agencies was designed to "make being looked at an aggressive act." The quote is from a talk Dick Hebdige gave at the University of Wisconsin in 1985 at the Center for 20th Century Studies.
10. See, for example, Lacan's discussion of signification in the process of analysis in *Ecrits: A Selection*, translated by Bruce Fink (New York: Norton, 2002), 88-90.
11. Perhaps this is the central concern of this essay, the very assertion "this is a true story": what, exactly, does truth amount to in fiction, in narrative, in theater? How can we believe anything, even our capacity to lie, given that deceit is the ground condition of consciousness? Even more distrurbing, how can you (the reader) believe what you are reading at this very moment? What are *your* (whose?) secret agendas, self-delusions, con-games? How can you, finally, even believe in the presence of deceit, if deceit is the condition of consciousness? What, in other words, we see in the primates' lies and deceits is being recapitulated at this very moment, in this very essay. What are we not telling you? What are we leaving out of the story? What theoretical niceties are we invoking, not to elucidate, but to, in essence, cover-up what we do not want you (or ourselves) to know or think about? Paranoia, or simply fear, of "being on the outside, being politically misaligned, not gettng tenure . . .".
12. The following baboon story is taken from Richard Byrne and Andrew Whiten, *Machiavellian Intelligence: Social Expertise and the Evolution of Intellect in Monkey, Apes, and Humans* (Oxford: Clarendon Press, 1988): Chapter 15.
13. Byrne and Whiten, *Machiavellian Intelligence*: front material.

WORKS CITED

Althusser, Louis. "Ideology and the State." *Lenin and Philosophy*. New York: Monthly Review Press, 1971.

Artaud, Antonin. "The Theater of Cruelty: First Manifesto." *Antonin Artaud: Selected Writing*. Ed. and introduction Susan Sontag. New York: Farrar, Straus and Giroux, 1976.

Blaha, Stephen. *Cosmos and Consciousness: Quantum Computers, Super strings, Programming, Egypt, Quarks, Mind Body Problem, and Turing Machines*. Auburn, New Hampshire: Pingree-Hill Publishing, 2002.

Blau, Herbert. *The Dubious Spectacle: Extremities of Theater, 1976-2000.* Minneapolis: University of Minnesota Press, 2002.

Butler, Judith. *Bodies That Matter: On the Discursive Limits of "Sex."* New York: Routledge: New York, 1993.

Byrne, Richard and Andrew Whiten. "Tactical deception of familiar individuals in baboons." *Machiavellian Intelligence: Social Expertise and the Evolution of Intellect in Monkeys, Apes, and Humans.* Ed. Richard Byrne and Andrew Whiten. Oxford: Clarendon Press, 1988.

Dennett, Daniel. *Consciousness Explained.* Boston: Little, Brown and Company, 1991.

Hedrick, Donald and Bryan Reynolds. "'A little touch of Harry in the Night': Translucency and Projective Transversality in the Sexual and National Politics of *Henry V*," in Bryan Reynolds, *Performing Transversally: Reimagining Shakespeare and the Critical Future.* Palgrave Macmillan: New York, 2003: 171-88.

——. "Shakespace and Transversal Power," in Hedrick and Reynolds Ed., *Shakespeare Without Class: Misappropriations of Cultural Capital* (New York: Palgrave Macmillan, 2000): 3-50.

——. *Machiavellian Intelligence II: Extensions and Evaluations.* Edited by Andrew Whiten and Richard Byrne. Cambridge: Cambridge University Press, 1997.

Haraway, Donna. *Primate Visions: Gender, Race, and Nature in the World of Modern Science.* New York: Routledge, 1989.

——. *Simians, Cyborgs, and Women.* New York: Routledge, 1991.

Reynolds, Bryan. *Performing Transversally: Reimagining Shakespeare and the Critical Future.* Palgrave Macmillan: New York, 2003.

Shakespeare, William. *King Henry V,* Ed. Andrew Gurr. Cambridge and New York: Cambridge University Press, 1992.

——. *Macbeth.* Ed. Kenneth Muir. London: Methuen, 1951.

——. *Hamlet.* The Arden Shakespeare. Ed. Harold Jenkins. New York: Routledge, 1989, 1990.

——. *Timon of Athens.* The Arden Shakespeare. Ed. H.J. Oliver. New York: Methuen, 1959.

2

Shakespeare's Construction of the Jew*

Mohit Ray

In *The Merchant of Venice* Shakespeare draws heavily on historical imagination rather than on historical reality in creating the character of Shylock and constructs the image in which the mythical Jew assumes the semblance of reality, an image that becomes the stereotype and historical image of a Jew. A close look however reveals that unlike Marlowe Shakespeare does not present a simplistic, monomaniac character like Barabas in *The Jew of Malta* but a character that is highly complex. While Shylock is a very powerful appropriation of the traditional image of the Jew that gets a local habitation and a name in Shylock, he is also a man of dignity, an astute man of business and pleads on behalf of his race and humanity. It would then appear that he is more sinned against than sinning, and that he is really as much "honest in his vices" as the Venetians and Christians are "hypocrites in their virtues" (Hazlitt; in J.R. Brown xxxiv).

* Reprinted from Coelsch-Foisner, Sabine/György E. Szöny. eds. *"Not of an Age but for All Time". Shakespeare across Lands and Age*: Essays in Honour of Holger Klein on the Occasion of His 66th Birthday. Austria: Braumuller, 2004.

In other words, Shakespeare seems to reveal through his treatment of Shylock the hypocrisy of the Venetians and the Christians. It would also appear that though Shakespeare apparently played to the gallery exploiting the audience's instinctive love of Jew-baiting his sympathy lies with Shylock. It is a matter of strange historical blindness that Shakespeare's sympathy with Shylock did not come to light till Edmund Kean in his famous presentation of Shylock on his first appearance in London on 26 January 1814 revealed the terrible energy of Shylock, his untold misery and his sufferings and the undeserved punishment that is inflicted on him.

In order to properly understand the various complex issues involved in the construction of Shylock it is necessary to understand first the traditional attitude to the Jew and the reason thereof. The Christian tradition looks upon Jewishness as a moral depravity because it chose Barabas and rejected Christ, chose the robber and rejected the Saviour, chose the flesh and rejected the spirit, chose the earthly pleasures and rejected the treasure of heaven. As the chooser of this world and the betrayer of Christ, the Saviour, the Jew is a type of Satan himself. Another reason for the hatred against the Jew was the practice of usury by the Jews. Christianity prohibits usury as an offence against the notion of charity. A man in distress must be helped but not out of selfish interest and money should not beget money as it is also against nature. Incidentally, in Latin, usury, usurers and the law concerning the loans are called "fenebris", from the word "fetus", since money or loan can give birth to money. But so far as Shylock or any Jew for that matter is concerned, he is well within his rights in practising usury because the Levitical law sanctions it. Secondly, and more importantly, as the Jews were uprooted from other trades by the flood of religious prejudices they were forced to turn moneylenders to make a living. In other words, this was the only opportunity open to them where they were not obliged to enter into an unhealthy and unfair competition with the Christians. Wronged and outlawed, the Jews pounced upon this only opportunity left open to them. The power of money derived from usury became thus an instrument of defence against restriction and persecution.

Now let us briefly look at some historical instances of persecution. Warner Martin and Muir tell us how after Jerusalem was captured from the Turks in 1099, and Godfrey de Bouillon was chosen as its ruler "the mere love of fighting mastered the Crusaders' heart. Even a good and virtuous knight like Godfrey, too pious to wear a crown of gold where Christ had worn a crown of thorns, had no spirit of mercy. He like the rest regarded himself as an avenger. Without shrinking, he took his share in the hideous massacres, even of women and children that followed the storming of Jerusalem. And this pitiless fury turned too against the Jews. Not merely in Palestine but in distant parts of Europe, they were plundered and ill-treated by kings and barons (Warner, Martin, Muir 123).

Raphael Holinshed chronicling the coronation of Richard I in 1189 describes how "King Richard, of a zealous mind of Christ's religion", abhorring the Jews commanded that no Jew should come within the church when he should receive the crown, nor within the palace when he was at dinner (Holinshed 477). In 1290 Edward I expelled the Jews from his kingdom. James Shapiro points out that the historical record is obscure as to the number of Jews actually expelled, and notes that the English wanted to regard their country as free of Jews rather than that Jews were truly absent. There must have been a significant number of Jews living in London before 1654 Whitehall Conference when the ban was lifted and the Jews were allowed to return to England. Even after expulsion there were some persons living in England descended from Jews who had converted to Christianity. They were called "New Christians" and they lived as Roman Catholics. But there were many among the converts who avowed Christianity but covertly continued to live as Jews practising various rabbinical rites and rituals at home. They were called *Marranos*. When the Jews were expelled from England most of them went to Spain and Portugal where there was a substantial Jewish population. But there also their lot followed them. In 1492 Ferdinand and Isabella expelled all the Jews from Spain and in 1497 all the Portugese Jews were forcibly converted to Christianity.

Now let us look at Shakespeare's presentation of the Jew in his plays other than *The Merchant of Venice.* In *The Two Gentlemen of Verona* (1591) Launce says that everybody was sad on his parting, "my mother weeping, my father wailing, my sister crying, our maid howling, our cat wringing her hands; yet did not this cruel-hearted ever shed one tear. He is a stone, a very pebble stone, and has no more pity in him than a dog. A Jew would have wept to see our parting" (Act I Scene III). Launce compares a Jew with animals and draws on the traditional image of a Jew as a ruthless person. The idea of "even a Jew" simply implies that. In another scene when Launce asks Speed to go with him to the alehouse he remarks, "If not thou art an Hebrew, a Jew, and not worth the name of a Christian". As Speed asks "Why?" Launce replies, "Because thou hast not so much charity in thee as to go to the ale with a Christian" (Act II Scene V). This short dialogue brings under sharp focus the bitter relationship and age-old enmity between a Jew and a Christian where a Jew is seen contemptuously as something like an anti-Christ. In *The Merchant of Venice* Shylock's refusal to dine with Bassanio, ("I will buy with you, sell with you and so following but I will not eat with you, drink with you, nor pray with you") makes it very clear that he will not have any association other than the commercial with a Christian, because he is fully conscious of the deep-seated hatred that Bassanio bears towards him. In *Much Ado About Nothing* (1598) when Benedick says to himself about Beatrice, "...if I do not love her, I am a Jew" (Act III Scene II), he actually draws on the traditional image of the Jew as a person devoid of tender emotions and thus a stranger to the feelings of love. In Henry IV Part I (1597) in contradicting Peto's remarks, "No, no, they were bound, every one of them, or I am a Jew else, an Ebrew Jew" (Act II Scene IV), Falstaff's utterance only reinforces the traditional image of Jew as an accomplice, if not an incarnation of Devil. The mythical transformation of the Jew through the medieval centuries and then three centuries following the Jews' expulsion by Edward I gave the Elizabethans, not excluding Shakespeare, their picture of Jewishness. They saw a Jew as an outsider, a strange creature, a walking, talking and acting phantom, a legendary creature thinly existent or even void of reality. Paradoxically, the Jews belonged to all states or no state. Even in countries like Spain or Italy they did not belong to those with whom or under whom they lived. A Jew was an outsider. He was compelled to live in a special part, the Jewish quarter or "Ghetto" (which literally means 'cut off') generally surrounded by a wall. In *The Merchant of Venice* Shylock is an outsider par excellence, enveloped in all the mysteries of the human creature that comes from outside and abroad. He is also an outsider in the romantic world of the play and is completely impervious to the romanticism of love, glory of Venice or even the joy of life. In the sixteenth century when increasing commerce and navigation brought England and the Mediterranean closer England was full of rumours and reports about Jews. But Shakespeare, it seems, was not so much interested in the dynamic role played by the Jews in controlling and wielding the social energy, as in the traditional image of the Jew. In other words, he dramatized what already existed in a nebulous form in the consciousness of the audiences, shaped Shylock out of the memories and conceptions of the past and presented him as a starkly realistic character, giving us a glimpse of the character who howsoever maltreated never loses his dignity. Shylock knows where he stands in the Christian society and therefore strictly adheres to his role as a moneylender. His very first speech in the play gives us an impression of an astute man of business. He repeats the amount he has to lend ("Three thousand ducats, well"), considers the time given ("For three months and Antonio bound"). He then examines the solvency of the guaranteer and the risks involved in maritime commerce("Ships are but boards, sailors but men, there be land rats and water rats, water thieves, and land thieves, I mean pirates..." Act I Scene III). In the same scene when Antonio enters we hear Shylock saying "aside": "I hate him for he is a Christian". But what he says immediately afterwards is more significant as it underscores the commercial aspect of his character: "But more, for that in low simplicity/ He lends money gratis and brings down/ The rate of usance here with us in Venice". The speech spoken aside and therefore frank and uninhibited makes two things clear. First, Shylock hates Antonio because he is a Christian and Shylock has suffered at the hands of the Christians as all the Jews have suffered and also because—as it will be presently clear from the conversation between Antonio and Shylock—he has personally been insulted and humiliated by Antonio on several occasions. Secondly, the Christian charity of lending money without interest affects him adversely as it cuts into his only means of living. Yet, in course of his conversation he politely but very strongly defends usury ("thrift is blessing if men steal not"). Antonio calls him a villain, "an evil soul producing holy witness", but in spite of sufficient cause of provocation Shylock keeps his cool, comes back to the business at hand and then as Antonio asks, "Well, Shylock, shall we be beholding you?" he gives vent to his feelings. At last he has got a chance to address the Venetians and state his case and express his genuine grievance. As a Jew he has to put up with wrongs, "For sufferance is the badge of all our tribe". The badge is not only metaphorical but also literal as well since the Jews had to wear a yellow cap in sign of their nationality. The wrongs that he enumerates present the Christians in general and Antonio in particular in a negative light: "You call me misbeliever, cut-throat dog,/ And spit upon my Jewish gaberdine,/... You that did void rheum upon my beard,/ And foot me as you spurn a stranger cur/ Over your threshold..." (96-105). Shylock has been treated like a street dog for no other fault than that he is a Jew, and so when he speaks he speaks not only on his own behalf but on behalf of his people. His arguments are based on human rights that need no bond to support them. By the end of his sarcastic speech, "Fair sir you spit on me on Wednesday last;/ You spurn'd me such a day; another time/ You call'd me dog; and for those courtesies/ I'll lend you thus much moneys?" The prevailing mood is no longer one of pathos but of a rebellious rebuff. It is the voice of a proud creature that triumphs over his adversary, lays bare the inhuman behaviour of the Christians and tilts the scale of audience response in his own favour. The next full opportunity for Shylock to state his case comes in the famous speech of Act III Scene I: "I am a Jew. Hath not a Jew eyes? Hath not a Jew hands, organs, dimensions, senses, affections, passions? Fed with the same food, hurt with the same weapons, subject to the same diseases, healed by the same means, warmed and cooled by the same winter and summer, as a Christian is? If you prick us, do we not bleed? If you tickle us, do we not laugh? If you poison us, do we not die?" Here Shylock claims a hearing on the grounds that a Jew as a man is like any other man, like any Christian for that matter. It logically follows, therefore, "If you wrong us, shall we not revenge? If we are like you in the rest, we will resemble you in that" (57-58). Repetition of the word "Christian" thrice with increasingly sneering emphasis on the word reinforces the idea of equality: hatred for hatred, revenge for revenge. In the inspired yet reasoned speech Shylock pleads for his nation. He pleads for the abolition of that injustice and oppression down the centuries that went into the making of Shylock. Here Shylock is no longer just a usurer or an individual Jew but a pure patriot aflame with the white heat of revolt against the wrongs mercilessly inflicted on his nation. Behind Shylock's fury lies a deep hate which is a curious complex of multiple motives: the hate of a Jew for the Christian, of the despised alien for the proud Venetians, and of the usurer for the generous man who brings down the rate of interest by lending money gratis. What fuels his fury is his impassioned diatribe against cruelty and injustice. In Act IV Scene I, Shylock will again cite another glaring and shameful instance of cruelty and abrogation of human rights evident in the Christians' treatment of the slaves like animals: "You have among you many a purchased slave/ Which, like your asses and your dogs and mules,/ You use in abject and in slavish parts,/ Because you bought them" (90-92). Shylock rebels against the inhuman handling of the slaves like animals and thus challenges one of the most important economic institutions of the medieval Christian world still persisting in the sixteenth century. In his bid to defend the legality of the bond he calls attention to the greater and more widespread injustice and mercilessness of the Christian world. Moreover, it is a cogent argument for Shylock to use, since a slave-trader may be said to be dealing in human flesh. Thus, we can discern that there are three distinct stages of Shylock's rebellion against injustice. In Act I Scene III, he refers to the ignominious and public insults he has suffered at the hands of Antonio as a Jew. In Act III Scene I, he speaks on behalf of all the Jews and in Act IV Scene I, he speaks on behalf of humanity.

Shylock is a much suffered man. He is an old man with a young daughter who elopes with a Christian. Not only that. She steals his money and the ring given to him by his beloved wife, and brazen facedly joins his adversaries, and promises to become a Christian. Shylock is a fair game for the young lovers. Not only his daughter. Even his servant leaves him and his friend Tubal plays with him in his misery. After the fiasco of the trial he is robbed of his fortune and the most cruel condition is given for his survival: he must become a Christian to avoid capital punishment. After the filial ingratitude, and the loss of his daughter, his fortune and his faith he is virtually annihilated. To become a Christian is a strange punishment for a Jew and certainly very hard for a man who has been so thoroughly a Jew. Still Shylock does not lose his dignity. Even after his daughter has run away with a Christian along with the valuables he does not parade his pain in public. He complains of the loss and expresses his shock only to his friend Tubal. That Shakespeare wanted him to maintain his dignity is evident from the fact that his lamentations are not presented on the stage but are reported by Solanio, and since Solanio's contempt for Shylock is manifest in his references to Shylock as "the villain Jew" (II, viii), "the dog Jew" (II, viii), etc., his report cannot be taken as a dispassionate, faithful one. As he chuckles at the discomfiture of Shylock his report is likely to be a biased, edited and exaggerated version of the actual situation.

A close reading of the play also reveals the moral decrepitude of the Venetians and the Christian characters. If Antonio rejects interest with moral scorn, his Christian friends in Venice have no hesitation in living upon "excesses". Venice in the sixteenth century was notable for its corruption through covetous pursuit of trade and venture. If Shylock's offence is greed and he is treated contemptuously for that Bassanio's first reference to Portia is: "In Belmont is a lady richly left" (I, I, 161). The first consideration that wells up spontaneously from the unconscious is the prospect of getting wealthy through marriage. Basanio is a prodigal gambler whose vast expenditure in wooing is laid out as a venture to win "a golden fleece", Portia's fair person and wealth. If the Christians find Shylock intolerable and detestable for his cruelty and mercilessness, the inhumanity and injustice of the Christians is writ large in the maltreatment of Shylock, their wild glee at the destruction of Shylock and their practice of slave trade.

It may be worthwhile to look briefly at this point at the situation prevailing in England in the late sixteenth century. In Elizabethan England a culture that officially condemned money-lending saw people growing rich in practising it, making what George Herbert described as "a Jewish choice", because it cherished the mundane. A culture that officially valued inheritance and continuity saw the lowborn rise to power and prominence. The identity of such people was self-created and was associated with the continental enterprise like foreign trade or money lending and thus anxiety producing. Bacon admits in "Usury" that making a profit is a goal that all men seem to desire even though the desire could appear a "Jewish choice". In an age of expansion and commercial prosperity one who controlled money also controlled the social energy. Deep down, therefore, lay the complex feeling of jealousy and allurement and fear of the self-fashioned Jews or the moneylenders who posed a threat to the social order determined by birth and continuity. The Christians saw how these people contained, controlled and wielded the social energy during the period of transition when the old feudal aristocracy was disintegrating grudgingly yielding place to the new rich mercantile class.

Shakespeare with his keen psychological insight and almost uncanny perception of the contemporary historical forces could clearly see the psychology of Jew-baiting. Through Shylock's speeches he lays bare not only the hypocrisy of the Christians but also the meanness, the inhumanity and the injustice perpetrated by the Christians on the Jews. He, therefore, takes sides. He is with Shylock and the Jews, the oppressed and the injured. But at the same time, howsoever sympathetic he might be towards the Jews, it was not possible for him to come out in the open and give the moral support to Shylock, because the audience in that case would reject the play. So the strategy that he adopts is to raise questions but leave them unanswered and thus create awareness among the auditors about the injustice done to the Jews. Thus when in Act I Scene I, Shylock appeals on his own behalf and on behalf of the race, and reminds Antonio how Antonio treated him like a despised animal, the words have no effect on Antonio who insolently threatens "to spit on thee again, to spurn thee too" (I, iii 126). The reaction of Antonio, his blatantly uncivilized behaviour, shows how impervious he is to the appeals of Shylock. Again, in Act III Scene I when Shylock, in a spirited defence of his stand ("Hath not a Jew eyes...") addresses Solanio and Salarino they do not reply to the Jew although they are otherwise quite vociferous. Shakespeare makes them leave the stage shortly afterwards, and Shylock's address remains unanswered. In fact, the parting remark of Solanio, on seeing Tubal entering ("Here comes another of the tribe: a third cannot be matched, unless the devil himself turn Jew") clearly indicates that Shylock's words have fallen on deaf ears. Even in the Court, in Act IV Scene I, when Shylock sharply points out the inhumanity of the slave trade, his attack on slavery remains unanswered. As the speech ends the Duke passes on to another subject: "Upon my power I may dismiss this Court,/ Unless Bellario, a learned doctor,/ Whom I have sent for to determine this,/ Come here today" (IV, i 104-07). The only possible explanation for all these silences may be that while Shakespeare, the humanist realized that something was seriously wrong with the Christian treatment of the Jews and took sides with the oppressed and the injured and upheld their cause, Shakespeare the dramatist, much too conscious of the contemporary audiences' prejudices against the Jew did not press the point too much lest the play be rejected by the audience. It is this very ambiguity and Shakespeare's ambivalent attitude to the Jewish question that makes Shylock a most complex character: a man of medieval origin putting forward arguments of a more progressive time.

In this connection it is necessary to remember the contribution of Edmund Kean in bringing out the terrible energy of Shylock whom he presented as a man stung to rage and who with sardonic, contemptuous scorn fought to the very last. Even Hazlitt who was in the audience on the first night (26 January 1814) conceded: "Certainly our sympathies are much oftener with him than with his enemies. He is honest in his vices; they are hypocrites in their virtues" (Hazlitt; in J.R. Brown xxxiv). Cowden-Clarke describes how Kean who took the stage by storm on his first appearance delivered the famous speech of Act III Scene I ("Hath not a Jew eyes..."):

> To those who...can remember Edmund Kean's delivery of this superb speech of wild wrath, pleading its claim to some show of justice, there is excitement in recalling the wonderful eyes flashing out their red sparkles, the body wreathing from head to foot, the arm thrown upward as witness to the recorded oath of vengeance. The attitude, as the voice, rose to a sublime climax when these words ("The villainy you teach me as I will execute, and I shall go hard but I will better the instruction" III, i 64-65) were uttered; then there was a drop, both of person and tone, as he hissed out the closing sentence by deep concentrated malignity. (Furness 129)

Shylock's sublime imprecation becomes the most eloquent plea that the human voice has dared to utter for a despised race. Through Kean's powerful acting one could see Shylock as the champion and avenger of his whole shamefully maltreated race. In his tones one could hear the protest crying to heaven, of human rights trodden underfoot. It is a protest against the hypocrisy of his oppressors, and as Francois Victor Hugo observed: "A pound of Antonio's flesh even if obtained could never outweigh, in the scales of reprisal, the millions of corpses heaped in the Christian shambles by a butchery of thirteen centuries" (Furness 128).

The trial in Act IV Scene I is a mockery of justice. The judge who admitted Shylock's right to cut a pound of flesh from the body of Antonio, by that very admission recognized Shylock's right to the blood inseparable from flesh. Furthermore, since he is entitled to one pound he can, if he likes, take less. But both the rights are denied to Shylock. In this connection Ihering's comments are worth quoting:

> And when under the weight of the decision of a judge who nullifies law by a miserable quibble, Shylock succumbs, and the butt of bitter scorn and jeers, totters away with trembling knees, who can help feeling that in his person the law of Venice is broken down, that it is not Shylock the Jew who staggers off but the typical figure of the Jew of the Middle Ages, that pariah of society who cried for law in vain. (Furness 410)

Shylock had a firm faith in law, a faith sustained by the judge himself until "the catastrophe strikes him like a thunderbolt, shivering his delusion to atoms, and teaching him that he is nothing but the despised medieval Jew, whose rights are in the same breath acknowledged, and by fraud, denied" (Furness 410).

Shylock had such a firm faith in law that he can hardly believe that he is receiving fair treatment. When Portia warns,— "if thou dost shed/ One drop of Christian blood, thy lands and goods are by *the laws of Venice* confiscate/ Unto the State of Venice" (IV, i 304-307 emphasis added) a nonplussed and bewildered Shylock asks Portia, "Is that the law?". Portia replies: "Thyself shalt see the act" (IV, i 310) but she never shows it to him. Shylock realizes the elaborate deceit so cunningly played on him, but he is helpless in an alien land and here is Hawkins's account of Kean's rendering of Shylock at the moment of his terrible abasement when the verdict has been passed on him:

> The sudden change of Shylock's whole appearance when the cause turned against him; the happy pause in 'I am —content' as if it almost choked him to bring out the word; the partial bowing down of his inflexible will when he said, 'I pray you give me leave to go from hence, *I am not well*'; the horror of his countenance when told of his enforced conversion to Christianity, and, to crown all, the fine mixture of scorn and pity with which he turned and surveyed the ribald Gratiano,—all exhibited a succession of studies to which words fail to do justice. He retired, as Shakespeare intended he should retire, with the audience possessed in his favour. (Furness 429)

After Kean Shylock has been played with special success by Macready, Charles Kean and Edwin Booth. It must, however, be noted that since the performance of Kean *The Merchant of Venice* has been Shylock's play, and although he appears only in five scenes it is he for whom people remember the play.

It is, however, a profound irony of literary history that in spite of Shakespeare's perceptive criticism of the maltreatment of the Jews by the Christians for centuries, and his presentation of Shylock not as evil by nature but made evil by the treatment to which he and his race have been subjected, Shylock has become a stereotype of a Jew, an embodiment of malignity, avarice, cruelty and inhumanity. To think of a Jew is to think of Shylock whetting his knife for a pound of Christian flesh. It is a strange case where the character does not mirror history but shapes it, and wrongly.

REFERENCES

Berek, P. "The Jew as a Renaissance Man". *Renaissance Quarterly*, (51) 1998, pp. 128-62.

Brown, J.R. "The realization of Shylock—Early Shakespeare". *Stratford-upon-Avon Studies*, 1961.

Cohen, W. "*The Merchant of Venice* and the Possibilities of Historical Criticism". *ELH,* (49) 1982, pp. 765-89.

Fiedler, L.A. *The Stranger in Shakespeare*. St Albany: Paladin, 1974.

Furness, Horace Howard[Ed.] The New Variorum Edition of *The Merchant of Venice*. New York, 1964.

Greenblatt, S. *Shakespearean Negotiations: The Circulation of Energy in Renaissance England*. Berkeley and Los Angeles, 1988.

Gross, J. *Shylock: A Legend and its Legacy*. New York, 1992.

Hazlitt, William. *The Chronicle* (6 April 1816); reprinted in *A View of the English Stage* (1821) pp. 226-27; quoted by John Russell Brown in the Arden edition of *The Merchant of Venice* (London: 1964). Rpt 1972.

Holinshed, Raphael. *History of England* (1577), p. 477. Quoted by W. Moelwyn Merchant ed. *The Merchant of Venice* (New Penguin Shakespeare). (London: Penguin, 1967).

Marlowe, C. *The Jew of Malta* (ed. N.W. Bawcutt). Manchester: The Revel Plays, 1979.

Prior, R. "A Sound Jewish Community in Tudor London". *Transactions of the Jewish Historical Society of England. TJHSE* (31) 1988-1990, pp. 137-52.

Roab, Theodor. "The Stirrings of the 1590s and the Return of the Jews to England". *TJHSE* (26) 1979, pp. 26-33.

Rotti, Cecil. *A History of the Jews in England.* 3rd edition. Oxford, 1964.

Shakespeare, W. *The Merchant of Venice.* (ed. J.L. Halio). Oxford, 1993.

——. *The Merchant of Venice.* (ed. W. Moelwyn Merchant). Harmondshire: Penguin, 1967. pp. 7-17; 61-63.

——. *The Merchant of Venice* . (ed. Bernard Lott). London: Longman (The Swan Shakespeare), 1964. pp. xxii-xxxv.

——. *The Merchant of Venice.* (ed. John Russell Brown). London: Methuen & Co. Ltd., 1964; rpt. 1972 (Arden edition). pp. xxxvii-xlvi.

——. *The Merchant of Venice* (New Variorum edition).

Shapiro, James. "Which is *The Merchant* here and Which is *The Jew*? Shakespeare and the Economics of Influence". *Shakespeare Studies* 20 (1980): 269-79.

Shatzmiller, J. *Shylock Reconsidered: Jews, Moneylending and Medieval Society*. Berkeley, Los Angeles and Oxford, 1990.

Sisson, C.J. "A Colony of Jews in Shakespeare's London". *Essays and Studies* (23) 1938. pp. 38-51.

Warner, George Townsend, C. Henry K. Martin and D. Erskine Muir. *The New Groundwork of British History.* (London: Blackie & Sons Ltd, 1943), p. 123.

Wolf, L. "Jews in Tudor England". *Essays in Jewish History*. London, 1934. pp. 73-90.

3

Shakespeare in Greece: A Study of the Athens Royal Theatre Plays

Maria Kladaki and *George Papantonakis*

Introduction

At the dawn of the 20th century, highly significant historical events and important developments at the economic, social and cultural level have a determining impact on the course of Greece, decisively contributing to its moulding into a modern State. 1897 is a rather clear starting point for processes that brought about changes not only in the operation of the Greek state, but also in the Greek intellectual conscience, as it ushered in a new era for thinking, literature and arts in the country. These times constitute an overall period of transition from tradition to modernist forms of art, which will actually manifest and be thoroughly cultivated in the historical conjuncture of the times that ensued, that is to say the Interwar. The period in question is characterised by the quest for a national point of reference in artistic form as well as the introduction of philosophical, socio-cultural views and art tendencies from Europe which influence in numerous ways the cultural and intellectual pursuits of the time. In essence, European trends are transfused to Greece through adaptations and translations by scholars of the time.

From as early as the period of the modern Greece enlightenment, historical works had been translated under the guidance of Korais, aiming at awakening the nation and boosting patriotic spirit. Subsequently, mostly after the state was established in Athens, we have the first attempts by Greek scholars and theatre people to "speak a national neohellenic drama language and dialect" (Fotopoulos, 2000: 13). As a consequence, in the early 20th century, it appears that the idea ripened to create a state theatre, that would be responsible for laying the foundation of a national dramaturgical tradition, as well as of the art of histrionics which until that time was characterised by amateurism and was largely based on empirical mutual teaching (*allelodidactics*) according to the opinion that the "Deck" (theatre stage) is the "School" of the art of Drama (Fotopoulos, 2000: 13).

It was to this request that King George I responded and, after receiving a 10,000-pound sterling donation from Efstratios Rallis (a Diaspora Greek), decided to build a National Theatre. In 1891, the foundation was laid for the theatre which was built after a design by Ernst Ziller, a German architect well-known from other notable public buildings. In 1900, Angelos Vlachos was appointed general director of the Royal Theatre, and Thomas Oikonomou was appointed stage director. In 1901, the Drama School commenced its operation with Thomas Oikonomou and Aristotelis Kourtidis teaching, while in November of that same year the Royal Theatre opened its doors to the Athenian public.

Royal Theatre Operation and the Role of the Court

The "Royal Theatre" was the first such institution to receive a state subsidy. King George I was essentially its owner and financial manager and also handled all sponsorships. He was in control of the theatre and assumed a leading role both in repertoire selection and in the Royal Theatre's overall mode of operation. A key example of the King's attitude and his propensity for self-promotion as an authority was his decision to put on a play he had written himself for the Royal Theatre's inauguration, in an attempt to place himself in the pantheon of classic European playwrights and categorically refusing to put on plays by modern Greek dramatists, deeming them unworthy of the Royal Theatre's grandeur. Contrary to the Royal Court, the scholars of the time, loyal to the ideals of the Enlightenment concerning national theatres as an institution, were of the opinion that the Royal Theatre should aim at creating national dramaturgy and enlightening the masses. However, this was a dispute won over by the Royal Court, resulting in the Royal Theatre being organised after the model of German Court theatres. In other words, theatre was considered a superior form of art that had to be kept away from the lower social strata.

The absence of a powerful bourgeoisie and the lack of cohesion between the bourgeois and the lower classes favoured the role of the Court, which used the influence of Drama to shape its public guise and consolidate its dominance, by ensuring that a specific theatre style, aesthetics and ideology were preserved (Patsalidis, 2000: 127, 134). The Royal Court used the only "mass communication medium" of the time in order to promote itself as the ideal social and economic model, cultivating conciousness. The participating bourgeois had the illusion of social advancement, as communicants of a spectacle largely directed by the Court. The King would declare the start of the play (Petras, n.d.: 53) and inspect the audience from his box, taking notes on attendance (Andreadis, 1993: 18).

This practice of using theatre as a socialising mechanism that conveys the rules and values of a given society's established class (Tsatsoulis, 1999: 14), had also been applied in the past in other European countries such as France and England (Wiggins, 1996: 26). Just like European theatres of the past, the Athens Royal Theatre presented creations of 'high' drama art like Shakespeare's works, right next to concealed "ideological practices of production and reproduction of these texts as carriers of power and submission" (Drakakis, 1998: 25). In other words, Shakespeare's plays offered themselves as the ideal framework for the Royal Court to accomplish its goals.

Shakespeare on the Royal Theatre Stage

In the eight years of the Royal Theatre's existence, six plays by Shakespeare were put on. This decision was by no means circumstantial; it was due, primarily, to personal choices of King George I, who followed the German model as pertains to the Royal Theatre. Shakespeare had a time-honoured presence on the German stage and was so loved that some (Hauptmann 1915, Fulda 1916) considered him the country's national poet (Hortmann, 1998: 3-4).

Apart from the King himself, another great admirer of Shakespeare's works was the Royal Theatre's German-educated director, Thomas Oikonomou. He was born in Vienna, where he attended the Drama School and assimilated the teachings of the Saxe-Meiningen Company, which played a prominent role in the shaping of directing in Europe in the late 19th century (Fotopoulos, 2000: 14). From his experiences there, it was only logical that he be influenced by the art trends that were established in the German scene with regard to Shakespeare's plays.

Although some scholars of the time—predominantly French culture sympathisers—were of a different opinion, the love for Shakespeare was manifest among the capital's audience, mainly for two reasons: Firstly, because the German model was widespread, while the French one no longer enjoyed the resonance it had during the previous decade (Puchner, 1997: 312); and secondly, due to the fact that according to the spirit of the times as well as the scholars associated with the Royal Theatre, the great classic playwrights of Europe were linked to the Greek nation through ancient Greek drama tradition. Also in Europe, from as early as the 19th century, one can observe a turn to classical antiquity, with a tendency to idealise it. The ancient Greek model was considered the cradle of European civilisation, or the matrix for the creation of all western peoples (Patsalidis, 1997: 121). In order to emphasize this historical continuity with the glorious past and the link between Greece and the advanced countries of the West, the plays selected for the Royal Theatre are the ones that have been put on in European stages—notably those of Germany.

1902 was the first year that a play by Shakespeare was performed on the Royal Theatre's stage. It was the "Midsummer Night's Dream", which would in fact be the most played one, since it was put on eight times, with only minor changes in casting. In 1903, the Royal Theatre featured "The Winter's Tale", which was subsequently put on another two times on site and twice more on tour in Cairo and Alexandria. The following year, it was the turn of the "Twelfth Night; or, What You Will". In 1905, the Royal Theatre features two of Shakespeare's plays: "The Taming of the Shrew" and "Othello". Both plays were put on later that same year in Alexandria during the Royals Theatre's tour. In 1906 we have the first performance on the Royal Theatre's stage of "The Merchant of Venice", a play that was performed again in 1908.

Looking closely at the Royal Theatre's list of plays, it is easy for one to perceive the distinct fondness of both the theatre officials and the audience for "A Midsummer Night's Dream", as well as for "The Winter's Tale". The two plays are characterised by a pronounced folktale motif combined with elements from legends and popular beliefs. So, this preference on behalf of the Royal Theatre in these plays may be interpreted as a return to popular tradition, a trend that was prevailing in Europe at the time. The following of this trend in Greece may not be construed as an opening towards the popular strata but merely as an element of the scenic phantasmagoria that was pleasant to the ownership of the Royal Theatre in terms of spectacle.

Of course, Royal Theatre officials did make an effort to combine what was traditionally Greek with all that was outlandishly European. It is under this scope that one may see the performance of "The Taming of the Shrew", which reflected the model of a patriarchal society and close family ties, thereby appealing to the Greek patriarchal ideology. Moreover, the humorous depiction of the shrew was also something familiar in Greek ethography. The Royal Court's intervention in the presentation of this and other plays by Shakespeare was to emphasise lavishness. Printed matter of the time specifically mentions the stage luxuriousness and wardrobe choices with a propensity to idealise them (Sideris, 1964: 37).

The trend for absolute verisimilitude on stage was utilised by Nikolaos Poriotis, who translated the play into the Demotic language. Although the first ever translation of this play into the simple vernacular added vividness to the stage performance and offered actors new possibilities of expression, it was not received positively by part of the press ("Acropolis" and "Empros") that focused on translator linguistic slips (Sideris, 1964: 37). The view that the *katharevousa* should be the language of choice when translating Shakespeare's plays into Greek enjoyed avid supporters, including the then general director of the Royal Theatre, Angelos Vlachos, who actually translated several works by Shakespeare into the *katharevousa*. As a matter of fact, he opted for his own translation when "Othello" was performed at the Royal Theatre in 1905. His views on using the *katharevousa* in Shakespeare's plays are stoutly outlined in the preamble of his first translation of "Romeo and Juliet". Therein, Vlachos maintains that the *katharevousa* is the most apposite language for translating these plays, since it abides by the rules of elegance, while the Demotic only satisfies the petty desires of the crowd (Shakespeare, 1905: 5-24).

The coexistence of scholarly and demotic language in the translations of Shakespeare's plays, combined with the presence of folktale motifs, myths and popular beliefs in the selection of works, occasionally underlined a lack of coherence in the choices of the Royal Theatre officials. However, the initial experimentation did not impede the use of Shakespeare's works to the benefit of the Royal Theatre's bourgeois audience that was struggling to establish itself by attending these performances and to solidify its identity by utilising the authenticity of popular culture, while at the same time maintaining a clear distance from the people. The unbridled luxuriousness in the stage performance of Shakespearean works was, in essence, an attempt to adapt classic theatre to those who were in power, by transforming these plays into a spectacle for a very specific social elite, which was using theatre as a means to consolidate its social status (Sinfield, 1998: 804-26; Žižek, 1998: 312-25). The bourgeois audience of Athens was very fond of attending the Royal Theatre's performances, without realising that drama—

through its aesthetic components and the power of imagery—can actually control the spectators and manipulate the audience (Styan, 1975: 4), or that it intrinsically constituted the Royal Court's means of power control.

It may be that the promotion of wealth and glamour through the luxuriousness of phantasmagorical sets and wardrobes was considered a key criterion in the success of a play (Sideris, 1990 Vol. A: 247), but what it actually served was the purposes of its ownership, the Royal Court, as it solidified the latter's economic supremacy over the bourgeois and the working classes, and underpinned the social struggle between the levels of bourgeoisie, by urging them to attend spectacles that would bestow prestige upon them and confirm their very bourgeois identity. The audience identified itself through its participation in such performances, which are the mirror of the society that produces them (Tatsoulis, 1999: 14).

Even the Royal Theatre's architecture accentuated social stratification and emphasised the prestige of the Royal Court. The pompous character of the building's exterior; its internal décor with the ornate ceiling artwork and the two velvet curtains with the gold embroidery (Fessa-Emmanouil, 1994: 309, 313); its capacity of about a thousand people; the clear seat/class distinction, all made it perfectly clear that there was no chance for its operation to be class-free. Besides, the Royal Court's unwritten rules only allowed a particular audience to attend the performances, thereby ensuring the King's favour. More to the point, the specific repertoire that excluded plays by modern Greek playwrights, the highly expensive (for its time) ticket and the requirement for formal attire dissipated any possibility for people from lower or working classes to see the performances. The social composition and luxurious apparel of the Royal Theatre audience was commented on by newspapers of the time (Sideris, 1964: V 35-46), while at the same time extensively referring to the performances' stage grandeur and opulence.

Indeed, the country's first theatre stage was particularly favoured, both in terms of luxury and material-technical support. The copious state subsidy allowed for extensive theatre maintenance and modernisation expenses (Fessa-Emmanouil,

1994: 303). All stage and theatre equipment was made to order from abroad, as was the wardrobe. From contemporary sources ("Acropolis" newspaper) one learns that the costumes for "A Midsummer Night's Dream" were ordered from in Vienna and cost one-third (1/3) of the total box-office receipts for the year 1902-1903 (Sideris, 1964: V 26-37). These costumes that were originally made for the Imperial Theatre of Vienna, the lighting and the music score that was a direct reference to European choices, all attested to the high level of stage organisation and were all conducive to a false sense of proximity to the West.

The state-of-the-art mechanical stage equipment that was (also) ordered in Vienna was akin to that used in the best German theatres. This equipment was first used in 1902, in the first performance of Shakespeare and played a decisive role in the luxurious and ingenious stage presentation of the play, earning them dithyrambic reviews (Xenopoulos, 1903: 2). The use of imported equipment, combined with the bonds of the Royal Theatre officials with Germany, created for the public the illusion of partaking in the practices of Europe and of being in direct contact with Western countries that served as points of reference on issues of national identity.

Shakespeare's Plays and the Creation of a New National Identity in Greece

Shakespeare's performances in Greece may be seen in the light of the country's agonising struggle to build a new national and bourgeois identity, which was based on uncritical copying of practices applied in Europe. The audience of the Royal Theatre was seeking its own identity within that phantasmagorical ambience; it was looking for points of convergence with the western model, so as to receive social recognition and feel self-justified, as participation in such events not only bestowed social status upon the partakers but also contributed in their being classified as "cultured persons" (Margolies, 51). The theatrical environment itself and the utilisation of works by the English poet in their entirety played their role in solidifying the idea in Greece that Shakespeare's plays are the exclusive privilege of the bourgeoisie.

Athens was not alone in using Shakespeare's works to help pass messages of a certain social or political ideology. The great English poet's plays contributed to the formation of national and literary traditions in many European countries (Shurbanov *et al.,* 2001: 13). Particularly in Greece, the efforts of the Royal Theatre's officials as well as of scholars of the time, were focused on the attempt to create a new national literary identity, one that would be directly linked to the country's historical past (Grammatas, 2002: 199). However, the difficult financial conjuncture and the lack of ideological cohesion in early 20th century Greece did not favour the correlation with the country's celebrated past. Consequently, the choices made by the Royal Theatre's officials were within the framework of their effort to make their artistic presence felt in European circles by convincing themselves and the others that they can in fact be worthy successors of a glorious past.

The Royal Theatre was considered the symbol of not just the creation of a new bourgeoisie, but also of the evolution of Greece from being a small nation, subjugated for centuries by the Ottoman Empire, to a geographically and socially new state that usurped Western practices, abhorring Eastern influence. The very presence of the English poet lent prestige to the country's official stage, as well as to the audience attending its performances. Nevertheless, this audience that comprised neo-bourgeois, could not comprehend that simply copying a foreign model—let alone one that comes at a high cost—alienates rather than helps its self-determination. And this was indeed the case, as the historical and social conditions in Greece at the time were entirely different to those in Europe, resulting in the imported drama practices not being assimilated by Greece within the framework of a cultural exchange that would enrich the indigenous cultural elements. On the contrary, these practices emerged as an externally imposed new ideal that in effect ostracised the local theatrical tradition. Gourgouris aptly describes this phenomenon as 'the colonisation of the ideal' in an attempt to state that Greece became trapped in the model that the West imposed on her. As a matter of fact, he compares the history of Greece to that of India, saying that "there is actually a point where the story of India and the story of Greece coincide. Both are burdened with a classical past, a similar trap for the nationalist phantasm: modern malaise to be overcome and ancient glory to be regained… . And in both cases, though in decidedly different ways, the trap is fed by Europe's own self-serving and autoscopic investment—*self-serving because autoscopic*" (Gourgouris, 1996: 6).

The Royal Court also played the role of the torchbearer of Western theatrical practices to Greece, unconcerned with whether such innovations would be assimilated and spur the revival of Greek dramaturgy. On the contrary, they used theatre to accentuate social stratification by addressing purely a small group that constituted a social 'elite', which followed the ideology of the Royal family, maintaining that Shakespeare represents high drama art, which in turn is distant from everyday life and its problems, and symbolises a spectacle that not all are capable of understanding and observing,—only the few chosen ones (Patsalidis, 1997: 225-26).

However, the Royal Theatre's hegemonic character and the deliberately luxurious performances of Shakespeare trapped the bourgeoisie as well, just as it was beginning to take shape in Greece. The bourgeois, in their effort to remain participants of the Royal Theatre's events and gain the King's favour, assumed the role of passive receivers, missing their opportunity to make their presence felt in a dynamic manner and claim substantial power in the political activities of the Athenian society. In other words, each spectator would see their participation in all that was theatrical as a means to promote themselves, thereby dissipating any and all possibility for a collective reaction (Patsalidis, 1997: 222).

The Royal Theatre suspended its operation indefinitely in 1908, after seven years. It was replaced—much later—by the 'Greek National Theatre', which was established in 1930. There is no doubt that the Royal Theatre not only made known the work of the great English poet in Greece, but it was the first official state entity to put on technically and artistically impeccable performances of Shakespeare, contributing decisively to the course of his plays and greatly influencing the way in which these plays were presented and received in Greece from the early 20th century onwards.

Naturally, the ruling class of the time did not leave Shakespeare's work separated from the period's political and socio-economic components. On the contrary, it attached to this work a purely political message in favour of the incontestable superiority of the Royal family, as well as a class message in favour of the established class. Moreover, its conveyance from the West without the slightest intention on behalf of the royal Theatres' officials and headship to have it assimilated, facilitated even further the objective of the aforementioned headship that was to keep theatre away from the lower social classes. This is how the system of values was built that served as the foundation on which Shakespeare subsequent stage presence was largely based.

Shakespeare's Plays at the Royal Theatre

PLAY	YEAR
A Midsummer Night's Dream Directed by Th. Oikonomou	1902
A Midsummer Night's Dream (repeat of the play with casting changes) Directed by Th. Oikonomou	1903
The Winter's Tale Adapted by F. Dingelstedt Directed by Th. Oikonomou	1903
Twelfth Night; or, *What You Will* Directed by Th. Oikonomou	1904
A Midsummer Night's Dream (repeat of the previous year's performance) Directed by Th. Oikonomou	1904
The Winter's Tale (repeat of the play with casting changes) Directed by Th. Oikonomou	1904

The Taming of the Shrew Directed by Th. Oikonomou	1905
Othello Directed by Th. Oikonomou	1905
A Midsummer Night's Dream (repeat of the 1903 performance with cast changes) Directed by Th. Oikonomou	1905
A Midsummer Night's Dream Starring: M. Kotopouli and E. Fürst	1905
The Winter's Tale (repeat of the 1903 show with casting changes) Directed by Th. Oikonomou	1905
The Merchant of Venice Directed by Th. Oikonomou	1906
A Midsummer Night's Dream (repeat of the 1902 performance with cast changes) Directed by Th. Oikonomou	1906
A Midsummer Night's Dream (repeat of the 1902 performance with cast changes) Directed by Th. Oikonomou	1907
The Merchant of Venice (repeat of the 1906 performance with cast changes) Directed by Th. Oikonomou	1908
A Midsummer Night's Dream (repeat of the 1902 performance with cast changes) Directed by Th. Oikonomou	1908

The Royal Theatre Performing Shakespeare on Tour

PLAY	CITY	YEAR
The Winter's Tale Directed by Th. Oikonomou	Cairo	1904
The Winter's Tale Directed by Th. Oikonomou	Alexandria	1904
The Taming of the Shrew Directed by Th. Oikonomou	Alexandria	1905
Othello Directed by Th. Oikonomou	Alexandria	1905

REFERENCES

Andreadis, A.M. *The Royal Theatre (1901-1908)*. Athens: D.N. Tzakas, S. Delagrammatikas & Co., 1993. Greek: Ανδρεάδης Α.Μ. Το *Βασιλικόν Θέατρον (1901-1908)*. Αθήνα: Δ.Ν. Τζάκας, Σ. Δελαγραμμάτικας και Σία, 1993.

Drakakis, Georgios. "Theatre, ideology and institution: Shakespeare and the road-sweepers". *The Shakespeare myth*. Ed. Graham Holderness, Manchester: Manchester University Press, 1988.

Fessa-Emmanouil, Eleni. *The architecture of modern Greek theatre 1720-1940*. Vols. A, B. Athens, 1994. Greek: Φέσσα– Εμμανουήλ, Ελένη. *Η αρχιτεκτονική του νεοελληνικού θεάτρου 1720-1940*. Τόμ. Α, Β. Αθήνα, 1994.

Fotopoulos, Vassilis. *National Theatre 100 years*. Athens: Latsis Group, 2000. Greek: Φωτόπουλος, Βασίλης. *Εθνικό Θέατρο 100 χρόνια*. Αθήνα: Latsis Group, 2000.

Fulda, Ludwig. *Deutsche kultur und Ausla?nderei*. Leipzig: S. Hirzel, 1916.

Grammatas, Theodoros. *The Greek Theatre in the 20th Century. Cultural Models and Originality*. Vols. A-B. Athens: Exantas. 2002. Greek: Γραμματάς, Θεόδωρος. *Το ελληνικό θέατρο στον 20° αιώνα. Πολιτισμικά πρότυπα και πρωτοτυπία.* Τόμ. Α–Β. Αθήνα: Εξάντας. 2002.

Gourgouris, Stathis. *Dream nation. Enlightenment, colonization and the institution of modern Greece*. Stanford: Stanford University Press, 1996.

Hauptmann, Gerhart. "Deutschland und Shakespeare" in *Shakespeare Jahrbuch* 51 (1915): vii-xii.

Hortmann, Wilhelm. *Shakespeare on the German Stage: volume 2, the twentieth century*. Cambridge: Cambridge University Press, 1998.

Margolies, D. "Teaching the handsaw to fly: Shakespeare as a hegemonic instrument". *The Shakespeare Myth*. Ed. Graham Holderness, Manchester: Manchester University Press, 1998. 42-53.

Patsalidis, Savvas. "Tensions and Dimensions". *Greek tragedy and the theory of the twentieth century*. Athens: Theatriki Paideia, Typothito, 1997. Greek: Πατσίδης, Σάββας. *(Ευ)τάσειςκαι (Δια)στάσεις. Η ελληνική τραγωδία και η θεωρία του εικοστού αιώνα.* Αθήνα: θεατρική παιδεία, Τυπωθήτω, 1997.

Patsalidis, Savvas. *Theatre and Theory. On (sub)text and (inter)text.* Thessaloniki: University Studio Press, 2000. Greek: Πατσαλίδης, Σάββας. *Θέατρο και Θεωρία. Περί (υπο)κειμένων και (δια)κειμένων.* Θεσσαλονίκη: University Studio Press, 2000.

Petras, Sotos. *Old Athens theatres and actors*, S. Petras Theatre Archives. Greek: Πετράς. Σώτος. *Θέατρα και Θεατρίνοι της Παλιάς Αθήνας,* Θεατρικά Αρχεία Σ. Πετρά.

Puchner, Walter. Texts and Objects. Ten essays on theatrology. Athens: Καστανιώτης, 1997. Greek: Puchner, Walter. *Κείμενα και Αντικείμενα. Δέκα θεατρολογικά μελετήματα.* Αθήνα: Καστανιώτης, 1997.

Shakespeare, William. *Shakespeare's Masterpieces: Romeo and Juliet, Hamlet, Othello, King Lear, Macbeth.* rhyming translation by Angelos Vlachos. Athens, 1905. Greek: Shakespeare, William. *Σακεσπείρου Αριστουργήματα: Ρωμαίος και Ιουλία, Άμλετ, Οθέλλος, Βασιλεύς Ληρ, Μάκβεθ.* κατ' έμμετρον μετάφρασιν Αγγέλου Βλάχου. Αθήνα, 1905.

Shakespeare, William. *A Midsummer Night's Dream.* Translated by Georgios Stratigis. All my life. Athens, 1910. Greek: Shakespeare, William. *Όνειρο θερινής νυκτός.* Μτφ. Γεώργιιος Στρατήγης. Όλη μου η ζωή. Αθήνα, 1910.

Shakespeare, William. *The Merchant of Venice.* Translated by Alexandros Pallis. Athens: Typografeio tis Estias, 1894. Greek: Shakespeare, William. *Ο έμπορος της Βενετίας.* Μτφ. Αλέξανδρος Πάλλης. Αθήνα: Τυπογραφείο της Εστίας, 1894.

Shakespeare, William. *The Tragedy of Othello, the Moor of Venice.* Translated by Konstantinos Theotokis. Athens: G. Vassiliou, 1915. Greek: Shakespeare, William. *Ο Οθέλλος, ο μαύπος της Βενετίας.* Μτφ Κων/νος Θεοτόκης. Αθήνα: Γ. Βασιλείου, 1915.

Shakespeare, William. *The Taming of the Shrew*. Translated by Nikolaos Poriotis. Athens: Govostis, 1938. Greek: Shakespeare, William. Το ημέρωμα της στρίγγλας. Μρφ. ΝικόλαοςΠοριώτης. Αθήνα: Γκοβόστης, 1938.

Shakespeare, William. *Twelfth Night*. Translated by Vassilis Rotas, Athens: Vivliopoleion tis Estias, 1938. Greek: Shakespeare, William. Δωδέκατη νύχτα. Μτφ. Βασίλης Ρώτας, Αθήνα: Βιβλιοπωλείο της Εστίας, 1938.

Sideris, Yiannis. "Shakespeare in Greece. Directors and performers in the 20th century: V". *Theatre. Bimonthly Drama Review* Sep.-Oct. 1964: 35-46. Greek: Σιδέρης, Γιάννης. <<Ο Σαίξπηρ στην Ελλάδα. Σκηνοθέτες και ερμηνευτές στον Κ' αιώνα: V>>. *Θέατρο. Δίμηνη Θεατρική Επιθεώρηση* Σεπτ.–Οκτ. 1964: 35-46.

Sideris, Yiannis. *History of the New Greek Theatre 1794-1944*. Vol. A. Athens: Kastaniotis, 1990. Greek: Σιδέπης, Γιάννης. *Ιστορία του νέου ελληνικού θεάτρου 1794-1944*. Τόμ. Α. Αθήνα: Καστανιώτης, 1990.

Shurbanov, Alexander & Boika Sokolova. *Painting Shakespeare red. An east European appropriation*. London: University of Delaware Press, Newark-Associated University Press, 2001.

Sinfield, Alan. "Cultural materialism, *Othello*, and the politics of plausibility". *Literary Theory: An Anthology*. Ed. Julie Rivkin, Michael Ryan. Oxford: Blackwell, 1998. 804-26.

Styan, John Lewis. *Drama, stage and audience*. London: Cambridge University Press, 1975.

Tsatsoulis, Dimitris. *Semantic approaches of the drama phenomenon*. thens: Ellinika Grammata, 1999. Greek: Τσατσούλης, Δημήτρης. *Σημειολογικές προσεγγίσεις του θεατρικού φαινομένου*. Αθήνα: Ελληνικά Γράμματα, 1999.

Wiggins, Martin. "The King's men and after. King and Parliament". Shakespeare: An illustrated stage history. Ed. Jonathan Bate, Russell Jackson. Oxford: Oxford University Press, 1996. 23-44.

Xenopoulos, Grigorios. "Review for 'A Midsummer Night's Dream', directed by Thomas Oikonomou". *Panathinea* 15 December 1903: 2. Greek: Ξενόπουλος, Γρηγόριος. <<Κριτικήγια το 'Όνειρο Θερινής Νυκτό', σκηνοθεσιας Θωμά Οικονόμου>>. *Παναθήναια* 15 Δεκέμβριος 1903: 2.

Žižek, Slavoj. "The sublime object of ideology". *Literary theory: An Anthology*. Ed. Julie Rivkin, Michael Ryan. Oxford: Blackwell, 1998. 312-25.

4

William Shakespeare on Womanhood and Motherhood

Chiara Biscella

Critics have always insisted on the relative absence of maternal figures in Shakespearean drama. This is to a certain extent, true: either maternal characters are completely absent from Shakespeare's plays, or instead they are strongly unconventional, sometimes even bordering on monstrosity. If this may be interpreted as Shakespeare's way of supporting male authority, it can also be seen as a means to disrupt the feminine stereotypes of docility and submission. Shakespeare's heroines, and Shakespeare's mothers among them, are indeed presented in a complex light and in their darker aspects, but also in their forceful opposition to a tightly-defined patriarchal system: being portrayed and looked at from a different angle, they thus acquire new strength and energy. Thus, although Shakespearean drama is never filled with maternal figures and mothers often remain on the margins of the plays, still Shakespeare, writing in a period, so full of contradictions as far as the condition of women was concerned, manages to hint at the important issues of femininity and motherhood, and to investigate the connection between women and power, even hinting, perhaps, at the necessity for women to develop a voice of their own.

Through a brief analysis of the condition of women in Renaissance England and of the Shakespearean ways to depict womanhood in his historical play Richard III, I intend to cast a light on all these aspects, showing how Shakespeare's portrayal of women is far from being stereotypical. Rather than describing submissive wives and mothers, Shakespeare seems to insist on women's liberty of thought and speech, thus offering today's women writers a vast heritage of crucial themes and concerns to consider and in some cases appropriate: as I will illustrate in the last part of this essay, recent works like Angela Carter's *Wise Children* (1991), and A.S. Byatt's *The Children's Book* (2009) find in Shakespearean drama a starting point to develop their own discourse on gender: concentrating on two fundamental, significant periods in the history of the "weaker sex", they both explore and interrogate the role of women—and of mothers—in society. Shakespeare's women hold a mirror to their modern descendants.

Beyond Renaissance Stereotypes

Fathers, either alive or dead, are always to the fore in Shakespearean drama, while maternal characters are, on the contrary, either relegated to secondary roles or completely absent. Such paucity of maternal figures has originated a certain reaction among feminist scholars, often focusing merely on women and on their conditions in history. Feminist critics, attaching a great significance to the issues of the numerical unbalance between Shakespeare's fathers and mothers, and underlining the important role that fathers play in Shakespearean drama, have indeed connected Shakespeare's paternal figures to the question of authorship. As Kate Webb writes: "It is this forever unresolved uncertainty about their role in biological creativity that has led men to create a mystique around artistic, and especially literary, creativity: ... the anxiety of paternity is translated into the anxiety of authorship" (Webb 300). If mothers, and women more in general, have always been linked to their capacity of giving life, men to a certain extent interpreted this same capacity exploring the possibility of writing, of freely expressing their opinions through the works they published, thus also managing to maintain their power over women.

However, such radical considerations somehow sound partial: it is true that in Renaissance England wives were still submitted to their husbands' authority and lacked economical independence; nevertheless, it must not be forgotten that it was precisely in this historical period that women slowly started their process of emancipation. As a matter of fact the economical, social and religious changes that characterized the English Renaissance could not but partially influence and modify the condition of women. Socially, the English middle class was expanding, because the quickly-changing economical condition of England had resulted in an increase of the number of craftsmen and tradesmen. Women, however, were mainly left out of public life to be instead confined to their roles of mothers and wives in the private, protected space of the house. If, from a religious point of view, the Reformation contributed to spread the stereotype of the silent and docile woman, whose virtues would guarantee the honour and the stability of the family, from a social and cultural perspective it promoted feminine literacy and supported egalitarianism between the two sexes, who were both given the right to read and interpret the Scriptures.

According to Tina Krontiris, Women did apparently exploit the contradictions in Protestant ideologies as well as the unsettlement of the religious situation itself. First, religion could be used by women as a permission to speak... . In the name of the word of God, women could and did claim their right to speak independently from men. They wrote, translated and published many religious works... . Religion gave them a legitimate voice and an opportunity to be heard. Telling about God's word became a sign of breaking the silence and often of disagreeing with men (Krontiris 10).

Religion remained however the main domain of women's expression in England. Appearing in print still meant, for a woman, to expose herself in public, which was considered highly immoral and inconvenient. Furthermore, a woman who desired to have her work published was perceived as sinning of presumption, since authorship had always been seen as a male prerogative. Therefore, the slow beginning of women emancipation as writers, which saw the publication of works by

Mary Wroth, Elizabeth Cary, Margaret Tyler among others, went hand in hand with an increase of pamphlets written by men and directed against such aspirations: reformers, who had at first promoted equality between men and women, were now afraid of losing control over the so-called weaker sex, whose strength was instead growing.

To complicate matters further, it must not be forgotten that Shakespeare's England was experiencing a peculiar situation, since it was a woman, Elizabeth I, who was sitting on the throne. Her role as head of the state and of the church was intensely problematic and paradoxical. If on the one hand, her femininity was strongly emphasized by a series of effective symbols and images (she was Astrea, Cynthia, and the Virgin Mary, these all mythological and biblical references that underlined her divine status), on the other, her potential masculinity was implicitly suggested by a number of epithets and emblems (one of which was the phoenix, the mythical bird associated to the masculine virtues of activity, vigour, and generative force). Moreover, Elizabeth did not hesitate to call herself prince, or even king, preferring these masculine designations to the more feminine and indeed more adequate attribute of queen. Elizabeth, the most powerful woman in England, was herself somehow split between a manifest femininity and a hidden, yet probably necessary, maleness. Renaissance England, as indeed Renaissance Europe, was an extremely paradoxical period for women: their struggle for emancipation was only moving its first, difficult and definitely unstable steps.

Richard III: Women Against

In a period during which the condition of women was marked by far-reaching contradictions, how did Shakespeare represent female characters? In Richard III, a play which was supposed to celebrate Elizabeth I through her ancestor Henry VII, the gallery of women is indeed rich and varied. Although the female characters of the play all belong to the aristocracy and gravitate around the court, Shakespeare depicts them first and foremost in their position of mothers, wives, and widows; if these women have lost their crown, even more their suffering is deeply rooted in the loss of their husbands and children. Characterized by constant ambiguity, their behaviour and language inevitably adds a layer of disturbance and discomfort to an already profoundly disquieting play.

It is common knowledge that Shakespeare's Richard III stages an exasperation of hatred, conflict and violence. The play describes a world dominated by appetites and fear, articulated by vicious plots, killings and bloodsheds so as to be almost unbelievable and unbearable. Strangely, its female characters are far from having a positive and reassuring role: they are indeed shown as contributing to the chaotic emotional and political condition of the whole play, as it is attested with their sometimes insane and always perverse relationship with Richard himself. Notwithstanding the repugnance they feel towards him, all these women in some ways contribute to his evil scheming: if Margaret, although always coherent in cursing him, does in fact nothing to prevent his abominable acts; even more shocking are the behaviours of Lady Anne and queen Elizabeth. The former, who is shown at the beginning of the play as she insults Richard for his 'flattering' proposal of marriage, is in fact later on depicted while preparing for the ceremony that, at Westminster, will make her his wife; although cursing her very self and crying over her destiny, Lady Anne is cast in the oxymoronic part of the widow who accepts to marry the man who had killed both her father-in-law and her own husband. Elizabeth, too, has all the reasons to hate Richard, as she herself tells him when he asks her the hand of her daughter:

> Send to her, by the man that slew her brothers,
> A pair of bleeding hearts; thereon engrave
> Edward and York; then haply she will weep:
> Therefore present to her,—as sometimes Margaret
> Did to thy father, steep'd in Rutland's blood,
>
> A handkerchief; which, say to her, did drain
> The purple sap from her sweet brother's body,
> And bid her dry her weeping eyes therewith.
> If this inducement force her not to love,

Send her a story of thy noble acts;
Tell her thou madest away her uncle Clarence,
Her uncle Rivers; yea, and for her sake,
Madest quick conveyance with her good aunt Anne.
(Richard III, 4.4)

Yet, surprisingly, distressingly, and notwithstanding such heated words, Elizabeth consents to the marriage between Richard and her daughter. Shakespeare's Richard III thus portrays the duke of Gloucester both as a centripetal and a centrifugal force: all the women in the play are at the same time attracted and scared by him; they know that he is evil and wicked, yet they are seduced by his alternating love promises and blackmailing menaces. The female characters seem to be truly animated by a sadomasochistic attitude that, persisting from the very beginning to the very end of the play, contributes not only to render Richard all the more unsettling, in spite or perhaps in virtue of his deformed and apparently unattractive figure, but also to make of the four women some extremely problematic characters, projecting them beyond any possible existing stereotype.

However, it must not be forgotten that these women, while they yield to persuasion in the end, still remain the only characters daring to directly oppose, by strength of words only, and from the very beginning of the play, the tyranny and the cruelty of the Duke of Gloucester. The historical drama thus triggers a deep and constant tension, rooted in the contrast between the women's actions on one hand and their language on the other. If their acts testify to their powerlessness and status as subjects inevitably driven to obedience, their words tend in the opposite direction: women are literally empowered by the verbal intensity of their resistance, a fact that also enhances their dramatic presence. As Kristin M. Smith wrote, the women's "linguistic command is an indicator of their transgressive behaviour" and indeed the symbol of a "(de)generative power" (Smith 144). Through words, women curse Richard and foretell his defeat; they somehow labour for the end of Gloucester's reign and help shape a new, different and more peaceful era for England. The most interesting aspect of the powerful means of expression practicsed by Shakespeare's women in Richard III, namely prophecy and curse, is that they are utterly feminine. Phyllis Mack clearly distinguishes the characteristics of male and female discourse, stating that:

> The kind of power associated with the social and political sphere, which was at least formally dominated by men, was power exercised in daylight: self-willed, rational, organized, and generally obvious. The kind of power associated with the spiritual realm, in which women often predominated, was...of a very different sort. Spiritual power infused and energized the body, it was polymorphous and morally ambiguous, either godly or demonic (Mack 45).

Thus, if Richard's discourse is political but also rhetorical, and consequently masculine in its convincing rationality, the voices of the women deploy on the contrary a deeply feminine energy: these feminine voices are spontaneous, instinctive, impetuous; they lack restraint but are instead the stark abrupt product of long-life sufferings, the genuine expression of anger, pain and rancour. They are voices that, imbued as they are with wrath and resentment, turn into "nonrational, non-cerebral, cryptic" utterances (Jardine 114). Women, deprived of political power, are compelled to show obedience and conformity; yet, they still possess freedom of thought and of speech, and they know how to use it. Exactly as it happened in Renaissance England, the language of women becomes their unique means to cry out their own truth, express their real feelings and even manifest their independence, albeit a fragile one. As Phyllis Mack writes,

> The common scold, the witch, the prophet, and the fine lady also shared a reliance on the power of words, rather than pens or swords, to make their wishes and ideas felt in a culture where the instrumental power of lustful or angry words or "heated speech" was perceived far greater than it is today (Mack 30).

Elizabethan audiences, accustomed to episodes of prophecy and witchcraft, could not miss the effect and the meaning of such "heated speech". Even more so if we consider that the disruptive voices of the four women, and Margaret's indisputably above all others, resonate throughout the whole length of the dramatic action. The women's curses, their bitter cries and their revengeful words indeed seem to constitute the sombre musical theme of the play.

> Richard: Foul wrinkled witch, what mak'st thou in my sight?
> Margaret: But repetition of what thou hast marr'd:
> That will I make, before I let thee go. (Richard III, 3.5)

Repetition is precisely what characterizes Margaret's and all the women's speeches: so, as the epithets devil, villain, slave, dog, regularly run across the play and become its violent refrain, the names of all the people Richard has killed are also continuously, almost ritually, evoked, as exemplified by the following lines:

> Margaret: I had an Edward, till a Richard kill'd him;
> I had a Harry, till a Richard kill'd him:
> Thoud hadst an Edward, till a Richard kill'd him:
> Thou hadst a Richard, till a Richard kill'd him.
> (Richard III, 4.4)

The repeated anaphora and Richard's name towering above the others, not only gives Margaret's voice a strong incantatory power, but concocts a musical partition that ominously defines the murderous course of the Duke of Gloucester's life. Inscribing in his play, and through the voice of its female characters, a powerfully anaphoric and rhythmic pattern of words, Shakespeare creates a real and effective alternative not only to Richard's dominant discourse, but also, and most importantly, to his sterile and wicked patriarchal system.

From Shakespeare to Contemporary Women Narrative

The women of Richard III (but this is true for many other Shakespearean heroines) definitely embody and give voice to a period shaken by a series of turbulences; a period in which cracks and fissures started to appear in the mechanisms of social, political and cultural control; a period, finally, that saw the condition of women change and evolve. No longer merely confined to the silent space of the house, women began to feel (and to feed) the need of expressing their ideas, of publishing their works, of participating in the political and economical life of Renaissance England, a nation that identified with the powerful and somehow androgynous body of Elizabeth I. Our contemporary epoch is similarly an age of turmoil, an age that still has not found answers to the many questions concerning the condition of women, even though they have achieved many a conquest. Women's submission to a masculine, patriarchal authority still appears to be the norm in various cultures, from the Middle-East to many European or African countries; the drama of the violence on women is far from being solved, and debates concerning the lack of equality between men and women —both in politics and in the workplace—are still extremely relevant.

It is thus not a coincidence that contemporary women writers often cast women and mothers at the very centre of their narratives, nor is it a coincidence that they look back at Shakespeare to trigger and problematize their discourse on emancipation and motherhood. The novels, *Wise Children* by Angela Carter, and *The Children's Book* by Antonia Susan Byatt can indeed be taken as examples: not only are they replenished with Shakespearean allusions (Shakespearean names, characters and quotations continuously crop up; Shakespearean plays are described, discussed and even staged by the characters; Shakespearean locations invade the narratives) but they are also set in two extremely intense periods of the history of Western women which marked important steps on the road towards female emancipation. Brimming with Titanias and Sycoraxes, staging Imogens, Hermiones or even Lady Macbethes, Byatt's and Carter's novels portray a violent and unexpected collision between Shakespeare's women struggling for a voice and an identity, and the contemporary culture and concerns of feminism.

The events narrated in Angela Carter's novel and gravitating around the two identical twins—Dora and Nora—take place between the First World War and the protagonists' 75th birthday, thus somewhere around the Nineties decades in which the condition of women was deeply altered. If the Suffragette Movement and with it the struggle for women emancipation had started well before the First World War, it was precisely during the war, with men at the front, that the role of women became crucial and that their economic importance was for the first time openly recognized; the war thus probably accelerated a process of emancipation that finally culminated with the universal suffrage of 1928. From that moment on, the condition of women began to change at a faster pace: women started to work, and not only in the extraordinary event of a war; the female branch of the British Army was formed; fashion started to change, bringing about shorter skirts and bikinis. In less than thirty years, the feminine condition had gone through a huge evolution; however, although the elements of liberation were many; and women were becoming new agents in the British economy and social life, their struggle for equality was not over.

Thus, in the Sixties and the Seventies, a new feminist wave spread throughout the United Kingdom and the United States of America, mostly articulated by the Women's Liberation Movement. Its members wanted to obtain equal pay, equal education and job opportunities, free contraception and abortion and free 24-hours help for baby-care; they founded the Women's Liberation Workshop and massively entered the publishing world. In the United Kingdom, the movement was not unsuccessful: the Equal Pay Act was passed in 1970, the Sex Discrimination Act in 1975 and the Domestic Violence Act in 1976; in 1974, what is more, the Women's Aid Federation was formed in order to support women and children suffering from domestic violence. Angela Carter's novel is somehow framed, through Dora and Nora's lives and careers as music-hall singers and dancers, by a time-span that, as far as the condition of women is concerned, can be considered extraordinary. Proud of their economic and professional independence, open-minded about love and sexuality, not ashamed of displaying their body but on the contrary using it to state their freedom and their liberation from a male-dominated society, the twin sisters definitely symbolize the emancipation of women. With them, Angela Carter ironically and lightly brings back to life years of struggles and conquests, a whole historical period that she herself lived as a committed feminist intellectual.

Antonia Byatt also entrusts her reflection on women mainly to the principal character of her novel: Olive Wellwood. Indeed, she is the real breadwinner of the family, managing to support her sister, children and husband even when this one decides to leave his job at the bank. As the narrator easily makes clear, Olive is extremely proud of her condition:

Olive resumed her unbuttoning. She stepped out of her underwear. "I shall write harder. I am doing better than adequately. I shall work harder." "You like that idea. The woman as breadwinner." "I do like it, yes. We both do, I think" (Byatt 67).

She is all the more so when she discovers that her husband has had an affair with a woman from Manchester, Marianne, who is got pregnant and who consequently expects to receive financial help for the baby. Even in this case, it is Olive who has to take control of the situation, giving her husband the money he needs and thus powerfully asserting, somehow, her own superiority over him:

> She took a curious pleasure in the power of independence when she gave him a cheque to meet the Manchester bills. You did not so much mind being—conventionally—betrayed, if you were not to be kept in the dark, which was humiliating, or defined only as a wife and dependent person, which was annihilating. (Byatt 178)

Associating a strong derogatory meaning to the word 'wife', Olive defines herself as an independent person, who earns her own money and chooses what to do with it. In this way, she is neither submitted to nor financially dependent on the traditional role of a husband who brings the salary home and runs the economy of the family. For Olive Wellwood, having a job, and a creative one for that matter, is not only a source of self-satisfaction, but something that defines her whole identity: she is not simply a wife, nor is she merely the "angel of the house"; her presence is not a silent one, nor does she spend her days confined in the nursery; indeed, if she did not have her profession she would not feel a complete human being: she is a wife and a mother, but she is first of all the author of tales for children. If Olive is definitely a driving force of the text, Byatt's novel is full of working women: from Philip's mother, who dies because of the unhealthy condition in which she had to work, to Marianne Oakwood, who earns a living by teaching in schools, to Elsie Warren, who slowly becomes conscious of the importance of getting an education, many are the figures of women whose salary is very often the sole income of the family. What is more, since the ideals of the Fabian Society are discussed in the novel, themes such as the equality between man and woman, the importance of education and the necessity to guarantee equal rights to all social classes come often to the fore. Staging various working women belonging to different social classes and each having to deal with different kind of problems on one hand, on the other discussing the matter from a theoretical and ideological point of view, Byatt moves from the particular to the general and from real life to abstraction, indeed offering the full size and full life picture of an age whose ideas and political fights contributed to shape the contemporary world.

If the women of Shakespeare's Richard III contrasted the tyranny of the evil Duke with the mere force of words and the vindication of their freedom of thought, women in Carter and Byatt are the reflection of years of struggles for emancipation: they are thus not only intellectually independent, but they share in the political life of the country, proudly support their families and are actors in the ongoing debate of ideas. Moreover, if the number of mothers that Shakespearean drama stages, is definitely inferior to the number of fathers; things are indeed different in contemporary narrative: as a matter of fact both *Wise Children* and *The Children's Book* depict not only traditional maternal figures, but are also filled with characters of adoptive mothers, stepmothers, and grandmothers, testifying to the importance that women nowadays have in the creation of the microcosm of the family as well as of the macrocosm of society. Shakespeare looms large in the background of these matriarchal worlds, a constant reference, foil and mirror, as if the doomed Margarets and Hermiones of the Renaissance have paved the way for liberated and sometimes even triumphant Doras and Olives who perhaps have started to defeat the patriarchal culture which had victimised and silenced their foremothers.

It comes therefore as no surprise that these newly born matriarchal communities should be located in spaces redolent of Shakespearean geographies. The woods in which large parts of both *Wise Children* and *The Children's Book* are set have the explicit flavour of two famous Shakespearean forests: the Forest of Arden, in which *As You Like It* takes place, and the wood near Athens that hides and confuses the lovers in *A Midsummer Night's Dream*. In both cases, woods are presented either as places of magic, secure hiding-spaces and idyllic landscapes ready to trigger love, or alternatively as locations dominated by irrationality and fear. Arcadian corners when flooded by daylight, Shakespearean woods turn into scary sites at night, when savage beasts and robbers often wait in ambush. In Shakespeare's narrative counterparts, the woods still convey such a strong dichotomy: apparently utopian places, they however conceal uncanny realities. In Byatt's *The Children's Book*, Olive and Humphry live in a house suggestively called Todefright:

> They took the train to Andreden, in the Kentish Weald, and took a fly at the station. Andred was the old British name for forest. Their house was called Todefright. They drove between hawthorn and hazel hedges, along curling lanes between overhanging woods of beech, and birch, and yew... Todefright was an old Kentish farmhouse, built of stone and timber. It had meadows and a river before it, woods rising uphill behind it, and a wide view to the high edge of the Weald across the river. (Byatt 17)

If the house suggests the commonplace quiet pastoral landscape of rivers, meadows and old cottages, its name seems on the contrary to hint at something frightening, dangerous, and uncomfortable. Similarly, the life of the Wellwoods is at first glance an idyllic one, with children leading a healthy and happy existence, carelessly spent between rides in the woods and meetings in the tree-house, and metaphorically ruled by Olive and Humphry who dress up once a year as king and queen of fairies during their familial representation of Shakespeare's *Midsummer*. Yet, precisely as the lightness of Shakespeare's Dream conceals much darker aspects, awful truths are slowly revealed in *The Children's Book*, disturbing the tranquil flow of life: doubts concerning Olive and Humphry's parenthood are raised, betrayals are more than common, fathers try to abuse daughters and the steady ethic principles of the Fabian societies suddenly stagger.

Woods and forests also offer Angela Carter a significant setting for Wise Children: in the central chapter, Dora and Nora travel to an aptly-named Hollywood, sleep in a motel called The Forest of Arden, and act as fairies in the film production of *A Midsummer Night's Dream* whose setting is naturally a huge, fake, wood. It is thus quite evident that Carter wishes to link her conception of the wood to Shakespeare and his plays; yet, the image of the playwright is translated in the narrative vision of a globalized, mass-industry Shakespeare, a literary myth to exploit in order to make easy money:

> Nora and I put up at the Forest of Arden. The legendary Forest of Arden, the residential motel of the stars, with its Old English motif. What could have been more appropriate, in the circumstances? All the little bungalows, half-timbered, thatched—replicas of Anne Hathaway's cottage—each one nestled under clematis, set in wee herbaceous gardens, tended with loving care by Japanese gardeners, and there were Warwickshire apple trees, imported oaks, you name it. (Carter 120-21)

Carter's Forest of Arden is an unlikely and humorous metamorphosis of its model which becomes a luxury motel and a prosaic replica of Shakespeare's home place. A fictional 'place' in Shakespeare's comedy, the Forest of Arden has been transformed by Carter into a fictional 'non-place', according to the anthropological meaning that Marc Augé attributes to these two words:

> If a place can be defined as relational, historical, and concerned with identity, then a space which cannot be defined as relational, or historical or concerned with identity will be a non-place. (Augé 77-78)

Carter's Forest of Arden is a space with no history, where relations are strictly commercial and where people—clients—are reduced to numbers, revealing the individualism and the capitalistic tendency of the contemporary Western society. Far from being a real wood, it becomes the impersonal non-place of Augé's super modernity, a space of luxury and "solitary contractuality" (*Ibid.* 94), which symbolizes the effects of globalization, mass-industry and mass-tourism on something that is instead often considered as exclusively literary. Shakespeare himself is thus somehow exposed to the risk of becoming a 'non-place': the dangerous forest of mass culture transforms him into a touristic destination and an easy product of the souvenir trade and of the film industry. At the same time, such a plastified Shakespeare is the theatre of livelihood and creativity, hinting not only at the playwright's desacralized transformation but also at his enduring creative function. This is similarly suggested by the presence of another wood in the novel, that of the movie production of *A Midsummer Night's Dream*. Angela Carter does not imagine a real forest as the setting of the film, but a fake, plastic one, as to underline, somehow, how much Shakespeare has been nowadays exploited, copied and abused; yet, by transforming a natural forest into a counterfeit one, Carter is once again exploring and exploiting the chameleonic qualities of Shakespeare, poking fun at the transcendent readings of the Bard and investigating the modes of his contemporary presence and fruitfulness. Significantly, the wood of the Midsummer movie points to the myth of yet another, much contemporary, wood: Hollywood.

And I no longer remember the set as a set but as a real wood, dangerous, uncomfortable...as if Hollywood was the name of the enchanted forest where you lose yourself and you find yourself, again; the wood that changes you; the wood where you go mad; the wood where the shadows live longer than you do. These days, half a century and more later, I might think I did not live but dream that night, if it wasn't for the photos, see? (Carter 157-58).

Paraphrasing one of Demetrio's last cues ("Are you sure/ That we are awake? It seems to me/ that yet we sleep, we dream." *A Midsummer Night's Dream*, 4.1), Angela Carter manages to juxtapose Hollywood, with its dreams of glory, fame and prosperity, and the disturbed dreams of love in

Shakespeare's Midsummer. In her witty and unusual comparison, she attributes the double nature of literary woods to the Hollywood environment: if it is on one side a place where everyone's dream of popularity and affluence may come true and where a kind of eternal life is guaranteed by the magic of the cinema industry, on the other it clearly represents a dangerous reality in which it is only too easy, as Dora says, to get lost.

With their explicitly Shakespearean settings, Carter's and Byatt's novels look back at the great British playwright to elaborate on the subject of womanhood, motherhood and matriarchy, historically defined by women's emancipation and feminist struggles. It is remarkable that these motives should be articulated in the shadow of Shakespeare's female characters and plays and in constant conversation with them.

Conclusions

Shakespearean heroines, all too often marginal, silenced, and submissive, have had their way. Reborn in the discourse on gender of contemporary women writers, they reveal first of all how unconventional and original Shakespeare was in the treatment of women. They also stand witness to the creative energy behind contemporary women's writing: Shakespeare is a safe harbour from which to leave and a set of established interpretations to contest; but equally a lively textual continent, the unlimited source of themes and issues, and in many ways the father of subversion and disobedience. Angela Carter seems to make it particularly clear in her novel *Wise Children*, whose protagonists live at 49, Bard Road, in the house they have inherited from their adoptive grandmother. Dora and Nora's home is the place to which all their souvenirs are attached, the one of which they think in a nostalgic mood after having spent too much time in dreamy, glamorous Hollywood:

> But I was pining away for home—for the whirr and rattle of the trams, the lights of Electric Avenue glowing like bad fish through a good old London fog, longing for rain and weather and bacon sandwiches, for the healthy chill of 49 Bard Road on a frosty morning, for the smell of home, the damp, the cabbage, the tea, the gin. (Carter 143)

Indeed, if 49 Bard Road is the place which the twins occasionally leave, it is also their refuge, the space to which they always return, significantly going back both to their adoptive mother and to Shakespeare. The house that Dora and Nora have inherited from Grandma Chance thus comes to represent on the one hand the power of matriarchy and the strength of maternal love, on the other, because of its address, it is also inevitably and explicitly connected to the immortal playwright. Shakespeare, in Carter's *Wise Children* but also in Byatt's *The Children's Book* and in many other contemporary novels written by women, ceases to be the symbol of a restrictive, suffocating patriarchy and morphs instead into a fertile literary mother.

WORKS CITED

Augé, Marc. (Non-Lieux, Introduction à une anthropologie de la surmodernité, 1992), *Non-Places, Introduction to an Anthropology of Supermodernity*. Translated by John Howe. London and New York: Verso, 1995.

Byatt, Antonia Susan. *The Children's Book*, 2009. London: Vintage, 2010.

Carter, Angela. *Wise Children*, 1991. London: Vintage, 2006.

Jardine, Lisa. *Still Harping on Daughters: Women and Drama in the Age of Shakespeare*. Sussex: Harvester Press. New Jersey: Barnes and Nobles, 1983.

Krontiris, Tina. *Oppositional Voices. Women Writers and Translators of Literature in the English Renaissance*. London and New York: Routledge, 1992s.

Mack, Phyllis. *Visionary Women: Ecstatic Prophecy in Seventeenth-century England*. Berkeley: University of California Press, 1992.

Smith, Kristin M. "Martial Maids and Murdering Mothers: Women, Witchcraft and Motherly Transgression in Henry VI and Richard III". *Shakespeare* 3.2 (2007). 143-60.

Webb, Kate. "Seriously Funny: Wise Children." *Flesh and the Mirror: Essays on the Art of Angela Carter*. Ed. Lorna Sage. London: Virago, 1994. 279-307.

5

Supernatural, Natural and Unnatural: From Shakespeare to the Lambs

Isabella Bruschi

> The terror which they put us in when reading, made them an object of belief,—when we surrender up our reason to the poet, as children to their nurses and their elders. (10)

In the above quotation from the essay *On the Tragedies of Shakespeare Considered with Reference to their Fitness for Stage Representation* Charles Lamb expounds on Shakespeare's power to make those readers endowed with the uncontaminated eyes of a child be filled with dismay before the supernatural beings of his creation as though they were real. Besides showing Lamb's unconditional admiration for the playwright and his Romantic sensitivity, those few lines contain, in a nutshell, the issues discussed in the present paper and aptly frame it within the questions around which it develops: how do the Lambs treat the theme of the supernatural—related to the Shakespearean concepts of natural and unnatural—in their abridgement of Shakespeare's plays? How does this theme combine with their declared, however, indirect pedagogical aim?

The pages that follow will try to find an answer to these questions by outlining the cultural context in which the Lambs lived and operated and through a comparative reading of *A Midsummer Night's Dream*, *The Tempest*, *Macbeth* and their prose versions by Charles and Mary Lamb.

The Context

It would be appropriate to say that *Tales From Shakespeare* is the result of the coincidence of two different but interweaving tendencies of the late 18th and early 19th century, that is, the growing enthusiasm for Shakespeare—a phenomenon later to be known as 'Bard-idolatry' or 'Bardolatry'—and a new conception of childhood. Both were connected to and depended on of the new European mood that gave birth to the movement of Romanticism.

As a reaction to the dominating canons of neoclassicism, based on the Aristotelian unities of time, place and action, which had caused the dismissal of Shakespeare's works as unsuitable and obsolete, in the second half of 18th century a considerable number of new editions of the dramatist's plays were published, many of them affordable also for the less wealthy. So much so that

> access to the texts within homes, schools and other venues with libraries or reading rooms was possibly a far greater factor in establishing Shakespeare's pre-eminent cultural status. (Young 32-33)

In line with this, another factor contributed to the renowned dramatist, the proliferation of magazine articles about his production. As Kathryn Prince states—

> in the nineteenth century, technological advances in printing combined with increased literacy rates in Britain, to make periodicals and newspapers an important medium for Shakespeare's unprecedented popularisation beyond the upper echelons of British society. (1)

His influence was so widespread and undiscussed that Shakespeare became a subject of conversation among the fictional characters of the age, as happens in Jane Austen's *Mansfield Park*.

The same decades witnessed a similar 'craze' for the Bard in theatres, thanks to new adaptations and, above all, to the success of such actors as David Garrick first, then Philip Kemble, Sarah Siddow and, later, Edmund Kean.

Shakespeare came thus to be regarded as the symbol of the British spirit, the paragon of propriety and decency, whose didactic and educational potential was highly valued.

It was however in the first years of 19th century that Charles Lamb himself (1775-1834), William Hazlitt (1778-1830), James Leigh Hunt (1784-1859) and Samuel Taylor Coleridge (1772-1834) opened new paths in the field of Shakespearean studies, informing their readings with Romantic principles.

The Romantics' attraction for traditional folklore, their consideration of fancy as a creative power and as the instrument of a 'superior' form of knowledge recognised in Shakespeare affinity with their own perception of reality and a fertile ground for exploration. They found in him the most elevated products of imagination and, among them, those aspects of supernatural and sublime without which—in their view—nature cannot be comprehended and reformulated. Jonathan Bates pointedly observes that not by chance, Shakespeare's eerie characters and situations—the witches in *Macbeth*, the fairies in *A Midsummer Night's Dream*, the ghost in *Hamlet*, and the magic in *The Tempest*—are the ones the painters of that age chose to represent more often than others.

Another distinctive feature of Romantic sensibility was the unprecedented attention paid to childhood. The importance of infants in Blake's and Wordsworth's thought and poetry is all too well known, but a new conception of children and their education went back to Locke and Rousseau. Both philosophers had a notable influence on the vast output of the children literature of the period.

One of the most debated topics in this field revolved around the nature of this kind of publications, namely whether they should be, in David Skinner's words, "instructional" (34), overtly educational and directly aimed at promoting practical and ethical behaviour, or whether they should include texts potentially but not explicitly didactic, carrying messages in more sidelong ways. This second option concerned folk and traditional fairy tales, narratives incorporating supernatural and fantastic elements, such as elves, ghosts and witches.

Charles Lamb sided with the latter stance and, though we have no first-hand testimony of Mary's opinion (women could aspire to write fictions, but didn't dare to step into the male domain of criticism yet), we might suppose she shared her brother's views.

In a letter to Coleridge, dated October 23rd, 1802, Charles deplored the pedantic didacticism of certain children literature and disapproved of those authors who had forgotten the educational value of "the old classics of the nursery", which enhance imagination and promote the growth of children into balanced men; he stressed the role of "Poetry" in upbringing. In his essay *Witches and Other Night-Fears*, he went so far as to aver that the supernatural, the frightening figures that often haunt a child's dreams may be given shape by "book, or picture, or the stories of foolish servants" (3) but they exist in the very essence of human mould, "they are transcripts, types—the archetypes are in us, and eternal" (3). They are part of a shared collective sub-conscious, as we would put it in psychoanalytic terms.

With such premises the stories told by Shakespeare must have appeared to the Lamb siblings the most appropriate food for young minds. Thus, when William Godwin asked them to adapt Shakespeare's plays for his Juvenile Library, they readily accepted[1] and set to the task. How difficult a task it was is something of which the Lambs were well aware, as it comes out from the affectionate picture Mary drew of herself and her brother at work:

> you would like to see us, as we often sit, writing on one table [...] I taking snuff, and he groaning all the while, and saying he can make nothing of it.[2]

or from Charles's essay on Shakespeare's stage representation which shows his insight into the problems implied in 'manipulating' Shakespeare. The idea underlying this essay is the impossibility of rendering the greatness of "our sweet Shakespeare" (7) on stage without dwarfing him. Shakespeare's fascination is lost "when the imagination is no longer the ruling faculty, but we are left to our poor unassisted senses" (9). No actor or actress—however clever they may be—can fully convey the subtlety and complexity of the poet which can only be grasped—according to Charles—through the communion between our imagination and his written texts, through what Coleridge would have defined "suspension of disbelief."

Finally the Lambs overcame the perilous straits of their task. Their tales were published in 1807,[3] immediately became very popular and are still considered a classic of English children literature.

Coherently with their view of this genre, the main point of the preface they appended to the book is their intent of introducing young people—especially "young ladies" (ii), who had a more limited access to family libraries than their brothers—to the study of Shakespeare. For this reason, in spite of having made "these Tales an easy reading for very young children" (ii), the Lambs affirmed that the poet's "words are used whenever it seemed possible" (i), even though they knew that "his language being transplanted from its own natural soil and wild poetic garden [...] must want much of its native beauty" (ii). Their foremost purpose in fact was not to provide moral teachings but to kindle the sparkle of the desire to read the original texts, because there lies the true lesson of "all sweet and honourable thoughts and actions" (iii).

Let's now turn to the texts and explore how the Lambs bring Prospero, the enchanter, the fairies of the midnight wood or the prophetic witches upto our imagination making them believable objects of wonder or scare, as it happens "when we surrender up our reason to the poet, as children to their nurses and their elders" (qtd. above).[4]

The Tempest

Unlike the Elizabethan romance, which plunges the readers into the midst of a tempest, Mary's tale opens with what Shakespeare's audience would learn in the second scene of act one through Prospero's words, namely with the description of the setting—"a certain island in the sea" (8)—and the introduction of its main inhabitants. Therefore a 19th century young reader would be informed of the fundamentals of the story since the very beginning.

As Shakespeare's Prospero repeatedly refers to his "secret studies" (1.2.73) as "my art" (1.2.24) or the "Liberal arts" (1.2.73), in outlining his character Mary associates him with his books, "which chiefly treated of magic" (8). The clause is immediately followed by an explanatory note, as it were,—"a study at that time much affected by all learned men" (8)—that, we surmise, she added to the benefit of her young readers, informing them of the fact that in Shakespeare's times the boundary between science and magic was not so clearly cut. To make things easier, she goes on to anticipate something that is not to be found in Shakespeare's play so explicitly, namely that "the knowledge of this art he [Prospero] found very useful" (8) to contrast the evil forces of the island.

We are then introduced to the former inhabitants of the island, the wicked witch and his son on one hand, the spirit Ariel on the other.

Not only does Shakespeare connote Sycorax by attributing her black magic powers, wickedness, mischief, and Caliban conveying the idea of ugliness ("freckled whelp, hag born"—1.2.283—"misshapen knave"—5.1.268), vileness, filthiness, treachery and lechery, but both of them are often indicated as bearing the 'unnatural' mark of those who are beyond, or rather below, in their case, human nature. So Caliban is "not honoured with a human shape" (1.2.83-84), he is "litter[ed]" (1.2.282) not born, he is named "savage" (1.2.353), in several instances "monster", and qualified as "brutish" (1.2.355), "devilish beast" (2.2.30), "demi-devil [...] bastard" (5.1.272-73). Sycorax in turn is a "dam" (1.2.320), not a mother, "terrible to enter human hearing" (1.2.164-65). More than that, Sycorax is defined "foul" (1-2-56) and Caliban "strange" (5.1.289), adjectives carrying devilish and outlandish overtones in Shakespeare's work.[5]

Although operating an inevitable simplification, Mary Lamb renders all the attributes of the two characters. In her tale Sycorax is a "bad witch" (11) and enchantress; her commands are "wicked" (7); her witchcraft "too terrible to enter human hearing" (11) as much as it was in Shakespeare's words. In order to depict Caliban's reluctance to obey his master's orders shown on stage, he becomes, in Mary's words "lazy and neglected" (8). Further on he is "a strange misshapen thing far less human in form than an ape" (8), the "ugly monster" (8, 17); he is given an "uncouth form and savage appearance" (17). As the quotations reveal, Mary manages to maintain the image of non-humanity of the two figures also by appropriating some of Shakespeare's words and phrases. The same concept is reinforced in Shakespeare and, faithfully, in Mary's text by associating Caliban with animals: in the romance he is compared to a tortoise (1.2.316) and his beastliness is comically underlined by Trinculo and Stephano, who see and smell a fish in him, in the prose version he is paralleled to an ape.

However much is lost of the depth of the character. In her abridgement Mary cuts the episodes of Caliban's alliance with Trinculo and Stephano which sustain the other side of the character, that of the slave-colonized rising up against his master-colonizer. Any reference to sex and Caliban's lustful nature—the hints at his birth from Sycorax and the devil's union, his assaults on Miranda's purity—is totally washed off, no doubt to be spared to the innocent minds of the addresses.

As for Ariel, Mary proceeds quite in the same way. She literally moves many of the adjectives and appellations we find in Shakespeare ("delicate"—10, "brave"—10, "dainty"—16, "my Ariel"—18, "bird"—18)[6] and she reproduces verbatim Ariel's song (18). When she reports the scene in which the spirit is turned into a harpy (15), she duly explains the meaning of the word to her young readers. She efficaciously conveys the idea of pertness in the paragraph (8) where she introduces Ariel, attributing it the qualities described in Caliban's soliloquy (2.2.4-17). To the ones employed by Shakespeare, she adds three adjectives—"lively"—(7), "little" (7), "wild" (18) that allow her to summarize some of the features of the Shakespearean spirit emerging from dialogue and action. So, if something of the linguistic brilliance of the playwright is necessarily lost (the shade of airiness and impalpability expressed by such words as "air", "a touch", "a feeling"—5.1.21), condensed in few lines as it is to the use of the little ones, the figure of Ariel is more effectively reproduced in prose than that of Caliban.

If the supernatural/unnatural qualities of the creatures of the island are by and large retained in Mary's tale, not the same can be said of their master Prospero's features. The most obscure facets of his personality (the neglect of his dukedom and his authoritarianism, pride, condescension, pitilessness at times), his failure in obtaining Caliban's obedience and gratitude, which at the end of the play he will acknowledge as part of himself (5.1.275-76), are greatly softened. The complexity of the character created by the Bard's pen, as in the case of Caliban, is decidedly simplified.

More specifically with regard to the implications concerning magic, a certain gap separates the two texts discussed. This aspect is doubtlessly to be found in Shakespeare; from him we learn that Prospero himself conjures up the tempest; we see him wear his "magic garment" (1.2.24), we hear him speak of "my charms" (5.1.69) and "spell" (5.1.254). Yet there are several instances in Shakespeare's play (the masque as a product of Prospero's "art"—4.1.41, his soliloquy in Act 4 and the epilogue he pronounces at the end) that lead us to interpret Prospero and his magic powers as a metaphor of the dramatist himself and of the strength of theatre. Thus Alonso's exclamation about the portentous events on the island—"there is in this business *more than nature*[7] (5.1.243)—takes on a double meaning: supernatural on the one side, and fictitious/theatrical on the other. These episodes are omitted in Mary's tale. Her Prospero, wielding the magic wand, though a learned man as she writes at the beginning of her narration, is closer to the traditional sorcerer of folk tales.

What Mary preserves instead is the dreamlike dimension, which more than once emerges in the play and is so powerfully epitomized in the famous line "we are such stuff as dreams are made of" (4.1.156-57), when she, like Shakespeare, makes

Miranda and Ferdinand doubt whether their memories and experiences were dreams or reality.

A Midsummer Night's Dream

Dream, natural and supernatural are constantly and closely knit together in *A Midsummer Night's Dream.*

The dimension of dream, on whose ambiguity all the occurrences of the play are based, is hinted at by Shakespeare since the beginning of the comedy when, to appease Theseus's impatience for their nuptials, Hippolyta says: "Four days will quickly steep themselves in night:/ Four nights will quickly dream away the time" (1.1.10-11, 30).[8] The word 'dream' recurs in the play in different contexts, referred to love (1.1), to nightmares and fear (2.2), to the charms of the enchanted wood several times (e.g. 3.2.), to the darkness in which goblins and fairies live (5.19) and to the play itself in Puck's final address to the audience. Oberon seems to preside over dream which is ultimately the induced and perceived effect of his spells both on the humans and the spirits. When the lovers wake up, cleared of the influence of the love-juice "all [...]/ Shall seem a dream and fruitless vision" (3.2.13-14, 65), and the same happens with Titania and Bottom: "Think no more of this night's accidents,/ But as the fierce vexation of a dream" (4.1.1-2, 71). Bottom himself, in his clumsy way, is made to mouth a reflection on dream.

Mary Lamb's tale starts as in *The Tempest*, supplying her readers with the general background. She introduces them to Athens and the law that will cause Hermia and Lysander to flee to the wood and set in motion the whole story. The word dream appears late in her text, when Oberon recommends Puck to amend the mistake made in pouring the love-juice into the wrong man's eyes, so that the four lovers "will think of all that passed a vexatious dream" (27).[9] The word occurs again when the lovers actually awake, their former feeling restored, doubtful whether their adventures "had really happened, or if they had [...] been dreaming the same bewildering dream" (30). Dream is also the word closing Mary's tale, when she condenses Puck's farewell in few graceful lines. It is rather obvious that Mary uses the word where it is functional, while she has to give up the multiple resonances and internal links that it generates in the Shakespearean play.

There is another point in which Mary sharply swerves from Shakespeare. She associates Lysander's retrieval of his love for Hermia with his having recovered his reason once freed from the spell, while reason is the faculty appealed to by Shakespeare in the reverse situation. These are the words Shakespeare puts in Lysander's mouth when he sees Helena and, by way of Puck's spell, falls in love with her:

> The will of men is by his reason swayed:/And reason says you are the worthier maid./ Things growing are not ripe until their season;/ So I being young, till now ripe not to reason/ And touching now the point of human skill,/ Reason becomes the marshal to my will/ And leads me to your eyes. (2.2.2-7, 45)

Shakespeare seems to reverse the current logic speculating about rationality in the very realm of the irrational, of desires, dreams and charms. Yet such are the things that come to pass in the wood where the spirits reign and the boundaries between dream and reality, credible and incredible, sense and nonsense are flimsy and porous. Mary, although opposing reason and dream, as Shakespeare does, reinserts it in the dominion of common sense. Also the pair reason/love has a different treatment in the two texts: in Mary's, as seen before, they go together, in the playwright's they contend with each other, as, in Bottom's words "reason and love keep/ little company together" (3.1.2-3, 51).

In the Shakespearean play all the supernatural events are given a specific location in place and time. The charms and spells (as both Shakespeare and Mary name the spirits' tricks) occur in the wood near Athens at night. The Elizabethan audience would hear the words "wood", "night" and "moon" repeated over and over.

Midnight is said to be the "fairy time" (5.1.1, 89). Day and night, darkness and light are often contrasted. Oberon, the

"King of Shadows" (3.2.23, 64), calls up darkness in order to bring his plans to effect. Puck is worried about the impending dawn, lest it dissolves the immaterial gossamer of their enchantments:

> My Fairy Lord, this must be done with haste,/ For night's swift dragons cut the clouds full fast,/ And yonder shines Aurora's harbinger. (3.2.21-23, 65).[10]

The mortals, on the other hand, are bewildered by night, their senses are impaired[11] and they perceive it as "weary", "long and tedious" (3.2.23, 67) while day is to them "gentle" (3.2.5, 67).

Similarly, we are constantly reminded of the place where the occurrences take place; flowers, fruit, plants, little animals are repeatedly mentioned and often combined in figures of speech. They may represent a threat to humans, but are instruments, the spirits have at their command, the elements they breathe with, so much so that, as Titania says, hers and Oberon's contentions alter the seasons to the amazement of the world. Shakespeare seems to suggest that the spirits of the wood are one with nature, they embody its forces, while "mortal grossness" (3.2.17, 51) can just figure them.[12] In spite of this human beings fret and pine for their petty affairs and Puck has enough ground to exclaim: "Lord, what fools these mortals be" (3.2.28, 56).

Although Mary's abridgement Mary's abridgement leaves out much leaves out much of this richness, her linguistic choices offer her young readers a good foretaste of the original text. The atmosphere of the Shakespearean enchanted forest is in fact recreated by a number of devices. Mary relies on the repetition of the words "wood", "night", "moonlight", "midnight"; Oberon maintains his appellation of "King of Shadows" (27); flowers, greenery and animals are in her tale as well. She employs the adjectives "delightful" (20) and "pleasant" (22) to qualify the wood and lend it the connotation of lightness and playfulness which pervades Shakespeare's play. When she narrates Hermia and Lysander's escape, she places the wood—the territory where Athens' "cruel law" (20) does not reach "beyond the boundaries of the city" (20), as to stress the fact that once that boundary is passed a different kind of order reigns. To the same purpose she keeps, almost verbatim, an exchange between Bottom and Titania that implies the change of logic within or without those boundaries: the mortal, feeling out of place, says, "if I have wit enough to find the way out of this wood, I have enough to serve my turn" (27-28), to which the Queen of the fairies retorts "Out of the wood do not desire to go" (28)[13] meaning that a step beyond its limits there is another world that would deny hers.

Also the treatment of the supernatural characters shows Mary's care in granting the flavour we relish with Shakespeare. The spirits and the fairies of the wood are often defined "little", an adjective that does not recur in Shakespeare and that summarizes an attribute the playwright repeatedly emphasizes throughout the play; to the same effect she reports some lines from the comedy almost literally: "her coverlet, the enamelled skin of a snake, which, though a small mantle, was wide enough to wrap a fairy in" or "wage war with the bats for their leathern wings to make my small elves coats" (23).[14] Titania's self-consciousness and stubbornness is reproduced in Mary's tale by retaining Shakespeare's words "I am a spirit of no common rate" (28)[15]; in the fury of their strife over the changeling, Titania and Oberon name each other "proud" and "jealous" both in the tale (21) and in Shakespeare (2.1.16-17, 34). Oberon's interest in the young Athenians' love affairs is made explicit in Mary's sentence "the fairy King [...] was always friendly to the lovers" (22). Further on Mary underlines Oberon's basically good nature by attributing him the same virtue of pity he is endowed with in the Shakespearean comedy and clarifies that Oberon's charm at Titania's expenses is a "merry contrivance" (29) far from any revengeful or malignant feeling. Thus, Mary manages to preserve the aura of mischievous jollity the King of Shadows has in Shakespeare. Puck's character as well is finely rendered by Mary Lamb. To outline his personality as faithfully as possible she paraphrases the passage about his impish tricks. Some of the appellations by which Shakespeare refers to the spirit, such as "merry wanderer of the night" (2.1.28, 33), "knavish sprite" (2.1.17, 33),[16] are adopted by

Mary, who adds more of them: “shrewd”, “light and airy form”, “fantastic shape” (21). What is lost of the comedy’s dialogues and actions is prettily condensed in Mary’s own creation: “Puck, who loved mischief to his heart, was highly diverted with this [the one at the expense of Titania] frolic of his master” (22).

One little word is worthy of reflections before taking leave from *A Midsummer Night’s Dream*: ‘strange’, which has to do with the wondrous nature of the story.

In Shakespeare’s play Hyppolita and Theseus comment on the four lovers’s tale of the night spent in the wood: “Tis strange, my Theseus, that this lovers speak of” (5.1.23, 77) one says and the other “More strange than true” (5.1.24, 77). The strangeness they are speaking of proceeds from the youths’ “seething brains” (5.1.26, 77) which Theseus parallels with the madmen’s and the poets’. What Shakespeare seems to imply here is that the lovers’ narration, which they perceive as inconsistent and beguiling as a dream, has the same substance of a lunatic’s ravings or a poet’s creation (the comedy’s itself!): all partake of imagination that gives form and shape to a world beyond common sense and is therefore ‘strange’, that is, extraneous to it. In Mary’s tale the word ‘strange’ occurs three times: once in the meaning of ‘surprising’ (“strange to relate”—24) and the other of ‘not known before’ (“his [Lysander’s] strange inconstancy”—29). The third and last time is included in the final paragraph, the one summarizing Puck’s final address:

> if any are offended with this story of fairies and their pranks, as judging it incredible and strange, they have only to think that they have been asleep and dreaming. (30-31)

The sense the adjective takes on here is rather ‘deviant’, ‘fantastic’, ‘unearthly’ and comes to coincide with what Hippolita and Theseus have in mind: here is reason, gross reality, out there, in the wood,—in William’s play or Mary’s tale—is dream, imagination, the lightness of the fairies’ world.

Macbeth

Also in *Macbeth* 'strange' is a key word related to the supernatural and unnatural deeds staged, which doesn't escape Charles Lamb's notice.

Comparing the play's and the tale's openings, it clearly comes out that Charles's abridgement reflects the pattern adopted by his sister. While Shakespeare's first scene shows the weird sisters working as a sort of chorus anticipating the underlying ambiguity of the play through the obscure sentence "fair is foul[17] and foul is fair" (1.1.11), Charles's narration instead is started by an introductory paragraph where Macbeth and Banquo are presented. The weird sisters follow in the second paragraph, where Charles dwells at length on their description, which he concludes with a sort of didactic note for the sake of his young readers: "the generals knew them to be weird sisters, or witches" (132), being witch, a word that never occurs in Shakespeare's text except in stage directions. The narrator assumes Banquo's role and depicts the sisters—much in the Shakespearean character's words—as "strange appearance", "figures like women except that they had beards", as having "choppy fingers", "skinny lips" and "wild attire [that] made them look not like earthly creatures" (132).[18] The witches' greeting to Macbeth, "prophetic" (1.3.78) in Shakespeare is further qualified in Charles's tale by the adjective "flattering" (133), as if to add an explanatory comment to the mysterious, puzzling salutations.

Further on in the tale Charles Lamb devotes an entire long paragraph (138) to the description of the blood-curdling ingredients the weird sisters stir in the cauldron out of which the ominous spirits will materialize. Apparently he considered the witches an attractive subject for children, since the detailed summary of the Shakespearean's characters's dialogue is not strictly functional to the development of the story line. Charles instead omits the figure of Hecate and all the references to Hell, the Devil or Belzebub made in the tragedy.

Macbeth and Banquo's bewilderment at the meeting and the sudden disappearance[19] of the sisters, mouthed in Shakespeare by the two victorious leaders, who doubt of their own senses and reason, is condensed by Charles in the word "strangeness" (132), which plainly denounces the outlandish, unearthly nature of the event.

When the first prophecy comes true and Macbeth is appointed Thane of Cawdor, the question of the opposition between evil and truth is raised, which echoes the sisters' mystifying motto ("fair is foul and foul is fair"—1.1.11) and mirrors one of the recurrent themes of the tragedy, namely the contention between truth and appearance. Thus Banquo's question "Can the Devil speak true?" (1.3.107) anticipates his and Macbeth's following discussion in 1.3.122-33. The importance of this exchange does not go unnoticed in Charles's reading who renders it faithfully paraphrasing some of Shakespeare's lines: "oftentimes these ministers of darkness tell us truths in little things to betray us" (133).[20]

In the same way, though unravelling the extreme density of the poet's words, Charles borrows them when Macbeth, at the sight of Birnam Wood moving towards his castle, realizes the emptiness of the weird sisters' promises; so, where in the play we have "I [...] begin/ To doubt th'equivocation of the fiend,/ that lies like truth" (5.5.44-45), in the tale we read "Macbeth now began [...] to doubt the equivocal speeches of the spirits" (141). Charles speaks of "hollow promises of the witches", of Macbeth's "false confidence" (140) and this is how he turns Shakespeare's famous lines:

> And be these juggling fiends no more believed,/ That palter with us in double sense;/ That keep the word of promise to our ear, / And break it to our hope. (5.9.19-22)

into

> let never man in the future believe the lying equivocation of witches and juggling spirits, who deceive us in words which have double senses, and while they keep their promise literally, disappoint our hopes with a different meaning. (142)

Not only do these few lines show Charles's ability in reproducing meanings, they also reveal his effort in keeping

Shakespeare's words as much as possible, even borrowing them from different lines—as is the case with "equivocation". A similar way of proceeding is applied to the phrase "riddling terms" (132) Charles uses at the very beginning of the tale drawing it out of Hecate's speech ("to trade and traffic [...] in riddles"—3.5.5).

Another issue Charles seems to have pondered over is the association Shakespeare establishes between the supernatural elements and Macbeth's mental workings, an aspect which legitimates the interpretation of the weird sisters and their prophecies as a projection of Macbeth's innermost desires.[21] The "horrible imaginings" (1.3.137) which the encounter with the sisters immediately generates in Macbeth's brain grow into dreadful visions, auditory hallucinations and dreams that haunt the protagonist and his wife all along the play. In this respect Charles reports also those episodes which are not so fundamental to the understanding of the story and yet they touch upon an important point in the tragedy. Thus the apparitions of the dagger as a "phantasm proceeding from his own hot and oppressed brain" (136) serves the purpose of connecting the portentous occurrence to Macbeth's disturbed mental state, as much as Shakespeare's lines do: "fatal vision, sensible/ To feeling, [...] art thou but/ A dagger of the mind, a false creation,/ Proceeding from the heat-oppressed brain?" (2.1.35-38). And again the "horrible imaginations" (136), "dreadful fancies" (138), the "wicked" (134) and "terrible dreams" (138) that afflict both Lord and Lady Macbeth in Charles's version go together with a "distracted state" (136), "distracted words" (138) and "disorder" (138). As observed before, this relation reflects Shakespeare's intentions and covers—however indirectly—the motif of illness which is part of the play's plot (the figure of the doctor is there to give it substance) and of its imagery.[22] On the contrary, there is no mark left of another view of Macbeth's predicament. In Charles's text in fact such definitions of his visions as "pictures", "a painted devil" (2.2.53-54), "the very painting of your fear" (3.4.60) are left out. In Shakespeare's play the words pronounced by Lady's Macbeth, besides further modulating her husband's hallucinations as 'material figments' of his terror, contribute to the understanding of her personality and to sustain the theme of the gap between truth and appearance.

The infirmity that, coming down from the fateful prophecies, overpowers the royal couple is reflected on a higher scale by the infirmity of the whole creation. The "sacrilegious" (2.3.65) breach of loyalty against the legitimate, "anointed" (2.3.66) king is not just a crime concerning the body politics, it brings disaster within the natural order of things. Shakespeare reminds his audience of the play throughout as shown in the few quotes—among the innumerable ones—related to Duncan's murder or to natural phenomena, to the general state of affairs in Scotland or to the conditions of the usurper and his wife:

> a breach in nature (1.5.137)—'tis unnatural (2.4.27)—a great perturbation in nature (5.1.9)—unnatural deeds/ unnatural troubles (5.1.68-69)

This also accounts for the occurrence of the adjective 'strange', meaning out of natural order, in Shakespeare's tragedy and, as seen before, in Charles's tale.

Nor does Charles forget to grant his young readers some of the flavour of Shakespeare's rich natural images. There are two instances, crucial as they contrast the atmosphere surrounding Macbeth's castle before and after the murder of King Duncan. The praise of the castle, voiced by Duncan and Banquo in the play, is entrusted by Charles to the narrator, who synthesizes the characters's exchange, keeping, as he often does, some of the playwright's words—"pleasantly", "sweet" (133) "delicate" (134) to which he significantly adds "wholesome" (133) that sends us back the idea of disease discussed before.

The second passage focuses on night and on the fatal overtones of the hour, which are maintained in Charles's tale, in spite of the radical simplification of Macbeth's soliloquy (2.1.48-60) from which all classical and mythological allusions are eliminated to facilitate comprehension.

In *Macbeth* more clearly than in *The Tempest* or *A Midsummer Night's Dream* Shakespeare seems to connect the supernatural to an inner drive which is all but too human—the protagonist's boundless ambition and thirst for power. The shadow of the dagger, Banquo's ghost and the weird sisters' prophecies seem to partake of the same immaterial substance, the one created by Macbeth's mind oppressed by horror and guilt. The promises of the three spirits turn out to be deceptive: the moving wood and Macduff's unearthly birth are explained with plain facts. Macbeth's claim to a "charmed life" (5.7.12)[23] shatters against reality, and the mystery, as Charles simply puts it for his little readers, "is easily solved" (141).

Conclusion

It would be pointless to evaluate the Lambs' tales in the light of Shakespeare's work. Nor did the siblings ever claimed this right.

As they declared in the preface to the book, they approached their "very difficult task" (ii)[24] in awe of the playwright's genius and with uncommon humbleness they recognized that their tales compare with Shakespeare's plays as "valueless coins" (ii) with "rich treasures" (i), or "faint and imperfect stamps" with a "matchless image" (ii).

Turning the dramatist's plays into short prose works[25] for children meant cutting, compressing, manipulating, changing their very narrative structure, as we have seen in discussing the openings of the plays and the tales here analysed. This implied the loss of suspense, of dramatic anticipation that Shakespeare's first scenes always carry. In spite of the fact that the Lambs, especially Mary, managed to embed direct speech in narration, the voices of the poet's characters are inevitably levelled in that of the 3rd person narrator they adopted.

Language was a particularly arduous point to tackle. The terms in which they wrote about it in the preface are rather unequivocal:

> the beauty of his [Shakespeare's] language is too frequently *destroyed*[26] by the necessity of changing many of his excellent words into words far less expressive of his true sense (ii).

They had in fact to simplify, explicate, explain to be comprehensible to their little readers; this of course evens off much of the fascination of Shakespeare's language, its complexity, ambiguity, multilayered meanings. Yet they did so unobtrusively, as shown in the examples given, adding little sentences as whispered as a short aside. In spite of the 'destruction' they spoke of, as a sort of apology or rather atonement for what they did, they made every effort to give their readers a taste of the dramatist's verbal wealth, keeping, sometimes relocating, his words wherever possible.

Dealing with *Tales from Shakespeare* all we have do is to assess its value in relation to the writers' aim.[27] And this was first of all the target they had in mind—children. In this respect the stories taken into account here are a good instance of their concern with them: convinced as they were of the instructive potential of folk and fairy tales, Mary and Charles found in *The Tempest*, *A Midsummer Night's Dream* and *Macbeth* those fantastic characters and situations capable to involve young readers and to teach them indirect lessons, which they managed to do finely passing on to them some of the ingredients that contribute to build up the atmospheres of the plays: the lightness and playfulness of their spirits, the horror and the fear of their enchanters, the magic of it all. In addition, despite the educational purpose of their book, never did they sound explicitly didactic or moralizing.

Mary and Charles just wanted to supply children with "some notions" (ii) of Shakespeare's stories; they wanted their tales "to prove delightful" (iii) so that their young readers might grow up with the desire of reading the original plays, the real "enrichers of fancy" and "strengtheners of virtue" (iii).

This is what Mary and Charles's "little book" (iii) still does nowadays.

NOTES

1. As their situation was far from prosperous, their interest in Godwin's commission was, no doubt, also financial, as is revealed in their letters.
2. Letter addressed to Sarah Stoddart, June 2nd 1806.

3. The volume includes 20 tales: the comedies and romances were Mary's work, the tragedies Charles's. However Mary's name did not figure in the first edition. If we know about her authorship, it is thanks to the Lambs' epistolary, where Charles not only recognises but repeatedly praises his sister's work.
4. We do not know if Shakespeare believed in witchcraft, ghosts or fairies; he certainly used them as dramatic devices to grip an audience for whom they surely had a more real existence than they have now or had in the Lambs' time.
5. Foul is the same adjective Shakespeare uses to qualify Antonio's deeds. His crime—the usurpation of his brother's dukedom—in fact is a crime against the natural order of the body politic and of family relationships.
6. Cfr. Shakespeare, 4.1.49, 1.2.206, 5.1.95, 1.2.215, 4.1.184.
7. My italics.
8. Since the edition I refers to numbers the lines per page, all quotations from Shakespeare will be indicated as follows: Act. Scene. line(s), page.
9. Mary's words are closely modelled on Shakespeare's, although his are pronounced by Titania: "think no more of this night accidents/ But as the fierce vexation of a dream!" (4.1.1-2, 71).
10. In the following lines Oberon claims his capacity to live under the sun's rays ("we are spirits of another sort"—3.2.31, 65). This connotes him and his court as white spirits. Nonetheless night cannot be dispensed with in case of spells.
11. Cfr. Hermia: "Dark night, that from the eye his function takes" (3.2.30, 58).
12. When Hermia declares herself readier to believe that the moon has usurped the sun's course (3.2.17-30, 54) rather than give credit to the fact that Lysander has deserted her, she is figuring an alteration of nature in hyperbolic terms.
13. Cfr. Shakespeare, 3.1.7-9, 51.
14. Cfr. Shakespeare, 2.1.24-25, 40 and 2.1. 11-12, 41.
15. Cfr. Shakespeare, 3.1.11, 51.
16. Cfr. Mary Lamb, 22 and 20.
17. Another key adjective that Charles borrows from Shakespeare.
18. Cfr. Shakespeare, 1.3.45-56, 1.3.44, 1.3.45 and 1.3.40-41.
19. The disappearance which Charles synthesises in the sentence "they then turned into air" (132), is debated by Macbeth and Banquo; they wonder about the state of the earth, which seems to have bubbles like

water, and about the faculty of their own minds. which seems to be altered by drugs (1.3.78-85).

20. Cfr. Shakespeare: "The instruments of Darkness tell us truths;/ Win us with honest trifles, to betray's/ In deepest consequence" (1.3.124-26).
21. This interpretation seems to be supported by Hecates's speech (which Charles, as seen before, escluded from his tale) when the devilish creature speaks of "artificial spirites", of "their illusion" and the "confusion" (3.5.26-28) they produce in Macbeth.
22. In Lamb's tale there is just one instance of such imagery in the phrase "Duncan's sound sleep" (134), in Shakespeare many of them are to be found.
23. Cfr. Charles Lamb, 142.
24. All the quotes in the conclusion are taken from the preface to *Tales from Shakespeare.*
25. The average length of each tale is approximately 15 pages.
26. My italics.
27. The same could be done through a comparative reading of the contemporary literature for children, which however is not the object of this study.

OTHER SOURCES

Lamb, Charles and Mary. *Tales from Shakespeare.* London: Nelson Classics, 1900.

Shakespeare, William. *The Tempest.* Oxford: O.U.P., 1992.

Shakespeare, William. *A Midsummer Night's Dream.* London: Penguin Popular Classics, 1994.

Shakespeare, William. *Macbeth.* Bungay: Arden Shakespeare, 1997.

WORKS CITED

Lamb, Charles and Mary. *The Works of Charles and Mary Lamb.* Vol. 5.

<http://www.gutenberg.org/ebooks/9365>

Lamb, Charles. *Witches and Other Night Fears.*

<http://www.angelfire.com/nv/mf/elia1/withches.html>

Lamb, Charles. *On the Tragedies of Shakespeare Considered with Reference to their Fitness for Stage Representation.* <http://www.angelfire.com/nv/mf/lamb/index.html>

Bate, Jonathan. "Il fenomeno Shakespeare." *Shakespeare nell'arte*. Ferrara: Ferrara Arte S.p.A., 2003, 21-41.

Skinner, David. *A Critical and Historical Analysis of Charles and Mary Lamb's Tales from Shakespeare and Thomas Bowdler's The Family Shakespeare*. University of Sheffield: 2011. <http://www.etheses.whiterose.ac.uk/2423/1/Skinner_David.pdf>

Prince, Kathryn. *Shakespeare in the Victorian Periodicals*. New York: Rutledge, 2008.

Young, Alan R. *Punch and Shakespeare in the Victorian Era*. Bern: International Academy Publishers, 2007.

6

Shakespeare Next: A Reappraisal: Focus on Bratya Basu's Adaptation of *Hamlet*

Amitava Roy and *Suchandra Ghosh*

Shakespeare "Next" Actually began right after Hamlet, i.e. around 1601 onwards. The Master achieved the impossible. He wrote 37 masterpieces by the time of his death. And did not leave much scope for others who followed to better his best. So other Masters (and less than Masters at times) did what the Germans did right after the Hamlet was performed in the 17th century—they re-wrote *Hamlet* as *Der Bestrafte Bruderumord*. Or what *Nahum Tale* did a little after the closed Jacobean theatres opened during the Restoration of 1660—rewrite *King Lear* with a happy ending. From thence grew and developed the new genre or sub-genres of Adaptations and Translations of Shakespeare, which soon became a torrent, a flood and finally a "new Shakespeare Industry". It was a creative infection that crossed all borders and seeped into the literary and cultural bloodstream of every country in the globe—Europe, the New World of the Americas, Asia, Australia, Canada, India, Africa, China, Japan—no one was immune from the Adaptation or Translation bug that germinated across cultures.

That is Shakespeare "Next"—every culture's graph of response and resistance to Shakespeare. If you cannot beat the Master, join him, collaborate with him, translate and adopt him for yourself and your times. So that, in a sense, you can go beyond Shakespeare and be the Shakespeare "Next", of the present and the future, his "next" in line to the master. Whatever translations, adaptations or performance of Shakespeare occurred after he himself wrote his texts, produced and performed (in a few of) them, constitute the canon of "Shakespeare Next". And unlike Shakespeare's fixed canon of 37 plays (give or take one or two either buried as Apocrypha or discovered and disinterred as latest adaptations) this canon of "Shakespeare Next" is an ever-expanding one that will continue on till the edge of doom. It is a global and international project that has successfully competed with the Master over the centuries and will continue to do so.

A major focus of this Adaptation Industry of "Shakespeare Next" has always been *Hamlet*. It has drawn adaptors and translators like a magnet and an enthralled world has gratefully received hundreds of translations and adaptations of this Mastertext in diverse forms and formats relocated into different cultural contexts and periods. Among its famed and renowned translators and adaptors in Western world have been—only to name a few—Turgenev and Pasternak (Russia), Holderlin, Goethe, Brecht and Heiner Mueller (Germany), Gide, LaForgue and Ionesco (France), Salvador de Madariaga, Garcia Lorca (Spain), Grotowski, JanKott (Eastern Europe). The list is endless.

In India too we have had a long, glorious tradition of Translations, Adaptations and Performance of Shakespeare and *Hamlet* from the 1850s up till today. A select lists of the notable *Hamlets* adapted and/ translated into Bangla from 1850s-2012 would include—*Amar Singh* by Promotho Nath Basu (adaptation), *Kirti Bilas* by Jogendra Chandra Gupta (adaptation), *Hori Raj* by Nagendranath Banbyopadhay (adaptation), *Hamlet* by Lolit Mohon Adhikari, *Chandi Prasad Ghosh*, by Haran Chandra Rakshit, by Ashok Guho, by Abu Saharear, by Sudhangshu Ranjan Ghosh, by Dattatreya Dutt (all translation). And finally the most current adaptation Bratya

Basu's "*Hemlat: Prince of Garanhata*" originally written in Bangla in 2006 and translated into English in 2012.[1]

Our central focus in this paper is Bratya Basu's *Hemlat: Prince of Garanhata*. But first, while dealing with the ideologies of Adaptation, the question that comes first is "what is Adaptation?" Adaptation is a kind of 'intellectual revisionism', to use Harold Bloom's phrase[2] that weaves past, present and future in one string of 'intertextuality'. Adaptation of Mastertexts as competing discourses from classical to medieval and Renaissance to the late modern times through phases of colonialism Imperialism and post-colonialism is one of the pivotal ideologies that focus on text, author, reader and the historical process. To put it simply: 'Adaptation' is a literary theory, initially, the fashion of changing names, titles and settings that help the work acquire a local colour and a sense of familiarity among the recipients of the target language audience.

William Shakespeare himself was a Master adapter who constructed a Universe of literary creations by adapting a wide range of ancient-medieval legends, combining the anecdotes and folklores of the West and the East. These source texts were transformed into great works of art that have influenced numberless works afterwards, inspired good many adaptation-translations century after century, across the globe.

But the contemporary adaptors take such bold steps further. They tear the concerned text (the Mastertext) from its cultural and historical roots and transplant the same on a different seedbed amidst a completely different socio-cultural atmosphere where the plant thrives into a big tree with a new set of branches—leading to a new hybrid form of literature. The writers of the later generation subvert the Mastertext by adapting-translating it. Although this practice has been viewed as parasitic or even as a cannibalistic approach as the adapting writer is supposed to ingest the Source Text, assimilate with his own thoughts as a parasite does, and thrives on it, yet the adapted text becomes something new. The adapter-creator develops something ingenious, often using the methods and techniques of parody, pastiche, collage, etc. At times the adaptor-translator hits back at his predecessor with his own version of the same thing. Sometimes he uses its analogue to suit his contemporary milieu, or to protest against his own situation, or to uphold his own ideology which may be at variance with the ideologies embedded in the text. Take for example, the *Bangla* translation and presentation of *Macbeth* by Utpal Dutt in 1975 (which was later published in book form in 2006). The performance was a political strategy of protest against the Emergency clamped on India (25 June 1975 to 21 March 1977), just as Ingmar Bergman had presented a version of the same play as a protest against the Fascists in the 1940s. Here in Dutt's play Macbeth's totalitarian rule over Scotland serves as an analogue for Indira Gandhi's totalitarian rule over India.[3]

Adaptation covers a large variety of modes of expression. The inter-textual relationship between the source and its versions may involve a complete replacement and demolishment of the original form, e.g., a play into a new format (poem, film or story). Thus a play-text may be used for a faithful stage production, a linguistic/trans-lingual translation, or a brand new play or even for any subjective/objective critical perspectives. To put it simply adaptation presents a text to a different kind of audience with different responses creating a different kind of aesthetic pleasure. As a case in point, Shakespeare had been introduced to the Colonized India as early as 1775 as a part of the Empire's cultural and political investment.[4] But was later utilized by Indian playwrights through translations and adaptations for their own and their Nation's purposes. This trend of re-writing the mastertexts of Shakespeare is seen in some plays of the second half of the 19th century. Jogendra Chandra Gupta's *Kirtivilas* (1852) is a Bengali play with unhappy ending highly influenced by *Hamlet*. *Amarsingha* (1875) by Pramathanath Basu; *Chandranath* (1894) by Siddhesvara Gupta; *Hariraj* (1895) by Nagendra Nath Chowdhuri are just some among the many that we have already mentioned. The founding and establishment of the National Theatre in Calcutta in 1872 came as a boon to the indigenous adaptations. It had two initial objectives:

1. To accommodate diverse traditions of the age old folk theatre.

2. To cater to the requirements of the larger audience who wanted to know about the Master Author, the great Shakespeare.

Almost contemporary interpretations in some other Indian languages may also be mentioned here, viz. the Marathi adaptations like *Vikarvilasita* (1883) and *Himmata-Bahadura* (1890)—which highlight the apparent inertia in Hamlet's character, while the Urdu plays *Jahangir* (1898) and *Khoon-e-Nahaq* (c. 1900) focus on the revenge motive. In the Blackwood's Magazine published in October, 1910, there appeared a report by R.E. Vernidy entitled 'Hamlet' at a Bengali Fair which spoke of one of the earliest Indian adaptations of Hamlet made in the 20th century, which is now not extant.

From 1800s to now Shakespeare has profoundly penetrated into the Indian consciousness, literatures and cultures. It is worth mentioning that every state in India, beginning with Bengal and Maharashtra, appropriated Shakespeare as the National Poet and Playwright of India as did the rest of the world. But, from about the 1970s there appears a revolutionary change in the people's perspectives, especially in theatre.

Theories of Adaptation

T. S. Eliot's essay *Tradition and the Individual Talent* (1919) may be seen as a major basis for the theory of literary adaptations. According to Eliot, the individual talent is always in a dialectical relationship of give-and-take with the tradition. He either absorbs the tradition and extends it further from the perspective of his time and consciousness , or, he challenges the tradition, subverts it and attempts to establish a counter tradition and 'makes it new', which in turn becomes part of the ongoing tradition of culture. Thus, the act of adaptation adds fresh trajectories of "inter-textuality" to the flow of tradition.

Adaptation may be viewed as an expression of Anxiety of Influence. Harold Bloom's well-known theory posits that a writer grows up in the cultural shadow of his Great Predecessor. Under the circumstances, one of his responses may be to accept the great authority and imitate him. But he soon finds that his own authentic voice is stifled under the overwhelming presence of the Mastertext. So the other response is to find his own voice in relation to the Master's voice and break away from the Master Text and assert his own self, own views and own perspectives. Freud gives this an Oedipal connotation that the child has to make an attempt to kill the father and become free. But this anxiety of influence, i.e., the continuing presence that haunts the writer throughout his life and his whole career may be seen as the map of a troubled relationship between the Master Text/Author and the individual writer himself/herself. Bloom sees further complications in this situation. His theory of 'Revisionism' holds that this is a deliberate 'misprision' (misreading) of a predecessor on the part of an artist of the later generation in order to clear out or carve out imaginative space for himself and in effect, for a new creation.

The fact is that the Mastertext uses the recurring patterns of historical events or fundamental feelings or human actions (viz. archetypes) with such force that it attains the status of a 'Text of Power', and remains relevant through time. Shakespeare himself was aware that there would be many adaptations of his master texts (e.g., *Julius Caesar*, 1599) because they contain certain archetypal forms relating to events, happenings, actions and characters that will be repeated in far off times and locales, in other contexts and texts, like the assassination of the head of a State—for instance Julius Caesar in Rome and Indira Gandhi in India nearly 2000 years later. But specifics, perspectives and ideologies will change according to the changes in time, place, culture, history and consciousness. This may be considered to be another theory of adaptation, observed by Shakespeare himself when he makes Cassius say in *Julius Caesar* (1599): "Stoop, then, and wash. How many ages hence/ Shall this our lofty scene be acted over/ In states unborn and accents yet unknown!" (Act 3, Sc .i).[5]

But the aspect of adaptation that attracts us the most is that it is an act of cross-cultural trans-creation. Critics and theoreticians like D.A. Shankar acknowledge the fact that translation and adaptation are major attempts on the part of one culture to come to terms with another, and therefore, it is not the fidelity to but the departures from the original texts that are significant. This is a new life that is created out of a cross-cultural intercourse (including 'assimilations', 'rejections' and 'modifications') between two different peoples of different nations. To quote Shankar: "...every culture consciously or unconsciously regards translation (and adaptation) as an agent which brings home both power and knowledge...and both are brought in a manner and a quantum that would benefit the receiving culture" (*Shakespeare in Indian Languages*, pp. 15-16).[6]

The cross-lingual and cross cultural transactions are made for various reasons. Various motivations may work behind the mind of the adaptor-translator:

i. **There may be some commercial reasons, i.e., popularity and easy accessibility**: the canonical position of the Mastertext entailing vast popularity and easy acceptability, may serve as a certainty of success. The adaptor shares the prestige of being a kind of co-author of the Mastertext;

ii. **Experimental creative modes**: the adaptor-translator's use of the canonical text offers him the scope of exfoliating and utilizing experimental creative modes like inter-textuality/parody/pastiche/collage;

iii. **The question of relevance**: the need to change time and place of the Mastertext in order to make a contemporary point and bring in contemporary relevance. This may be summarized as the attempt to make 'Shakespeare our contemporary'. We may recall what Jan Kott observed in his book *Shakespeare Our Contemporary* (1967) with reference to *Hamlet*: "Shakespeare has written/ rewritten an old scenario, and the parts in it. But he did not distribute the parts. This has been done anew in every age. Every age has its own Poloniuses, Fortinbrases, Hamlets and Ophelias" (pp. 52-53).[7]

The post-War adaptations of the canons have challenged the traditional values and perspectives of the Mastertexts. In our transformed global scenario resulting from the great upheavals in our history (death of God, Authority and traditional Institutions, the Wars, the economic Depressions, Globalization and its discontents, recurring Capitalist crises) the writers and thinkers were led to review, re-interpret and at times challenge the Mastertexts and the Great Books which had been hitherto considered to be the humanist basis of civilization and culture in new and emerging perspectives focusing on 'Power' and 'Domination'. The politics of power and the politics of sex became central to most of the Shakespeare adaptations made by Bertolt Brecht (*Coriolan*, 1952-55), Charles Marowitz (*The Marowitz Hamlet*, 1965), (*A Macbeth*, c. 1969), Tom Stoppard (*Rosencrantz and Guildenstern are Dead*, 1967), Edward Bond (*Lear*, 1971), Arnold Wesker (*Shylock*, 1976), Heiner Mueller (*The Hamlet Machine*, 1977), Eugene Ionesco (*Macbett*, 1972), (*Exit the King*, 1988), et al. These works may be called collectively the 'Shakespeare factory' which generates multiple adaptations of the mastertexts. *Hamlet* (perhaps due to its complexity and globally renowned position), has been much appropriated by modern adaptors both from the West and the East where the Medieval-Renaissance protagonist of Elsinore may be hardly recognizable. The modern dramatists from the mid 20th century onwards relocate and re-contextualize *Hamlet* into modern contemporary terms.

The Bengali and Indian stage with its rich tradition of culture and dynamism, felt the tremendous impact of this intellectual revolutionism. Accordingly we find a number of master texts of Shakespeare which have been adapted in *Bangla* theatre where the great artist has been relocated, reinterpreted and remodeled into contemporary Bengali Indian terms and perspectives. *Hemlat, the Prince of Garanhata* (2006) and *Kolkatar Hamlet* (1989), among others represent this great destructive-constructive tendency that propels adaptations. Mumbai based theatre group the Company theatre's presentation *Hamlet the Clown Prince* is another creation of this genre.

As evident from its title, *Hemlat, the Prince of Garanhata* is a Bangla adaptation of Shakespeare's *Hamlet* (1602) re-locating it in a different time and a different place, or more precisely, a subversion of the medieval Renaissance tragedy into contemporary times. The Medieval-Renaissance "rotten state of Denmark" which is an oblique re-creation of London of the early and ferocious capitalist ethos, is re-located in Basu's play into Bengal/ India in general and Kolkata and Garanhata in particular. Shakespeare's time and ours are different but similar too except that the glory and grandeur of Hamlet is purposefully diminished.

This kind of relocation is seen in Asit Basu's *Kolkatar Hamlet* (1971) too where the playwright with communist inclination presented this city as a slaughter-house of new life and new dreams. Burning on the pyre of the Naxalite Movements and the state's ruthless means of domination this Kolkata became a replica of Hamlet's 'rotten state of Denmark' where the cloud of conspiracy, suspicion, espionage looms large; where bullet is the final authority; where the dream and aspiration of bringing about something 'new' is destroyed every moment with the budding youth being murdered at every turning of the road. The spirit of Shakespeare's Hamlet appears before the protagonist Abhi and exclaims:

> My prison was Denmark... I see that Denmark has spread through the entire world like a fatal ulcer! Your country, too, I see, is just like my Denmark. (*Kolkatar Hamlet*, pp. 100-01).[8]

Abhi, the urban *Arjuna*, the young intellectual 20th century reincarnation of Shakespeare's *Hamlet* is caught between Naxalite extremism and quietitude. On this postmodern *Kurukshetra* of unequal battle between protesting idealism and capitalist realism, he gropes for the right action in theatre, in politics, in personal relations, in morality and ultimately gives us a quest for the meaning of life. Through the political and psychological, external and internal struggles of the protagonist, and his quest, the playwright holds up a mirror to Kolkata and India of the 1960s and 1970s.

Re-locating Shakespeare to *Garanhata*, Kolkata 2006

As we have observed, the post-war world saw a multitude of bold adaptations of the great canonical texts which at times have challenged the traditional values and perspectives of the Master Texts. The political upheavals, economic depression, social degradations—resulted in an overall despair, faithlessness and monotony in human life. The Master Works of art and literature that had hitherto been accepted as the basis of human culture and civilization, began to be reviewed, challenged and reinterpreted in the new and emerging perspectives focusing on 'Power' and 'Domination' in a transformed world scenario. Theatre and film being the most popular media which can reach out to thousands became the chief platforms of protest.

The wave of intellectual revolutionism had touched the Bengali stage and other Indian theatres with tremendous impact and this resulted in creating a very rich tradition in adaptations especially of Shakespeare's works. Attempts at adapting the mastertexts of Shakespeare have been successfully made in *Bangla* theatre where Shakespeare has been relocated, reinterpreted and remodeled into contemporary Indian terms and perspectives.

Hemlat as an Example of a Remarkable Indian Adaptation of *Hamlet*

Hemlat, the Prince of Garanhata (2006) is a Bengali play[9] written and directed by the renowned Bengali dramatist Bratya Basu enriching this tradition of adapting a 'great book' in contemporary colours. The playwright who is an accomplished actor-director and renowned educationist is currently the Education Minister of the TMC government, a pioneer and architect of the radical change or '*parivartan*' in the State of Bengal—the new dawn that the play looks forward to. The play as evident from its title, is a Bengali adaptation of Shakespeare's *Hamlet* (1601), re-locating it in a different time and a different place. With its eleven scenes the play 'subverts' the Mastertext and makes it contemporary. Through transculturation both the texts taken together, focus on the competing multiple theatrical discourses. Bratya Basu's India (Bengal and Kolkata) and Shakespeare's Denmark and London are both under the grip of globalization and capitalist discourse. Shakespeare's time and ours are different but similar too except that the glory and grandeur of Hamlet is purposefully diminished by relocating it from Denmark and London to Garanhata in Kolkata abutting on the city's red-light area and burning ghat. In the post colonial squalor of a decadent capitalist Kolkata Shakespeare is consciously diminished and downscaled.

This diminishment is perceivable from the very nomenclature used for the characters, e.g. Hamlet becomes '*Hemlat*', Claudius '*Kodu*', Polonius '*Pol*' or '*Paul*' and Ophelia becomes '*Shefali*' (Shephalia) which recalls the name of a famous nightclub dancer of Kolkata of the 1970s, to mention some. This paper seeks to find the vibrant echo of the great bard as it has resonated in the creative text of the Bengali playwright of today and also the angles where the two depart.

The setting is the 21st century Garanhata, a locality of north Kolkata amidst all its '*para*-cultures' and gossips. The protagonist is Hemlat, a 30-32 years old young man of a declining middle-class Bengali family. His experience resembles to some extent those of the Shakespearean Hamlet as his father has been killed by his opportunist uncle who has a secret and mysterious intimacy with Hemlat's mother, Monorama. Quite similar to the Shakespearean plot Hemlat's uncle Kodu wants to usurp the house and sell it to a promoter for big personal profits. Hemlat considers himself as an incarnation of Hamlet, the prince of Denmark and calls himself (in scene 2) 'the Prince of Garanhata' while his dead father Sadhan is, according to him, 'the original king of Garanhata'. As Hemlat explains "That's why I am Hem. I have drunk from a laat's dugs, Laat, Laat Hemlat...."[10]

Hem: On the one hand your drunken, worthless father; on the other the corruption and rottenness in my house—what will I do with this life of mine, Shefali? O, Shefalia.

Shef: Don't worry. Everything will turn out well at the end, Hemlat. Tell me what you want, shall we have a son or a daughter? [Hemlat frees his hand from Shefali. Stares strangely]

Hem: *Amavasya*, the fortnight of the dark moon is coming on again. I will go out once with the guards at night. Alone.

Shef: Why?

Hem: If it can be seen again. My father. The original King of Garanhata.

Shef: What good will come of seeing him? You will suffer so much. What does it profit you to take on the burden of agony anew? I cannot endure seeing you suffer. I feel that it does not matter how I live as long as you are happy. That you do not suffer agonies.

Hem: No, no. I must know. That rail yard, that Ganges strand, that burning ghat, the fire of the funeral ovens, the pyre, the confetti, the incense mingling with the astonishing scent of *ganja*[11]—I must know out of what ashes my father's ghost will rise as smoke and materialise as an image and confront me in what form and manner? How will he whisper in my ear 'did you want this rotten ruinous existence, Hem?' This lot, this destiny? At this time, this juncture? Father, speak to me. 'Speak my son of the Lat, Hemlat'?

Shef: You are mad again, Hemlat, crazy.

Hem: What does my father wish to tell me? What does he want me to know? What new information is there left for me to know? For us to know? Life whispers the prophecy of our ruin, our destruction daily into our heads! What is happening, what is to happen, what is now and what is to come are all astonishingly known to all of us. [Pauses]. Look Shefali—perhaps even now my father, mingling with and riding the wind all burnt into utter blackness, is looking down at me. Looking at me, overseeing me, me, me. And as he looks on his peaceful eyes are sparkling like stars in the dark vault of the sky. (*Hemlat* Act 5. pp. 41-42)

The revenge theme is highlighted in the 2nd scene where Hemlat, left alone in his room, takes out a tin-sword from under his bed and revolving it in the air speaks to himself:

> Hemlat, the Prince of Garanhata. Garanhata. I don't care any doubts. One day I'll stick this in the entrails of that swine. Otherwise I'm not Hem. *The Master of my lot*. Hem-lot. Filthy bustard! O wicked soul! (c. 2, p. 81)

The outline plot construction of the play follows the basic storyline of Shakespeare. In the same manner as in Shakespeare the hero comes across the spirit of his dead father, who reveals the truth and incites Hemlat to avenge the murder. But in the course of the play he withdraws, commits suicide and bequeaths the task to the generation next.

The Diminishment and Descaling in Bratya Basu Operates at Many Levels

First, as we've said earlier, in the nomenclature of the characters themselves. As the names of the dramatis personae reveal: King Claudius becomes '*Kodu*', Hamlet is equal to '*Hemlat*', Polonius is '*Pol*', etc. The names of the characters in *Hemlat*...are not just Bengali—Indianised versions of the original but reveal a conscious and inevitable degeneration and diminishment. The wicked, corrupt Claudius becomes Hemlat's "*Kodu Kaka*"—"*Kodu*" bringing with it association of "*kada*", i.e. mud, slush and mire. Similarly "*Paul*" or "*Paulda*" is the drunkard father of Hemlat's sweetheart, the Polonius of the original who is always over-vigilantly protecting his daughters from infamy. Here is a vulgar, loquacious patriarch who is over-embroiled in squabbles with his children. Hemlat comments on the tensions and conflicts within "Pauls", i.e. the parrot's house thus: "This goes on all the time in their family" (To Harish-Horatio, Sc. 4, p. 32).

The heroic grandeur attendant upon Shakespeare's Hamlet is similarly subverted in Basu's adaptation. In Shakespeare Hamlet, the prince of Denmark is "the courtier's, soldier's, scholar's eye, tongue, sword;/ The expectancy and rose of the fair state,/ The glass of fashion and the mould of form,/ The observed of all observers" (Act III, sc. 1, ll. 151-54). In Basu, he may be basically a good man fallen into evil times, but is otherwise consciously diminished to a man of no importance, an unemployed Bengali middleclass youth of some education and decadent family who struggles in vain, fitfully and feebly to reveal the truth about his father's death, to take some kind of revenge for that, to regret his inability to fight against all the corruptions around him, and to save his ancestral old, crumbling house from the greedy promoter's grasp set up by uncle Kodu. This is Basu's Hemlat, the prince of Garanhata, far removed in status and charisma from the prince of Denmark.

The passive and exploited Ophelia is here in Basu split into two characters—the sisters *Shefali* and *Mantali*. Shefali is perhaps the most positive character in the play, who as Hemlat's partner, is far removed from the submissive Ophelia. As Harish-Horatio observes about Shefali's gutsy opposition to her father's tyranny:

> Just wait and see how Shafali gives it to Paulda. He's all swaggering on the outside, but before his daughters just a mouse. (Sc. 4, p. 32)

While Ophelia succumbs to authority and the pressures of her "rotten" society, Shefali stands up against them and fights. Her name does contain resonances of immorality as Shefali was a night-club stripper who danced on the Bengali stage of Kolkata of the 1960s-1980s; and offers a kind of parallel to the mad Ophelia's sexually explicit flower-dance in front of King Claudius, Queen Gertrude and the leering Danish court in Act IV of *Hamlet* after Polonius' murder by the prince.

Yet Shefali as Hemlat's Ophelia functions in Basu's play as Hemlat's wife and surrogate-mother who at play's end decides to raise Hemlat's children (real and symbolic—meaning the next generation) and acts as midwife to the hoped—for future revolution that will bring in the great "*parivartan*" or transformation in our society as well as our state.

The degeneration of Hemlat's situation and his post-colonial world of Bengal-India of the late 20th and early 21st century is powerfully and consciously presented in Basu's play. The public and political conflict in Shakespeare's *Hamlet* is between two opposed royal powers represented by Hamlet and Claudius fighting over the fate of Denmark. Here in the Bangla adaptation the Danish state and Elsinore have become a crumbling old mansion with greedy promoters led by *Kodu*-Claudius squabbling and fighting over its acquisition, to raze the property to the ground and construct a high-rise building in its place.

The conflicts are also about the political turf-war between opportunistic parties and infighting among major political ideologies that are going bankrupt. This crisis-time is perhaps just the right historical moment for emergence of a third force and for ushering in something "new", an overwhelming change in society and the nation (*parivartan*). The third force is never mentioned by name specifically as the *Trinamul Congress*. Yet there are strong, perceptible hints and observations on the development of a third force drawing within its ambit most of the disillusioned masses. The hope and promise of a new dawn, a new age of radical change reverberates through key moments in the play. "The time is out of joint", but it must "be set right". In Sc. I, the two night-guards, actually two frustrated, unemployed youths, Basu's version of the Danish guards on the battlements of Elsinore at midnight (*Hamlet*, I, Sc. I) discuss this idea in their own way:

> Bimal: "'New' means 'new'. That something new when it appears will make everyone run like mad... Right now it's all the same every day. Everything's stale and bloodless, anemic. Everything's useless."
>
> Ponkoj: "It'll never come. Nothing's ever going to happen to us bums. Nothing is going to happen."(Sc. I, p. 77)

The night-guards in their alternation between desperate hope and abject despair seem to be echoing the accents of the two tramps—Vladimir and Estragon in Beckett's *Waiting for Godot*.

The Setting: Denmark and Kolkata (Garanhata)

"Something's rotten in the state of Denmark" (*Hamlet*, I, iii, 90) reverberates in Garanhata too. The squalor of this Red-light district of Kolkata and the piled up corruption of this crumbling, decadent late 20th century post-colonial erstwhile capital city of India is brilliantly caught by Basu in *Hemlat*. Shakespeare's London represented by corrupt Denmark of the Medieval-Renaissance period is re-created and re-located into the decadent circle of Garanhata. Garanhata teems with illegal trespassers and immigrants across the Bangladesh Border who eke out a living in the slums; the middle-classes with little property and less money who had once seen better days; the rising money-grabbing promoters and land-sharks trying to be the *nouveau riche* new middle and upper classes; dishonest politicians; businessmen on the make, small-town shop keepers; students, the unemployed, pimps, prostitutes, drunks and drug-addicts—all of whom combine to constitute the post-colonial derelict face of Kolkata, Bengal and India in the late 20th century capitalist phase of our history.

Revenge Theme and Popular Culture/Hindi Movies

At this point we may take a look at Basu's use of popular culture represented here by Hindi films that mesh in with the revenge motive and themes of corruption and decadence of the harrowing present moment of our history and culture. This interlinking of revenge, decadence and popular culture is highlighted in the telling utterance of Hemlat's father's ghost who screams out to his unbelieving son these words in Hindi:

> *Paap se dharti fatti...fatti...fatti...*
>
> *Adharma se asman...man...man...* . (*Hemlat*, sc. 6, p. 101)
>
> ("The earth is fissured and broken apart with sin, impiety is erupting across the skies...*in man, in man, in man...*")

The ghost's screams haunt the entire play and the characters and serve as a reverberating curse in and through the world of *Hemlat*. The ghost is the restless spirit of Sadhan, Hemlat's father, called "*Sadhu jatha*" or "*Sadhan uncle*" who speaks out to the night-guards and later to his son and to all who may listen in fear and trembling the lines of *Tridev*, a mainstream superhit Hindi movie of the 1990s. I quote:

> "Paap se dharti fatti...fatti...fatti...
> Adharma se asman...man...man...
> Atyachar se kampi insaniyat
> Raz kar rahe hawaan...
> Jinki hogi takat apurv —
> Jinki hoga nishana abhed...
> Jo karenge inka sarbanash —
> *Who kahelayenge Tridev... Tridev...Tridev...*" (*Hemlat*, sc. 1, pp. 6-7)

As Sadhan utters this *mantra,* in the background we hear the theme music from *Tridev.* Following this comes the second installment from Sadhan's ghost:

> *"Mhatre naam hain mera – Bhikhu Mhatre... yeh akkha Mumbai ke Don hoon main... mhatre—Bhikhu Mhatre."*

All of us here can easily recall Manoj Bajpei in the Bollywood hit *Satya*—a hit film on corruption and violence in society and in politics. The degeneration and decadence in our body politic (and in England and in Denmark) are focused upon again as Sadhu's ghost (a unique take-off from Hamlet's father's ghost) jumps from film to film both Hindi and *Bangla* quoting scraps from each to ram home the theme of corruption and revenge.

The two night-guards, Hemlat and others who hear of these strange *mantras* coming from Sadhan's ghost may appear to be far from apprehending them in their depth and totality; but it leaves everyone pondering and meditating on the words and on Hemlat's father's addiction to Hindi films when he was alive. Meanwhile, the words *"Paap se dharti fatti... fatti... fatti..."* ring on like a terrible refrain throughout the text and throughout Hemlat's and our worlds and lives.

Such frequent use of popular films, colloquial slang and subversive obscenities throughout the text help to make Hemlat's tragedy relevant and accessible to everyone of us. Hemlat in that sense becomes Everyman.

Language in the Play

The language used in *Hemlat* undergoes a conscious diminishment. We do have some intense passionate passages but the magnificent linguistic splendors of the original are here dislocated into vulgarity, obscenity, slanguage and the common language of the common man. Among proliferating instances we include the following examples:

(i) A character says to one of the night-guards:

"You'll get a whammy of a kick up your backside, you motherfucker... ." (*Hemlat*, sc. 1, p. 2)

(ii) Hemlat himself can give as good as he gets:

"You, son of a bitch! You show me your teeth once

> more and I'll kick your balls in. you dog, You whoreson dog. Go; show your teeth to your father in law. You black dog, you!" (*Hemlat*, sc. 3, p. 23)

Hemlat, like Shakespeare's *Hamlet*, was not written for an academic audience or for professional university-based critics, but for the "*aam-janta*" (the people); and *Hamlet*, though now the world's greatest play, was in its time the most popular revenge tragedy of the Elizabethan-Jacobean period. Bratya Basu's play too is a most popular play dealing with things both "high and low" and he consciously re-creates the *Hamlet* model in every aspect. The veteran Bengali playwright weaves Shakespeare's *Hamlet*, his own and many more future Hamlets to come in Hemlat's agonized, tormented inclusive visions throughout the play; but perhaps most tellingly so in the concluding scenes.

In a bizarre remix of Shakespeare's *Hamlet* in the ninth scene of the play Basu makes Sadhan's ghost berate his son Hemlat's delay, ridicule "his almost blunted purpose" and attack him for selling out to the devil and to his land-grasping uncle Kodu:

> Sadhan: "Is your soul also sold out to the devil, Hem? Everyone's been bought over. Will there be no dreams left in anyone's eyes and hearts, Hem? Everyone will have to suffer all the crimes in silence? All of you want to go on living by selling out to others all the time? Shop-keepers all? Will all of you go about with price-tags on your backs?"
>
> [Hemlat screams out at every question. Now he stops and speaks:]
>
> Hemlat: "Yes, father. I have dreams in my heart. Only I am retching and writhing inside. The worms are biting into my entrails and vitals. When I go to kill Kodu I see my fingers ooze pus and melt. Always and ever this sullied flesh oozes and melts. We are all illegitimate children of our fathers—we are all Bastards, father. There is nothing legitimate about our births. We are all bastards."
>
> [Kodu tries to stop every utterance of Hemlat.

Monorama-Gertrude tries to restrain him.]

Kodu: "shut up, you bastard. Stop it, you son of a gun. One more word out of you and I'll smash you to bits. Stop. Stop, I say. (Kodu screams on.) I admit I have killed my elder brother. Murdered him. One more word out of you and I'll murder you too." (Monorama exits wiping tears. Hemlat speaks to Sadhan in a quiet tone)

Hemlat: "I've become a *hijra*, father. A eunuch. I'll no longer be able to take my revenge standing on the shores of my times. Nothing means anything to anybody now. I no longer feel any hesitation. Doubt, anger, hurt, feelings and emotions all are the same to me now. Cast in the same mould. We, our generation, will no longer feel any response to anything. We are all reaction-less, un-revenging machines. Robots. Robots. We have no anger left, we feel no pain, and we know no way to transcend ourselves. I am an emasculated *hijra*, father. A defeated, expressionless eunuch.

Sadhan: No. No. Kill him, Hem. Fill his mouth with poison. Stick your sword into his guts. *Paap se dharti fatti - fatti - fatti.* Don't spare him Hem. At least *you* don't let him go.

[Exits while speaking. Kodu falls at Hemlat's feet and grabs him.]

Kodu: Forgive me, Hem. Forgive me. Just for some money—o ho-ho-ho—just for a few pieces of gold...forgive me. What, you are shaking with fever. Your body is burning. You are on fire!

[Music plays. Hemlat extricates himself from Kodu and comes front stage. At the back, the silent procession goes on its way. Hemlat picks up a tinsel sword, speaks—

Hemlat: Bring me to the test and see I am not mad. What I have said before and what I am saying now I'll knit them together into one harmony. Only confess

> everything to God. Repent all your sins committed in the past. Turn away from the fruitless and unwanted future. In these lust-obsessed pursy times *Dharma* will come and stand beside *adharma*. With folded hands and bowed head *Dharma* will plead to *adharma* for permission to pray for the good of all. Virtue itself of vice must beg pardon. Hamlet. Third Act. Fourth Scene. (i.e. *Hamlet*, III, 4. ll. 140-54) [Music returns] (*Hemlat*, Sc. 9, pp. 62-64)

Adaptations, re-creations, re-locations and re-mixes and analogues like *Hemlat* carry on a continuing, combative dialogue with the dead and here we have a marvelous dialogue of competing discourses between Hemlat, who himself gives the scene reference to the master text, Hamlet and all the Hamlets past, present and to be written. Hemlat speaks Hamlet's tirade against Claudius, Gertrude and the pursy times with his own *Bangla* variations and telescoped quotes, and creative additions relevant to our times, while himself speaking out the source: "*Hamlet*, Act 3, Sc. 4".

Both Hamlet and Hemlat struggle desultorily and through fits and starts "to take arms against a sea of troubles". Both stumble tragically as they vow revenge. Hamlet achieves revenge, if at all, accidentally while Hemlat takes sleeping pills and attempts and commits suicide. In the eleventh and last scene of the play Hemlat reappears on an empty stage. Behind him stands his father Sadhan in front of the burning pyre. Only the sound of the wind blows as a small boy plays with a toy sword. Hemlat speaks directly to the audience:

"I could not do it. My sword is broken. You cannot kill Time with it. Rather one can pull Laertes' sword towards one's own heart. This is what always happens. But this I know, that our failures will not be seen as important on another day. Those failures will be superseded and transcended by many, many successes. The successes of my children. My son's achievements. I know he will succeed. Shefu (Shefali) will teach him how to succeed and win. Harish, Paulda, uncle, my mother, Lacchu,

Ponka all of them together will teach and train him. Then come, let's go, go. But before I leave let me give you this advice—press your lips with your index finger and be silent. Do not say anything. Express nothing. Our times are bad. As if the time is out of joint. O hate, have I been born only to embrace hate, malice and revenge? Come, come, let all of us go now."

The play ends as a smiling Sadhan places his hand on Hemlat's head, and Hemlat with a fixed gaze places his hand on his son's head, and all freeze.

The three generations stand one after another in line consoling us that in every age, time and again, whenever corruption and depravity engulf humanity, Hamlets will be born and re-born to avenge the wrongs and purify society and the state. They will appear and re-appear in various shapes and forms—sometimes as a Prince in the rotten state of Denmark, sometimes as an urban *Arjuna* caught between Naxalite extremism and quietitude, sometimes as the head of a corporate group caught up in the dirty world of business and high-finance, sometimes as a weak, depressed youth trapped in a devastated post-war world, sometimes as Hemlat. They will end their benighted lives so full of potential—sometimes by the prick of Laertes' envenomed sword, sometimes commit suicide with sleeping pills. They will have to bequeath their superhuman task to their successors and succeeding generations to accomplish, just as Shakespeare's Hamlet left the cleansing of Elsinore to Fortinbras. With the hope, desperate but essential, that what they could not, their successors will achieve. And this is the eternal cycle of civilization; this is the way our lives will go on. Caught in the squalor and injustice of life and the world the Hamlets will grope for solutions. While Shakespeare's *Hamlet* ends in "silence", Bratya Basu's *Hemlat* offers a kind of hope and resolution leaving the ever-unfinished task to his children and the future generations to come. Thus Hamlets, and we, their children and children's children, will be condemned to make the attempts to make a better world weaving and knitting the past, present and future into a rhythm of dissonance and harmony.

Notes and References/Books and Editions Used

All references to Shakespeare's *Hamlet* are from the Arden edition: W. Shakespeare, *Hamlet*. Ed. Harold Jenkins. UK: Arden Shakespeare, 1982.

All references to Bratya Basu's *Hemlat: The Prince of Garanhata* are from the English translation, published in 2012: Bratya Basu, *Hemlat The Prince of Garanhata*; Edited and translated into English from the original Bengali with Annotations, Commentary and Introductory Essays by Amitava Roy, Tapu Biswas, Suchandra Ghosh. Pub. 2012.

NOTES

1. Ranu Pramanik, Shakespeare: Bangla Anubade/Shakespeare in Bengali Translation (1852-2007) Avantgarde Press, Kolkata, 2008.
2. Harold Bloom, *Anxiety of Influence: A Theory of Poetry*, (NY: OUP, 1973).
3. Samik Bandyopadhyay, William Shakespeare *Macbeth*, trans. U. Dutt, (Kolkata: Thema, 2006).
4. Presidential Address in Colonial and post-colonial Shakespeares, edited by Amitava Roy, Krishna Sen, Debnarayan Bandopadhyay. Avantgarde Press, Kolkata, 2001, p. 2.
5. S.C. Sengupta, ed. *Shakespeare's Julius Caesar*, (Calcutta: A. Mukherjee & Co. Pvt. Ltd., 1958).
6. D.A. Shankar, *Shakespeare in Indian Languages*, (Shimla: Indian Institute of Advanced Study, 1999).
7. Jan Kott, *Shakespeare Our Contemporary*, (USA: Methuen & Co. Ltd., 1967).
8. Asit Basu, "Kolkatar Hamlet", *Kolkatar Hamlet: Ramtar Mukut*, (Kolkata: Jatiya Sahitya Parishad, 1989).
9. B. Basu, "Hemlat, the Prince of Garanhata". *Natak Samagra* Vol. 2. Kolkata: Ananda Publishers Pvt. Ltd., 2006. 73-122.
10. Laat's dugs—Laat is the colloquial term for the Viceroy, the lord who rules over the polity. The '*Laat Sahab*', is the owner of the land. The word is derived from the practice of dividing land into separate plots or lots (Lots later becoming Lats in oral speech) which were sold by auction to highest bidders. The British govt. taxed the land owners

according to the amount and numbers of Lots (or Lats) held. Hence whoever owned a large amount of Lots or Lats was an important, rich zamindar. Obviously the Viceroy who owned all of India was referred to as the great *Laat Sahab* and the others as the smaller or "Chhoto" *Laat Sahab*.

11. Ganja: A popular addictive soft drug in India, smoking of which is illegal in many countries across the world. Technically known as *Cannabis indica*.

7

Shakespeare among the Cows

Carole Rozzonelli and *Alessandro Monti*

We will focus on a few cinematic adaptations of Shakespearean dramas, with some considerations concerning in a concise way its heritage back to colonial days. Our main concern will deal with a process of nativization—one which might as well view the Minute (1833-34) by Macaulay as its point of beginning. This seminal start implied the institutional discarding of Indian traditions and culture, in favour of a full Victorian syllabus in education including English literature and its masterpieces, foremost Shakespeare's theatre.

The first contact between Shakespeare and Indian students aroused on the part of the English, either in India or at home, reactions of funny parody. As a matter of fact the Shakespearean discourse was thought to be polluted by Indian backwardness and ridiculous assimilation of English. Consequently its migration within the crude pale of 'Indianness' gave birth in the colonial and Anglo-Indian background to an endless repertory of jokes, grounding on lexical misunderstandings or on hilarious native performances.

With reference to the sometimes confused comprehension of Shakespeare and his sonorous language we would refer to the notorious so-called Baboo English, a bombastic and often semantically surprising Indian version of Victorian English, brought again to light by Amitav Ghosh in *Sea of Poppies* (2008), possibly as a counterpart to the crazy and crippled rendering of native languages by the Anglo-Indian sahibs.

Among the wealth of anecdotes relating the supposed villainous English spoken by the miscreant educated users is worth remembering the sad case of the student whose intensive, but perhaps a bit chaotic, cramming obviously included Hamlet and also Darwin. Requested to comment upon the scene of the ghost in Hamlet the unhappy boy so explained the line in which the prince of Denmark exhorts his father to "unfold your [his] tale". The student apparently understands "tail" instead of the phonetically similar "tale" and so explains that since according to Darwin our ancestors were monkeys, Hamlet's honoured father sported a tail that he is urged to uncoil. The probably apocryphal story was meant to illustrate the uselessness to introduce Shakespeare to the rustic sons of zamindars and the like, given how they would spend all their lives among cows and illiterate peasants in backwood places.

However, we would claim the mofussil imagined displacement of Shakespeare and his language to measures, initially perhaps a bit objectionable but spontaneous, of native relocations of his dramatic environment, in particular if we consider the regional rustic setting in North India of *Omkara* (that is *Othello*; the film has been directed by Vishal Bhardwaj, 2006). Omkara reveals as it were its transgressive ancestry not only by migrating the plot, but also in its treatment of the badly concealed rivalry which opposes the Anglo-Indian ("Anglo", in the filmic text) avatar of Cassius, together with the college version of the native Desdemona, to the coarse embodiment of plotting evil and unchecked rancour for missed power that rakes Iago.

Such a reinterpretation points at a hint of revenge against the Victorian amused consideration of the Indian Shakespeare *wallah*. This reassessment signifies many-layered terms of adherence to Indian basic customs and manners (also in the matter of regional language) with a redeeming evaluation of the much despised mofussil background. The growing into an Indian, or indigenous location, of the Elizabethan Shakespeare introduces us to a qualified awareness of what we should intend by nativization. It is a reinterpretative device different from a simple revisited version of an original text, following measures of contemporaneity (for instance, Julius Caesar replacing the black shirts for the Roman togas, or even the musical metamorphosis of Romeo and Juliet into West Side Story).

To understand the process we have to move back again in time to the colonial age. Then an earliest rough process of nativization did not modified the text, but just adopted performative strategies of everyday local familiarization, a practice however already current in Victorian England and in North America, in matters of scenery, dresses, manners and the like. These rather amateurish performances catered mostly for a low-class audience, often one belonging to specific, and in various ways marginalized groups. In colonial India, however, they were usually patronized by would-be anglicized rajas or nawabs, presumably as a sign of assimilative distinction and/or of *chamcha* attitude towards the English.

Instead of a basic but appealing popularization of Shakespeare, such as witnessed in the West, we should speak of an initially untutored des reshaping of the Elizabethan background, as understood hegemonically in the West. This process led to final terms of thoughtful, and not merely assimilative, approach and then to the partial abrogation of a pristine impositive literalism (via college curricula) in handling the cultural heritage constituted by the Shakespearean canon. Of course such hybridizing representations of Shakespeare in the colonial age were meant for a select (and pre-cinematic) Indian audience, whereas a philological correct interpretation held a parallel sway in colleges, following what happened, and still happens, in the English schools.

A good case in point is given by "Hamlet at a Bengal Fair", a passage taken from Robert E. Vernède, An Ignorant in India (William Blacwood and Sons, Edinburgh, England, 1911), here quoted from British Life in India, Raymond V. Vernède ed., Oxford University Press, Delhi, 1997 (1995), pp. 229-41. The performance is organized by a local raja, in the occurrence of an up-country fair in Bengal. The description of the performance is intended in a tongue in cheek mode. A native orchestra (a harmonium and a tom-tom) plays on the stage, "what—it may be asked—had this orchestra to do with Hamlet? What—as far as that goes—has any orchestra to do with Hamlet?". This notation endorses the judgement that Hamlet "in Bengali is—if my attempt a definition—a musical imbroglio" (p. 235).

A printed synopsis ("The Plot in Short") is given to the Western guests, in order to make them understand what is happening on the stage.

The first scene opens with the King chatting with the Queen in a room in the castle. He then feels drowsy and subsequently falls asleep; whereupon the Queen sends for her husband's brother Farrukh and induces him to drop poison in his ear. The King dies of its effects, and the Queen gives out importunately attributing the cause to a serpent's bite. Jehangir mourns his father's death and Aktar, his friend and associate comforts him.

This delocalization of Shakespeare entails a seminal change in the communicative order of the story, by focusing first on the murder (but the Italian director Franco Zeffirelli misbehaved in a similar way, when his opening scene features the King's funeral, in the presence of Hamlet). However, to displace means to relocate. For instance to attribute the death of the king to a serpent's bite introduces a consistent local notation,

This, it will be observed, is Shakespeare, though not in the order we know it. Liberties have been taken, but what actors have not taken them? The point to be noticed is that the plot serves India admirably. Look at the Queen importunately attributing her husband's death to a serpent's bite. It is thoroughly Bengali. Official returns of today attribute an enormous proportion of deaths among the natives to snakes-bite; individuals say that the variety of snakes is a human one (p. 236).

As a matter of fact this Bengali Hamlet is represented according to a picturesque canon, I have never heard anyone so nasal as Hamlet. He reminded me sometimes of a Swiss jodeler [...], sometimes of a Venetian boatman singing 'Funicoli-Funicola' [...]. He never reminded me of Hamlet (p. 236).

The apex is reached by Meharbano/Ophelia, when she drops her handkerchief, "Absent-mindedly she put out one big toe at it gracefully, half-raised it, and then had the mortification of seeing it fall again. She had forgotten her stockings, prisoned in which her prehensile toe had lost its cunning" (p. 238). The point is that "In Bengal, when you drop a thing, there is no bothering to stoop and pick it up. You use your foot" (p. 238).

A somewhat ludicrous phase of exterior assimilation is witnessed by the "sporting" costume donned by Hamlet, "he wore rowing shorts, puttees and a pair of football boots; also a big pistol in his girdle, such as highwaymen used to carry and, fully exposed like a decoration, a large gun-metal watch and chain over his heart [...]. Well, Hamlet wanted to make quite sure that it was the very witching time of night when he could drink hot blood, and he consulted the gun-watch accordingly" (pp. 236-37). Jehangir (that is Hamlet) stands as an unaccomplished imitative assimilation of British wear meant for a school sports day. This awkward assemblage of clothes mimicking college garb for the playing field or a rowing race (Hamlet was a student after all) leads morphologically to Omkara, when Kareena Kapoor (in the role of Desdemona) learns painfully from the "general" (Cassius) an English song, so as to please her husband.

This act of mimicry updates as it were the blurring divide between assimilative practices and abrogation, between a failed or faked passage in-between cultures and its re-interpretative transformation into an autonomous elsewhere. The same happens with the plot, whose events (not only their sequence) intimates a drastic departure from the original. However, what may seem mere extravagance should be more fruitfully understood as a pre-cinematic treatment of the script, these features including outbursts of romancing passion, some comic relief and even a dancing interlude. Act II is turned into a true passion play, Bombay style.

At the opening of the second act, Farrukh in court putting on the guise of anxiety for Jehangir's safety shows concerns and inquiries. Mansoor the Wazirzada falls in love with Meharbano. Suleiman enters and a conversation passes on. Akhtar recounts the accident of the grave to Suleiman. Seeing Jehangir entering, Suleiman withdraws. Akhtar questions Jehangir who confides him with the disclosure. Mansoor in frenzy declares his love for her (p. 234).

Revenge and the emphasis on the culpability of the Queen (for instance, the love-story with Claudius, alias Farrukh, is more than explicit. In a scene "we come to a room where the Queen is seen merrymaking with Farrukh" constitute further elements of nativization. After the ghost has prompted Hamlet to vengeance, the prince "Roused by his tale did a sword dance, preparatory to taking vengeance. It was a great effort, that dance, lasting roughly for ten minutes, Hamlet doing Indian clubs with his sword and shrieking at the top of his voice" (pp. 239-40). As a matter of fact the sword dance might have remembered the Anglo-Indian writer more properly of a Morris dance (a traditional English country dance, performed by men carrying sticks and wearing costumes with bells and ribbons attached). It should be noted that Morris derives from Morys, that is Moorish or Moor.

In the end a feeling of estrangement prevails: India and Shakespeare belong to different and unassimilable worlds, "The stars glittered from a black velvet sky, and in the starlight, as we drove back, we could see the shrouded Bengalis shuffling home along the dusty road. Though we had all been seeing Shakespeare's Hamlet, I had the strange feeling that we were moving in some time and place that were pre-Shakespearean" (p. 241).

The late presence of Shakespeare on the Indian stage within this double context, of educated and feudal-like elite, is well witnessed by the Ivory film Shakespeare Wallah (1965), which is about the twilight of a wandering British company—they did not leave India after Independence and are faced with the declining interest for British literary culture. The private performance for an anglicized raja, another figure historically on the wane, the half-accepted performance in a school, the representation in a nostalgic club from the Raj, and as such a further relic of the past are the melancholic stages of the growing regret for a bygone age, now lost for ever. In a highly meaningful suggestion college schedules show a lukewarm response to the dramas of Shakespeare, these being now replaced by the rising mania for the practice of cricket, another English heritage however.

A further cause of obsolescence is induced by the ascent of cinema and stardom—a rampant mass cult whose cheap priestess is embodied by the filmi dancing heroine, also a disturbing rival in love with the young Lizzie, and to make matters worse one which causes a major inconvenience during a public performance of the company. Lizzie, English born and living in India, has a truncated brief love-story with an Indian who jilts her (he refuses flatly to marry the girl)—she leaves for England never to return. This separation marks definitely the doomed distance, apart any possible merging between different identities and cultures, even suggesting a reversal of hegemonies.

The juxtaposition of commercial cinema and Shakespeare is taken up again by Rituparno Ghosh in *The Last Lear* (2007), a film in which an ageing Shakespearean actor is induced by a director to play in his film, *The Mask*, the role of a murderous and disfigured clown. His character is shot down a cliff in the last scene, and he refuses to be replaced by a professional stuntman. He survives a first fall, but the unsatisfied director tricks him into repeating the scene, with the result that the old actor is seriously injured to a comatose state. He will die on the night of the première, with Shakespeare's words on his lips.

He had quit the stage several years before, because someone had unpleasant words against the woman he lived and lives together, and on the eve of performing Prospero in *The Tempest*, to crown his career. Nowadays nobody seems to care for Shakespeare, in a society ruled pitilessly by selfishness and jealousy, competition for success and human insensibility. The solitude of women is a leading submotif as well in the film—both the night nurse and the model turned to actress (to whom he has taught the magic of Shakespeare) share a crumbling and unhappy affective life—in a sad correlation with the loneliness of a betrayed and finally unfulfilled King Lear.

The germs for the cinematic craze may also trace back to the pre-bourgeois Parsi theatre, whose stage mixed freely action, passionate love, dance and song. Perhaps its performative range helped to shape some des features in the cinematic translations of Shakespeare—foremost the handling of passion and betrayal, on the corporate background of a struggle for power (within a closed community), one which does not attain a metaphysics of culpability and bitter isolation, but instructs the drama of an overflowing self, also in terms of excessive individual wish, because bounded by a society (as it happens in *Omkara* and in *Maqbool*, Vishal Bhardwaj, 2003) in which corruption and violence are the everyday behaviour and rule. The focus here is not exclusively on usurping individuals, whose rise in authority is finally nullified by growing feelings of culpability or unsteadiness in character. It rather concerns the institutional mechanics which allows or even promotes such heavy infringements against public or domestic morality.

In the Indian context it is quite impossible to separate the representation of individuality from a public and shared discourse of control and approbation—so in films like *Omkara* and *Maqbool* the acts which claim desire, not always in simple intimations of power, are obliged to deny it, given the all-absorbing interconnection between the simple self and the hyperstructured dimension or extended nexus-like structured body of society. So the normative violations nurtured by individual self-desire are always liable to be twisted into a grid of punishing agencies, many of them in their turn outside the pale of the legal sphere of authorization.

The notion itself of a split in authority opens the way to a wild decentralization of conflictual powers, whose symbol of rupture and fragmentation is given by the crumbling unity of the gangs in *Omkara* and *Maqbool*. The different, and often antinomic, individualities of their members mimic, or rather mock, the very concept of the nation-state and of its achieved unity in multiform difference. Instead of an inclusive national body (one once featured originally in cinema by *Dharmaputra*, Yash Chopra, 1961) these films focus pitilessly on a state of disorder and unchecked rivalry. It is a long way from the eulogic patriotic and hopeful films of the fifties (*Mother India*, Mehboob Khan, 1954), with their village controlled inclusiveness and their anti-vigilante or dakoit bias, such as expressed against the rebellious son, in an achieved harmony of aims and means between the basic domestic domains within the village and a central authority.

The emphasis laid on domestic order and nationhood modifies in the Indian cinematic versions of Shakespeare the Elizabethan notion of ruling power, viewed as the descending reflection of the coordinated movement originating in the heavenly spheres. Its metaphoric representation equated the sophisticated dancing at court, with its exact measures and geometries, to the divine harmony of stars and planets. A poem by John Davies, Orchestra or A Poem of Dauncing—1596/1622, imagined the Queen sitting in the middle of the room, a mirror in her hand to reflect her harmonizing visage towards the dancing courtiers.

The Indian refiguration of this archetypal flowing of symbols between sky and earth through a royal person in power is supplanted in the Indian cinema dealing with Shakespeare by a hierarchy of correlated clusters, progressing upwards from family (this also implying further links as gotra and caste) to village and nation. The corporate and aggregating structures in *Maqbool* and *Omkara* proceed functionally like this: at the bottom the extended in-group formed by the gang (that is a family-like circle), then the corrupt police-wallahs (who should ensure the joint respect of the specified standard of behaviour, a task achieved in Mother India by the village), at the top the inter-conflicting politicians, whose selfish greediness and murderous lust for power disrupts and authorizes as a consequence shocking disorder instead of a well-regulated mechanics in the institutions.

As a side effect this disintegrating frame collapses as well the eulogic link with the morally beautifying landscape of the Indian nation. For instance in *Jis Desh Mein Ganga Behti Hai* (Radhu Karmakar, 1960) the lyrical sublimation of a shared Indian motherland reintegrates the outlawed gang of dacoits into the fold of nationhood, in a way that runs against the successive evolution of the subgenre, at least in *Bandit Queen* (Shekhar Kapur, 1994) and in *Paan Singh Tomar* (Tigmanshu Dhulia, 2012), the latter a film in which the honoured service to the nation does not help to achieve justice in the general corruption of the village landlord and of the district powers.

The Indian version in cinema of *Othello* (*Omkara*) and *Macbeth* (*Maqbool*) are branched off from the so-called crime, or dacoit, film, in their representation of patriarchal dons and their evil nexus with badnaam politicians and police-wallahs. This transformation of Elizabethan drama in des terms which cast a critical eye on contemporary Indian society includes as well romancing in standard measures of contrasted or transgressively-conquered mutuality within the tabooing bonds of a close and hierarchic community. So Maqbool exasperates the dangerous effect of sexual, or erotic wish, and recuperates fatherhood as a token of acquisitive masculinity—Maqbool becomes the supposed father of a son, actually the possible offspring, and the future leader of the gang, generated by the previous don Abhaj, killed and replaced by him.

This patriarchal imagination illustrates how the dramatized search after power (one which implies the fall of princes, according to the English Medieval and non-Aristotelian definition of tragedy) calls for inflected rationales of gender and family relationships. The first issue endorses feminine culpability, particularly in the seductive behaviour of Abbaj's wife, and also in the professional characterization of the don's lover, a suggested tawaif role, one which elaborates on the dancing and naughty actress in Shakespeare Wallah, and more overtly in the item girl which sings and dances with lascivious extravaganza throughout a couples of scenes in *Maqbool*.

For the second issue the qualifiers of customary domesticity in traditional rural areas are openly instructive in *Omkara*, also given the transition from the urban setting and Muslim milieu of *Maqbool* to the Hindu rustic background of *Omkara*. Here the racial marginality of *Othello* (the Moor in the text), metaphorically the barbarian within the walls, is structurally evoked by the unmodernized transferred location of the events to somewhere presumably in North India's badlands, a place suggestive of violence and backwardness, ridden with dacoity and murderous political intrigue.

The family clan in *Omkara* (one which is paralleled by the representation of the rustic patriarchy in *Shakti—The Power* (Krishna Vamsi, 2002) stands for the closed military establishment in Cyprus, an interface of depersonalising sites that in both dramas moulds a personal and long-standing resentment into a crafty and shattering revenge. Both *Maqbool* and *Omkara* move as a matter of fact on the fringe of the revenge play—they explore exploded individual subjectivities within the unchecked borders of domestic-like communities which deregulate the rule of shared belonging into interrupting outbursts of conflictual energy.

In particular Omkara not only shifts the narrative of the family feud from the domestic circle to the gang (a transition not attained in *Shakti—The Power*, which just denounces the authority of backward patriarchy) but instructs a series of implied links which connect together a multifaceted discourse on power. It ranges from discarded conjugality, corruption in politics, the goonda gang which is seen as a tainted symbol of infection within the collapsing body of the Indian nation. Consequently the claim of des values and styles of life, which was central in the early cinema of the new India (*Andaz*, Mehboob Khan, 1949; *Amar*, Mehboob Khan, 1954) becomes in *Omkara* a motif of dissolution and the rupture of the conjugal pact which was instrumental in raising and maintaining the identity of India after Independence.

Consequently, the personal feeling of malevolence and grudge which acts behind the revenge in the film feels its objective substance (that is, nationalist) in the largely shared resentment among the members of the gang against the Anglo heritage. This is the weak spot in Omkara's love, in a way that transcends the individuality of reactive jealousy. If in *Andaz* the believed culpability of the woman was meant to preserve national cohesion through the defence of unpolluted conjugality, in *Omkara* it operates as an agency of ruin and doomed destiny, one indicative of a public disturb.

A kind of punitive balance is finally restored in the film through a standard ritual evocation of avenging feminity—Konkona (who plays the role of Saif's, that is Iago, wife) kills her husband. She takes for a while the identity of a furious Devi, but immediately afterwards becomes again the Hindu wife, a desperate and sobbing sati, not purified by fire, one who is going to throw herself into a well.

However, such a numinous double quotation marks the collapse of the corporate national frame, both in the public and private spheres. It is something different from the Shakespearian "fall of princes" or the failed integration of the foreigner into the receiving city. It stands as an uncouth dispersal of decentralizing powers rather than for an unauthorized usurpation, a theme which is central to *Macbeth* and *The Tempest*. In *Omkara* a kind of political communalism (murders included) controls and endorses through violence the ascent and the fall of the ruling authorities. This hellish background of noxious institutional and degenerated behaviour was absent in the patriotic films of the fifties.

Mother India, for instance, emphasized the self-governance of the archetypal Indian village (a sort of rustic but spontaneously tutored swades) as the normative power, either against the excess of individualism or the still early stage of the personalized social rebellion (later, the vigilante hero). The only sign here of an authorized power outside the village is given by the framing caterpillars that dig a canal to irrigate the land. If *Omkara* constitutes a salient instance of reversal, since the previous correlation of powers between a centre and its many peripheries yields to the successive fragmentation hitting at a shared identity, the tragedy of usurpation in *Maqbool* recuperates through its prevalently Muslim setting and its feudal-like ambiance a pre-modern notion of royalty, but a self-authorizing one, in the petty court of the don.

In the film the tearing fight for power and, outside the gang, hegemonic control in the urban area articulates a shattering of clans reciprocally hostile one another and instructs individual revenge as the only possibility of survival within the group. The numinous and specifically folkloric resorting to uncanny prophecy and ambiguous predestination which in Macbeth acts as a chorus that unveils to the audience the inner feelings and unconfessed purposes of the ambitious usurper is reshaped halfparodically in *Maqbool* though the funny personae of the two corrupted officers of police. In particular one of them draws continually horoscopes (a recurrent item in Indian culture), not to address or reflect the action, but as an external voice that conveys comedy and popular superstition in lieu of dark comedy. Instead of premonitions which echo back the hidden wishes of Macbeth, in *Maqbool* the initially firm loyalty of the hero is slowly and almost painfully shaken over by the seductive insistence of the Don's wife. Here again the culpability of the woman (whose passion is a mix of lechery and long-standing resentment against her unfaithful husband) is emphasized as the founding behavioural framework which gives the action a destructive push forwards. The paradigm usurpation-fall acquires in *Maqbool* a domestic turn, but also disarticulates at the same time desire through its simplification, one that causes male disempowerment because of feminine sexual overflowing. The excessive disclosure of female unbridled desire redefines the inner codes of the Shakespearian original in a way which introduces confusion and internal feud into a precariously set hierarchy.

We should consider the discourse of infringing seduction which takes place in *Maqbool* simultaneously with the suggested evocation of the Sita myth longing for the skin of the golden deer, an act of female greed which courses havoc also in *Omkara*. The shakhi steals out of vanity a precious family heritage belt, and the theft will be used by her scheming husband as the proof of the adultery which constitutes the turning point in the events. Both films foreground feminine transgressive subjectivity—a feature which generates through its narrativization of reifying desire, both in women and consequently in men, an institutional crisis which illustrates a fall in power.

A rhetoric centering on biographical drama (one replacing domesticity and conjugality for the throne) accomunates in this purview *Omkara* and *Maqbool* to the intimate drama of Hamlet, given its traumatic separation between individuality and power, by means of a blurring and devastating tale of adulterous lechery and usurpation. Indian cinema adapts Shakespeare to the evils of its country and age, in an accomplished fusion of domestic tragedy and of a mirror for the magistrates.

8

Lust for Life: Life for Lust: Shakespeare's Examination of 'A Natural Guiltiness' in *Measure for Measure* and *Antony and Cleopatra*

Niranjan Goswami

> To't, Luxury, pell-mell!
> For I lack soldiers. (*King Lear*, IV.vi.116-117)

Measure for Measure is one of the many works of the Jacobean period reflecting the sombre Puritanical mood of the times ruing over the spread of corruption and vice in London. Shakespeare's focus in this play is not only upon the ruler's dilemma over meting out justice and mercy[1] in the face of proliferating crime but also on the interpretation of such universally hated sin as lust. In sonnet 129 Shakespeare presents an unmitigated picture of lust as 'perjur'd, murderous, bloody, full of blame,/ Savage, extreme, rude, cruel, not to trust' that can only bring madness and lead to hell.[2] *Measure for Measure*, however, is a more complex work and gives a nuanced representation of lust, which is not just one of the seven deadly sins in the medieval tradition but from a post-Lutheran consciousness is an important ingredient necessary to a degree to constitute love and pleasure that finds its civil and religious sanction in matrimony. In order to understand what 'lust' may have meant for Shakespeare in these two plays we will have a brief look at the history of the concept since the middle ages.

In translations of the *New Testament*, the word 'lust' often translates the Greek word 'epithumeo': "Ye have heard that it was said by them of old time, Thou shalt not commit adultery: But I say unto you, That whosoever looketh on a woman to lust after her ('epithumeo') hath committed adultery with her already in his heart." (Matt. 5:27–28).[3] In Roman Catholicism Pope Gregory I made a list of the seven deadly sins in which 'luxuria' (original meaning was extravagance) came to stand for lust. St. Thomas Aquinas defines the sin of lust in his Summa Theologia Questions 153 and 154 (www.sacred-texts.com/chr/aquinas/summa/index.htm). Aquinas says the sin of lust is of "voluptuous emotions," and makes the point that sexual pleasures, "unloosens the human spirit," and set aside right reason. Aquinas restricts lust's subject matter to physical desires specifically arising from sexual acts, but he does not assume all sex-acts are sinful. Sex is not a sin in marriage, because sex is the only way for humans to reproduce. If sex is used naturally and the end purpose is reproduction there is no sin. Aquinas says, "[I]f the end be good and if what is done is well-adapted to that, then no sin is present...." However, sex simply for the sake of pleasure is lustful and therefore, a sin. A man who uses his body for lechery wrongs the Lord. Sex may have the attributes of being sinless; however, when a person seeks sex for pleasure, he or she is sinning with lust. Lust is best defined by its specific attribute of rape, adultery, seduction, unnatural vice, and simple fornication, etc.

> In one of his sermons Wyclif wrote that lust awakens in man as a result of lack of faith:
>
> Some failen in beleve, for their beleve slepith, and other thingis waketh that thei trowen more; and thus failith ech man that is overcomen with synne; for lust wakith in hem to whiche the synne moveth hem, and peyne and drede of his synne is leide asleepe; and thus failen in trouthe the more part of men. (Wyclif 70)
>
> His use of the word 'lust' is in a quite indeterminate sense. It is clearer in another sermon:
>
> Here men may touche many synnes that rengnen amonge

> men and specialy synne of clerkes that lyven in lustis of food and lustis of atire contrarie to Joon Baptiste. (Wyclif 73)

The reason of this could be that in the medieval conception, lust, gluttony and sinful attire—all were bound up together because one deadly sin encouraged another.

Even an early reformer like Latimer looks upon lechery as a sin prompted by the devil. In one of his sermons he says:

> So likewise when we be in health, the devil moveth us to all wickedness and naughtiness, to whoredom, lechery, theft, and other horrible faults; putting clean out of our mind the remembrance of God and his judgments, insomuch that we forget that we shall die. Again, when we be in sickness, he goeth about like a lion to move and stir us up to impatiency and murmuring against God; or else he maketh our sins so horrible before us that we fall into desperation. (*The 7th Sermon upon the Lord's Prayer, 1549)*

The line between physical desire that is love and physical desire that is lust is often a thin and wavering one. Robert Burton in his *Anatomy of Melancholy* writes that he will examine "all the kinds of love, his nature, beginning, difference, objects, how it is honest or dishonest, a virtue or vice, a natural passion or a disease" (III, 473). Burton discusses all kinds of love following the division of it into Natural, Sensible, and Rational Love. Both the degree to which man is inflamed and the object of his desire seem to distinguish love from lust for Burton. If it "rage, it is no more love, but burning lust; a disease, phrenzie, madness, hell" (III, 499), and he proceeds to catalogue all of the horrors that result from lust. He admits that there is "an honest love, I confess, which is natural, laqueus occultus captivans corda hominum, ut a mulieribus non possint separari; a secret snare to captivate the hearts of men, as Christopher Fonseca proves, a strong allurement, of a most attractive, occult, adamantine property, and powerful virtue, and no man living can avoid it" (III, 501). He tells us that "this nuptial love is a common passion, and honest, for men to love in the way of marriage" (III, 501). But the passion that is "immoderate, inordinate, and not to be comprehended in any bounds. It will not contain itself within the union of marriage, or apply to one object, but is a wandering, extravagant, a domineering, a boundless, an irrefragable, a destructive passion: sometimes this burning lust rageth after marriage, and then it is properly called Jealousy; sometimes before, and then it is called Heroical Melancholy" (III, 502). David O. Frantz writes that "the issue is complex, and in determining what is glorified physical love and what is lust in literature we also face some hazy boundaries." (159 note 6)

In this context we may observe that Calvin's idea of lust was in conformity with the medieval attitude. In one of his sermons while deliberating on how one should dress he comes upon the theme of lechery:

> Howsoever the world go, let us learn that God will have us not only to be pure and clean from all lechery, but also to prevent all inconveniences. As for example, when he saith, Thou shalt not commit adultery: that commandment hath an eye to this present text. I have told you already, that all the laws which are written here, concern manners, & are rules of good life, & are to be referred to the ten commandments: For God hath not added anything to those ten sentences. Therefore whereas in this text it is said that the man shall not wear the apparel of the woman; doth God set down an eleventh commandment? (www.truecovenanter.com)

Lechery, for Calvin has many manifestations and some human conducts may encourage man in lechery. In this sermon Calvin's example is that of cross-dressing:

> And therefore let us mark, that to keep ourselves from such dangers, and from defiling our bodies with lechery, and other infections; we must eschew evil occasions, and not meddle with anything that may allure us to any wicked lust of lechery, or otherwise, but apparel ourselves soberly and necessarily. Thus ye see in effect, how we ought to put this commandment in use. (www.truecovenanter.com)

On the one hand the Reformers condemned lechery but on the other they also acknowledged the importance of marriage and lawful pleasure in sex. The key text in this respect was *Genesis: 9:7*:

> And you, be ye fruitful, and multiply; bring forth abundantly in the earth, and multiply therein. (*Genesis* 9:7).

Such was God's advice to Adam after his fall and to Noah after the Flood. Edmund Leites refers to a Roman Catholic Catechism that incorporates the Counter-Reformation ideas of marriage according to which the first of the appropriate ends of marriage is

> [The] very partnership of diverse sexes—sought by natural instinct, and compacted in the hope of mutual help so that one aided by the other may more easily bear the discomforts of life and sustain the weakness of old age. Another is the appetite of procreation, not so much that heirs of property and riches be left, but that worshippers of the true faith and religion be educated . . . And this is the one cause why God instituted marriage at the beginning. . .The third is one which after the fall of the first parent was added to the other causes,... [for man's] appetite began to fight with right reason; so indeed he who is conscious of his weakness and does not wish to bear the battle of the flesh may use the remedy to avoid the sins of lust.[4] (Leites 383-384)

In *De Genesi ad Litteram Libri Duodecim, 9. 7* Augustine concludes that woman is of use to man because of her child-bearing capacity. However, he is silent on the question of pleasure of companionship (Leites 384). By making companionship the first end of marriage, the authors of the Catechism go beyond Augustine. St Thomas Aquinas finds that companionship makes marriage an essentially human union because it assumes equality between the monogamous partners. "The greatest friendship" seems to be between spouses, Thomas writes, for husband and wife "are made one not only in the act of carnal intercourse, which even among dumb animals causes an agreeable fellowship, but also as partners in the whole intercourse of daily life: so that, to indicate this, man must leave father and mother (Gen. 2. 24) for his wife's sake"[5] (Leites 385).

In the Renaissance the debate centred around the question of the comparative superiority of celibacy or chastity over marriage. Erasmus strongly spoke not only in favour of marriage but also pleasure in sex. Erasmus says, "the most holy kynd of lyfe is wedlocke puerly & chastly kept." And in this bond, duty and pleasure need not be enemies (Leites 386): [6]

> ...[I]f the most parte of thynges (yea whyche be also bytter) ar of a good man to be desyred for none other purpose, but bycause they be honeste, matrimony doutles is chefely to be desyred whereof a man may dout whether it hath more honesty than plesure [.] For what thynge is sweeter, then with her to lyve, with whome ye may be most streghtly copuled, not only in the benevolence of the mynd, but also in the coniunction of the body.[7] (Leites 386)
>
> On the question of sex Erasmus is quite straightforward in acknowledging its relevance:
>
> [It has]...bene rightly everywhere pronounced as a proverbe, that *god nor nature have made no thynge frustrate nor in vayne* / why (I pray you) hath god geven us these members? why these pryckes and provocations? why hath he added the power of gettynge, if bachelarshyp be taken for a prayse?" (Leites 386) [8]

Of course this went against the vain of Roman Catholic monasticism which glorified celibacy and Erasmus's *Encomium Matrimonii* was quickly put on the Index of prohibited books. On the continent, the Council of Trent declared the view that marriage is superior to celibacy "anathema" (Leites 386). The Puritans also did not believe in the virtue of celibacy. William Secker wrote:

> When all other creatures had their mates, Adam wanted his: Though he was the Emperor of the Earth, and the Admiral of the Seas, yet in Paradise without a

> companion, though he was truly happy yet he was not fully happy; Though he had enough for his board, yet he had not enough for his bed; Though he had many creatures to serve him, yet he wanted a creature to solace him; when he was compounded in creation, he must be compleated by conjunction; when he had no sinne to hurt him, then he must have a wife to help him; *It is not good that man should be alone.* (Leites 387)[9]

Martin Luther's rejection of celibacy and his marriage with Katherine von Bora in 1525 was not only a refusal to obey canon law but a severe critique of Roman Catholic ideology on the issue of marriage and sex.[10] Thomas A. Fudge writes:

> Luther insisted that priests ought to be allowed to marry in order to avoid temptation and sexual misconduct, and saw the vow of chastity as a "devilish tyranny," which no bishop had the right to require. Luther refused to take a position on whether individuals ought to marry or remain single, preferring to leave such decisions to the judgment of each person. Nevertheless, he felt certain that it was wicked to live licentiously or in concubinage, and better to enter the legitimate state of matrimony. According to Luther, "salvation ... is more important than the observation of tyrannical, arbitrary, and wanton laws that are not necessary to salvation or commanded by God." (323)

Luther was biting on the monastic vow of chastity:

> I fear that greed is a cause of this wretched, unchaste celibacy. As a result, everyone has wanted to become a priest and everyone wants his son to study for the priesthood, not with the idea of living in chastity, for that could be done outside the priesthood. [Their idea is to] be supported in temporal things without work or worry, contrary to God's command..." (Fudge 323 n. 25)[11]

For Luther, marriage was not just about sex, but about salvation, and in this way the religious nature of marriage was emphasized. Four hundred years earlier, Peter Abelard may have argued for the goodness of sexual intercourse in its own right, but not one of the reformers of the sixteenth century, save Bucer, ever completely separated sinfulness from sex.[12]

Even before Claudio's offence is named in *Measure for Measure* the conversation of the low characters Pompey, Mistress Overdone, the two Gentlemen and Lucio lightens the offence by alluding to the irreverent flouting of the Ten Commandments in Vienna, the whorehouses, and venereal disease. In such context Pompey refers to the offence as 'Groping for trouts in a peculiar river'. This harmless piscatorial image lessens the gravity of the offence. Later charged by Lucio to mention the offence, Claudio imagines it to be too grave an offence to be named and has instead Lucio name it.

> Lucio. ... What's thy offence, Claudio?
> Cla. What but to speak of would offend again.
> Lucio. What, is't murder?
> Cla. No.
> Lucio. Lechery?
> Cla. Call it so. (*M for M*, I. ii.126 – 129)[13]

It is not Shakespeare's purpose here to make light of lechery, a deadly sin. However, we must remember the peculiar circumstances of the couple. Claudio and Juliet were bound by the marriage law of *sponsalia per verba de praesenti* (Lever liii-liv);[14] their marriage was only to be completed by church announcements. This marriage would hold good under the eyes of canon law and therefore Claudio is right in claiming "she is fast my wife,/ Save that we do the denunciations lack/ Of outward order." (*M for M,* I.ii.136-138.) However, sexual union between partners before the marriage is solemnized in a church would attract the sin of fornication in a Catholic dispensation and Juliet's pregnancy makes it an established fact. It would of course be deemed otherwise in the Reformed circles because Luther held the view that sexual intimacy during the period of "engagement" was absolutely permissible and did not constitute fornication and he himself probably did the same with Katherine von Bora. (Fudge 332)[15] But even though Angelo is sketched in puritanical terms, the dispensation in Vienna is not Reformist. That Claudio and Juliet are held guilty of fornication shows that the law against fornication is an outdated one as the religious doctrine behind it has been proved to be outdated by Protestant reformers. The 'puritanical' Angelo is therefore not a Puritan but a Roman Catholic in sentiment.

If Claudio and Juliet have committed any crime, by the Duke's own admission he is complicit in that crime: "for we bid this be done,/ When evil deeds have their permissive pass,/ And not the punishment." (*M for M*, I.iii.37-39) While the Duke appears contrite at his past leniency, Claudio in a mood of despondency tends to believe himself a sinner and gives expression to the traditional view of lechery: "Our natures do pursue,/ Like rats that ravin down their proper bane,/ A thirsty evil; and when we drink, we die." (*M for M*, I.ii.120-122) It is interesting to note how many characters in this play lack self-knowledge apart from the two 'puritanical' characters Angelo and Isabella. These two characters are presented as virtuous, possessing chastity, the opposite of lust. It is important for the dramatist to contrast the general venality of Vienna with the superhuman chastity of Angelo and Isabella. The Duke refers to Angelo as "A man of stricture and firm abstinence" (*M for M*, I.iii.12); "Lord Angelo is precise; / Stands at guard with Envy; scarce confesses/ that his blood flows." (*M for M*, I.iv.50-52) Later Lucio says about Angelo: "a man whose blood/ Is very snow-broth; one who never feels / The wanton stings and motions of the sense" (*M for M*, I.iv.56-58); whereas he calls Isabella "a thing enskied and sainted" (*M for M*, I.iv.34). When Isabella is first introduced we see her finding the discipline and restraint imposed upon the nuns at Saint Clare too liberal rather than strict. To the surprise of the nun she tells her: "I speak not as desiring more, / But rather wishing a more strict restraint / Upon the sisters stood, the votarists of Saint Clare" (*M for M*, I.iv.3-5). Angelo and Isabella are extremists in their notion of virtue and self-deluded. Luther's objection was against such hypocritical celibacy of the monks and nuns. As soon as the opportune moment of temptation arrives such hypocrites fall. Whereas Angelo's fall in this play is spectacular and exemplary Isabella's silent acceptance of the Duke's proposal at the end of the play that has baffled many critics is in fact the proper logical consequence of her past delusional chastity.

As Erasmus held, sexual desire is natural to man[16] and Shakespeare poses the idea in a straight-forward manner through an exchange between Pompey and Escalus:

> Pom. Does your worship mean to geld and splay all the / youth of the city?
>
> Esc. No, Pompey.
>
> Pom. Truly sir, in my poor opinion, they will to't then. (*M for M*, II.i.227-230)

The universality of desire in man is brought out most piquantly in Angelo's temptation and fall. Isabella pleads to Angelo who is resolved to execute her brother:

> Isab. Go to your bosom,
> Knock there, and ask your heart what it doth know
> That's like my brother's fault. If it confess
> A natural guiltiness, such as is his,
> Let it not sound a thought upon your tongue
> Against my brother's life.
> Ang. She speaks, and 'tis such sense
> That my sense breeds with it.—Fare you well.
> (*M for M*, II.ii.137-144)

In a single phrase 'natural guiltiness' Shakespeare captures the dichotomous moral judgement on sex of the times: it is both natural and thus should be condoned and there is a guilt about it. The striking use of 'sense' with different meanings (the first 'sense' stands for 'rightness/meaningfulness', whereas the second 'sense' stands for 'sensual desire') further enhances the ambiguity; not just literal ambiguity but also moral ambiguity in Angelo's position.

Among the various trials in this play Angelo's trial is of the greatest consequence. In a sense the whole play is Angelo's temptation and trial. However, Angelo is only saved by the bed-trick conjured up by the Duke. The bed-trick was necessary as cohabitation would turn Angelo's marriage with Mariana as per *sponsalia per verba de futuro* to a fast marriage according to canon law. Secondly, because of this trick Angelo's fornication with Isabella did not materialize as is argued and pleaded by Isabella to seek the Duke's pardon for Angelo: "For Angelo,/ His act did not o'ertake his bad intent,/ And must be buried but as an intent/ That perish'd by the way." (*M for M*, V.i.448-451)

If *Measure for Measure* is about correctly judging or measuring the love/lust complexity *Antony and Cleopatra* is about Antony's "dotage" over Cleopatra that "O'erflows the measure." Antony's "dotage" in the second line corresponds to the "gipsy's lust" in the ninth line of the play. Shakespeare in this play takes up 'luxuria' not only in the sense of lust but in the older sense of extravagance or abundance as well. In fact, the whole play turns upon the polarities of Rome and Egypt, West and East, reason and passion, male and female and so on (Payne 266).[17] If there is no limit to be set on desire, as Antony says "There's beggary in the love that can be reckon'd," (*A and C*, I.i.15) then the boundary between love and lust becomes invisible.

Love and lust are intrinsically bound up with pleasure in the 'epicurean' economy of this play.[18] In a moment of reflection after Fulvia's death Antony recognizes the transience of pleasure: "The present pleasure,/ By revolution lowering, does become/ The opposite of itself: she's good, being gone,..." (*A and C*, I.ii.121-123). This could mean Antony's growing unease with his slothful life with Cleopatra at the cost of neglecting duty to the empire; this could also suggest that absence of the object of love makes one pine for it (as in the case of Antony for Fulvia). Either way, one must pursue one's desire and take on one's stride the consequences of such pursuit. Interestingly, both Epicureanism and Stoicism advised against *luxuria;* Stoicism suggested that one must practice *apatheia*, i.e. not being overwhelmed by any passion and according to Epicureanism one should aim at a balanced and calm state of mind or *ataraxia*.[19] Such a man, however, could be no Shakespearean hero or heroine. Antony and Cleopatra are drawn oversize, their dimensions are beyond the ordinary and they are great-souled or magnanimous in the Aristotelian sense. An indifferent observer like Enobarbus can make out that Cleopatra's "passions are made of nothing but the finest part of pure love" (*A and C*, I.ii.144-145). The contradiction between this "pure love" and "gypsy's lust" is never resolved in the play.

Caesar's criticism of Antony is direct: "If he fill'd / his vacancy with voluptuousness, / Full surfeits, and the dryness of his bones / Call on him for't." (*A and C*, I.iv.25-28) Antony should be chided like little boys who "Pawn their experience to present pleasure, / And so rebel to judgment" (*A and C*, I.iv.32-33). The word 'pleasure' continues to reverberate in the next scene as the eunuch Mardian asks Cleopatra "What's your highness' pleasure?" She replies churlishly, "Not now to hear thee sing. I take no pleasure / In aught an eunuch has..." (A and C, I.v.8-10). Cleopatra's aggressive sexuality is pitted against Mardian's sexless nature; however, she is troubled by the absence of Antony and asks Mardian "Hast thou affections?" Does "affections" stand here for love or lust? Cleopatra is clearly thinking here in sexual terms. Her lines "Stands he, or sits he?" and "O happy horse to bear the weight of Antony!" (*A and C*, I.v.19-21) give it out.

Pompey's description of Antony in the next act presents the negative interpretation of Antony's character in full:

> Let witchcraft join with beauty, lust with both,
> Tie up the libertine in a field of feasts,
> Keep his brain fuming; Epicurean cooks
> Sharpen with cloyless sauce his appetite,
> That sleep and feeding may prorogue his honour,
> Even till a Lethe'd dulness-
>
> (*A and C*, II.i.22-27)

Cleopatra is here associated with the powers of dark magic, beauty and lust to seduce Antony; Epicurean (associated with hedonism in the common misunderstanding of the term) feasts, sleep, feeding and dullness complete the arraignment of the deadly sins of gluttony, lechery and sloth. Pompey believes that it would be crediting themselves with too much to imagine "that our stirring / Can from the lap of Egypt's widow pluck / The ne'er-lust-wearied Antony" (*A and C*, II.i.36-38). The last phrase with reference to Antony is particularly damning. But Shakespeare has many other speeches up his sleeve to present the heroic picture of Antony sufficient to deify him.

The hedonistic and slothful life in Egypt finds a reference again later in the conversation between Maecenas and Enobarbus:

> Eno. Ay, sir, we did sleep day out of countenance; and made the night light with drinking.
>
> Maec. Eight wild-boars roasted whole at a breakfast, and
> but twelve persons there; is this true?
>
> Eno. This was but as a fly by an eagle: we had much more monstrous matter of feast, which worthily deserved noting. (*A and C*, II.ii.177-183)

In consonance with the rioting and feasting with which Antony and other Romans like Enobarbus indulged in Egypt, the first description of the queen in the barge scene is a riot of the senses:

> Eno. Her gentlewomen, like the Nereides,
> So many mermaids, tended her i'the eyes,
> And made their bends adornings. At the helm
> A seeming mermaid steers: the silken tackle
> Swell with the touches of those flower-soft hands,
> That yarely frame the office. From the barge
> A strange invisible perfume hits the sense
> Of the adjacent wharfs. (*A and C*, 206-213)

The mythological allusions to Nereides and mermaids metamorphose Cleopatra and her maids into creatures of another world; the senses of vision, touch and smell are all assaulted by a riot of pleasant stimuli associated with the orient. Antony is so transformed by the over-indulgence that "Being barber'd ten times o'er, goes to the feast; / And for his ordinary, pays his heart, / For what his eyes eat only." (*A and C*, II.ii.224-226) In Act III Caesar speaks of Antony's lust (*A and C*, III.vi.60-61) and Maecenas calls him "the adulterous Antony" (III.vi.93). As the war drums start rolling, the language of love and lust is replaced by that of war and politics.

We may abstain from following the ups and downs of the love story of Antony and Cleopatra of which Shakespeare exploits the dramatic potential fully. The betrayals, misunderstandings, quarrels and patching up between the two carry forward the plot through the thick of battle. What elevates them beyond ordinary mortals is the vehemence of their passion and their loyalty to each other till the end make it a story of love than lust. I will just briefly note that the death scene of Cleopatra conveys an all-out message of love. Cleopatra addresses dead Antony as her husband whose courage she wants to emulate:

> Cleo. Husband, I come:
> Now to that name, my courage proves my title!
> I am fire and air; my other elements
> I give to baser life. So, have you done?
> Come then, and take the last warmth of my lips.
> Farewell, kind Charmian, Iras, long farewell.
> [Kisses them. Iras falls and dies.
> Have I the aspic in my lips? Dost fall?
> If thou and nature could so gently part,
> The stroke of death is as a lover's pinch,
> Which hurts, and is desir'd. (*A and C*, V.ii.286-295)

Cleopatra transcends the bounds of human glory and the fear of humiliation at her death not because her lust has turned into love. By kissing her loyal maids she remains true to her nature as the goddess of passion and power, as Isis. Death cannot come to her in any other form than a "lover's pinch." The aspic's poisonous kiss transmutes her nature—she is all fire and air and has relinquished the earthy and watery elements to baser life. Lust produces life and life makes one a votary of love. More than Antony's apotheosis in this play Cleopatra's transformation at the end strongly reinforces our belief in what we had always suspected. Shakespeare examined lust in his mature works and found the magic formula to transform it into love.

NOTES

1. On the theme of justice and mercy in the play see Ernest Schanzer, *The Problem Plays of Shakespeare: A Study of Julius Caesar, Measure for Measure, Antony and Cleopatra*. London: Routledge, 1963. Rpt.2005; A.P.Rossiter, *Angel with Horns*. London: Longman, 1961; J.M.Nosworthy, ed. *Measure for Measure*. Harmondsworth: Penguin Books, 1969; Wilbur Dunkel, "Law and Equity in Measure for Measure." *Shakespeare Quarterly* 13 (1962); Harry Keyishian, "Henry de Bracton, Renaissance Punishment Theory, and Shakespearean Closure." *Law and Literature* 20 (2008): 444-458.
2. Sonnet 129

   The expense of spirit in a waste of shame
   Is lust in action; and till action, lust
   Is perjured, murderous, bloody, full of blame,
   Savage, extreme, rude, cruel, not to trust,
   Enjoy'd no sooner but despised straight,
   Past reason hunted, and no sooner had
   Past reason hated, as a swallow'd bait
   On purpose laid to make the taker mad;
   Mad in pursuit and in possession so;
   Had, having, and in quest to have, extreme;
   A bliss in proof, and proved, a very woe;
   Before, a joy proposed; behind dream.
   All this the world well knows; yet none knows well
   To shun the heaven that leads men to this hell.

3. *The Holy Bible (King James Version)*. Philadelphia: National Publishing Company, 1978. All quotations from the Bible are from this edition.
4. Quoted by Edmund Leites. "The Duty to Desire: Love, Friendship, and Sexuality in Some Puritan Theories of Marriage." *Journal of Social History* 15 (1982): 383-408; http://www.jstor.org/stable/3787154. Accessed: 19/01/2013. Original in *Roman Catechism* of 1566: 2. 8.13,14.
5. Leites. The Duty to Desire. Original in *Summa Contra Gentiles* 3. 123.
6. Leites. The Duty to Desire. Original in Erasmus, *Epystle*.
7. Leites. The Duty to Desire. Original in Erasmus, *Epystle,* sig. C6r.
8. Leites The Duty to Desire. He cites Erasmus, *Epystle*, sig. B7v.

9. Leites. The Duty to Desire. Original in William Secker, *A Wedding Ring for the Finger* (London, 1658).
10. According to Fudge "all of the major reformers rejected the principle of clerical celibacy and numerous reformers married in the early years of the movement: Philip Melanchthon in 1520; Justus Jonas in 1522; Johannes Bugenhagen, Andreas Karlstadt, Martin Bucer, Wenceslas Link, Thomas Muntzar, Wolfgang Capito, and Matthew Zeil in 1523; Ulrich Zwingli in 1524; Michael Sattler and Johannes Oecolampadius in 1528, to name a few."
11. Original in Martin Luther, "To the Christian Nobility of the German Nation concerning the Reform of the Christian Estate," in *Works*, 55 vols., ed. Jaroslav Pelikan and Helmut Lehmann (St. Louis: Concordia; Philadelphia: Muhlenburg, 1955-86), 44:176.
12. Herman J. Selderhuis, Marriage and divorce in the thought of Martin Bucer Translated by John Vriend and Lyle D. Bierma. Kirksville, Mo.: Thomas Jefferson University Press at Truman State University, 1999.
13. J.W. Lever, ed. Measure for Measure. London: Methuen, 1965. Rpt. Routledge, 1994. All quotations are from this edition.
14. See Ernest Schanzer, "The Marriage Contracts in Measure for Measure." Shakespeare Survey 13 (1960): 81-89;

    T. G. A. Nelson, "Doing Things with Words: Another Look at Marriage Rites and Spousals in Renaissance Drama and Fiction." Studies in Philology 95 (1998) 351-373; Subha Mukherji, Law and Representation in Early Modern Drama. Cambridge: Cambridge University Press, 2006.
15. Fudge cites "On Marriage Matters". Martin Luthers Werke. Kritische Gesamtausgabe, 114 vols. (Weimar: B?hlaus, 1883-1999) 30/3:226-27.
16. Eramus tells a friend who is unwilling to marry, "Bachelershyp, is a forme of lyvnge bothe barren and unnaturall," whereas nothing could be more natural than wedlock, so much so that all peoples, no matter how barbarous, deem it holy. Leites cites Erasmus of Rotterdam (1530). A Right Fruteful Epystle . . . in Laude and Prayse of Matrymony, trans. of Encomium matrimonii by Richard Tavernour (London, 1530), sig. A3r.
17. See also James Hirch, "Rome and Egypt in Antony and Cleopatra" in Sara Munson Deats, ed. Antony and Cleopatra: New Critical Essays. Routledge: New York, 2005.
18. See Donna B. Hamilton, "Antony and Cleopatra and the Tradition of Noble Lovers." Shakespeare Quarterly 24 (1973): 245-252; Graham

Storey, "Love and Sex in Antony and Cleopatra: A Stylistic Interpretation." Alif: Journal of Comparative Poetics (1988): 88-100; Jonathan Gil Harris, "Narcissus in thy Face": Roman Desire and the Difference it Fakes in Antony and Cleopatra" Shakespeare Quarterly 45 (1994): 408-425.

19. See Don Cameron Allen, "The Rehabilitation of Epicurus and His Theory of Pleasure in the Early Renaissance." Studies in Philology 41 (1944): 1-15; J. Leeds Barroll, "Antony and Pleasure." Journal of English and Germanic Philology 57 (1958): 708-720.

WORKS CITED

Aquinas, St. Thomas. http://www.sacred-texts.com/chr/aquinas/summa/index.htm. Accessed: 14.02.13.

Burton, Robert. *Anatomy of Melancholy (1621)*, Reprint. London: B. Blake, 13 Bell Yard, Temple Bar, 1838.

http://books.google.co.inbooks?id=4rvhM56lsn8C&printsec=frontcover&dq=robert+burton+anatomy+of+melancholy&hl=en&sa=X&ei=11UeUc7wIouJrAffpoHQAQ&redir_esc=y Accessed: 14.02.13.

Calvin, John.

http://www.truecovenanter.com/calvin/calvin_sermons_deuteronomy_22_05etc.html. Accessed: 14/02/13.

Erasmus of Rotterdam. *A Right Fruteful Epystle . . . in Laude and Prayse of Matrymony, trans. of Encomium matrimonii* by Richard Tavernour (London, 1530).

Frantz, David O. "Leud Priapians" and Renaissance Pornography." *Studies in English Literature, 1500-1900* 12 (1972): 157-172; http://www.jstor.org/stable/449980. Accessed: 19/01/2013.

Fudge, Thomas A. "Incest and Lust in Luther's Marriage: Theology and Morality in Reformation Polemics." *The Sixteenth Century Journal*.34 (2003): 319-345. http://www.jstor.org/stable/20061412. Accessed: 19/01/2013.

Holy Bible, The. (King James Version). Philadelphia: National Publishing Company, 1978.

Latimer, Hugh. *The 7th Sermon upon the Lord's Prayer*; http://articles.ochristian.com/article10756.shtml. Accessed: 14.02.13.

Leites, Edmund. "The Duty to Desire: Love, Friendship, and Sexuality in Some Puritan Theories of Marriage." Journal of Social History 15(1982): 383-408; http://www.jstor.org/stable/3787154. Accessed: 19/01/2013.

Lever, J.W. Ed. *Measure for Measure*. London: Methuen, 1965. Rpt. Routledge, 1994.

Payne, Michael. "Erotic Irony and Polarity in Antony and Cleopatra." *Shakespeare Quarterly* 24 (1973): 265-279. http://www.jstor.org/stable/2868352. Accessed: 24/01/2013.

Wyclif, John. *Select English Works of John Wyclif*, ed.Thomas Arnold. Vol 1 *Sermons on the Gospels for Sundays and Festivals*, Oxford: Clarendon Press, 1869. http://books.google.com/ Accessed: 14.02.13.

9

The Crises of Succession in William Shakespeare's *King Lear*

Kenneth Usongo

Shakespeare's (1564-1616) *King Lear* can be read as a play that interrogates sovereignty via the challenge to the rule of Lear by Goneril and Regan, as well as drama that problematizes, through the action of Edmund, the issue of inheritance in Jacobean England. In this essay, I intend to demonstrate that the crises over succession (at both the state and family levels) not only bring to focus dominant traits of Shakespeare's protagonists in *King Lear*, but also engage in the questioning of the Jacobean order of succession. Put differently, the quest for political power or influence helps to externalize some of the hidden traits of the characters. Moreover, investigating the theme of succession is relevant because *King Lear* anticipates recent political upheavals such as the Arab spring.

During the reign of King James I from 1603 to 1625, he emphasized, among the English, the idea of respect for the monarchy and its sovereignty over everybody, including the church. In 1609, James addressed the British parliament thus:

Kings are iustly called Gods, for that they exercise a manner or resemblance of Divine power upon earth: For if you will consider the Attributes to God, you shall see how they agree in the person of a King. God hath power to create, or destroy, make, or unmake at his pleasure, to give life, or send death, to judge all and to be judged nor accomptable to none: To raise low things, and to make high things low at his pleasure, and to God are both soule and body due. And the like power haue Kings. (307-8)

The above speech shows James's concern with asserting his authority within his kingdom—an issue that Lear would most likely agree with. James was quite anxious about his security as noted in the witch trials that were rife during his rule. For example, he was personally involved in the North Berwick witch trials of 1590, which implicated seventy people from East Lothian, Scotland, of communicating with the devil and attempting to sink the king's ship.

Among other concerns, *King Lear* foregrounds the vanity and credulity of Lear and Gloucester before their offspring. These weaknesses are exploited by their antagonists—Goneril and Regan, and Edmund—to bring about the downfall of Lear and Gloucester. For his part, Lear's controversial decision to relinquish power and share out his kingdom among his three daughters paves the way for the politically ambitious Goneril and Regan to begin hatching a plot against him. Although Lear asks his daughters to declare their love to him, he appears to be more interested in promises from them that they would grant him some freedom from the burden of leadership, which he hopes to be still symbolically in charge. However, by abdicating the throne before his death, Lear violates the king's two bodies (natural and political), which ought to remain inviolate because it is only after the king's demise that the body natural is separated from the body politic. In fact, as Emily Sun rightly argues, the "doctrine of the king's two bodies insists on the immortality of the body politic that survives the finitude of successive kings" (43).

Similarly, Gloucester's gullibility in accepting what Edmund tells him about Edgar's "dishonesty" lays the foundation for Edmund's malignity. Edmund begins to hatch a plot against Gloucester and Edgar by making a prayer to nature:

Thou, Nature, art my goddess; to thy law
My services are bound. Wherefore should I
Stand in the plague of custom and permit
The curiosity of nations to deprive me?
For that I am some twelve or fourteen moonshines
Lag of a brother? Why "bastard"? Wherefore "base"
When my dimensions are as well compact
My mind as generous, and my shape as true
As honest madam's issue? Why brand they us
With "base," with "baseness" "bastardy"? Base? Base?
Who in the lusty stealth of nature take
More composition and fierce quality
Than doth within a dull, stale, tired bed
Go to th'creating a whole tribe of fops
Got 'tween asleep and wake? Well, then,
Legitimate Edgar, I must have your land.
Our father's love is to the bastard Edmund
As to the legitimate. Fine word, "legitimate"!
Well, my legitimate, [*takes out a letter*] if this letter speed
And my invention thrive, Edmund the base
Shall to th'legitimate. I grow, I prosper.
Now gods, stand up for bastards! (1.2.1-22)

Edmund's intention to justify his claim on inheritance on grounds that all individuals, legitimate or illegitimate, must be judged according to their capabilities, merits, careful examination. His claim that he is badly treated within his family because of his bastardy seems lacking in credibility. There is hardly any evidence to support Edmund's allegation of discrimination against him. Instead we understand that Gloucester treats Edmund fairly as evidenced in the pride with which he introduces him to Kent: ". . . there was good sport at his making" (1.1.20). The suggestion of Edmund being left out of inheritance, by Jacobean standards, is not sufficient to justify any malignity on his part given that he is not the eldest son. Thus, Edmund's prayer represents a flagrant denunciation of the moral law and an endorsement of the law of the jungle, or survival of the fittest. However, by laying his claim to inheritance, Edmund, according to John Danby in "Edmund and the Two Natures," is seen as belonging to a new age of scientific inquiry, of the new man [sic] in an era of individualism, suspicion and glory (53-54). Thus, in his prayer, Edmund rejects the thinking that social order and human identity are predetermined and argues instead for people to pursue their individual aspirations.

Throughout his soliloquy, Edmund strenuously attempts to justify his intentions of supplanting Edgar and climbing socially. He is disgruntled that, according to him, he is badly treated in society because of his illegitimacy. Edmund is unhappy that he has all along been slighted by his father. His ideas on legitimacy and inheritance question how a culture invents and perpetuates itself. He sees moral conventions as social constructs designed by a culture to protect its vested interest and proscribe competition. It is, as Millicent Bell remarks, "by invoking an anarchic nature and by ignoring the rule of custom that Edmund justifies his plot against brother and father" (173). By stating that he owes his services to the Nature goddess, Edmund announces his creed that "Nature sanctions ruthless competition in which the race goes to the swiftest". (Bevington 142)

Edmund pursues his scheme of inheritance by secretly writing a letter in the name of Edgar, in which the latter purportedly plans the death of Gloucester. In order to make Gloucester believe in the authenticity of the letter, Edmund further reveals to him that he picked it up from the window of his private room, allegedly thrown there by Edgar. Gloucester is so moved by Edmund's disclosure that he begins to think of Edgar in terms of an "Abhorred villain," "detested, brutish villain," and "abominable villain" (1.2.73-75). Like Iago in Shakespeare's *Othello*, Edmund instructs Gloucester to consider Edgar innocent till when Edgar can be apprehended contemplating villainy. Reminiscent of Iago's action to Othello, Edmund promises to place Gloucester where he can hear Edgar speaking ill of Gloucester. Alone on stage, Edmund scoffs at his father's credulity and superstition in relating Edgar's "crime" to recent eclipses which Gloucester is convinced, points to impending moral decay. Mischievous as he is, Edmund informs Edgar of Gloucester's anger against him and urges him to stay away from Gloucester. He also intends to place Edgar where the latter can hear Gloucester denouncing him. In a suggestive soliloquy, Edmund reveals his evil intention: "I see the business./ Let me, if not by birth, have lands by wit./ All with me's meet that I can fashion fit" (1.2.169-71).

On his part, Lear, who has misjudged Cordelia's love for him and subsequently rejected her, begins to feel the pangs of his rash and unjust decision. The Fool, who does not appear foolish but rather fits as Lear's conscience, advises Lear in these telling words: "Have more than thou showest,/ Speak less than thou knowest,/ Lend less than thou owest,/ Ride more than thou goest,/ Learn more than thou trowest,/ Set less than thou throwest" (1.4.108-13). Unfortunately, these edifying words are ignored by Lear in his dealings with his daughters. However, sanity appears to return to him when Goneril rebukes him for keeping a large retinue of knights and for laying claim to authority which he had wilfully given up. According to her, Lear is an "Idle old man" (1.3.17), who naively thinks that he is still enjoying power that he had relinquished. Goneril compares old people, her father as an example, to babies who require not only comforting words, but also sharp rebukes when they err. She is so blunt that she states that if Lear does not welcome her attitude to him, he can go to Regan where, she is convinced, he will be accorded similar treatment. Goneril goes as far as instructing her servant, Oswald, to attend to Lear and his entourage unenthusiastically in order that if he objects to this conduct, she will have an excuse to take tougher action against him. It is ironical that Goneril, who got political power through flattery, now shows no qualms in tormenting her father.

Goneril's rebukes against Lear reflect her heartlessness and complete disregard for the Order principle which states that fathers should be obeyed and held in esteem. She has no limits in humiliating Lear: she reduces his retinue to fifty knights and reproves her husband, Albany, for being soft-spoken towards Lear. The reduction of Lear's entourage constitutes an affront to his dignity and personality; it is a symbolic attempt to curb his authority and to remind him that he is no longer in control of affairs. Exasperated by Goneril's challenge to his authority, Lear curses her by invoking Nature to render her sterile:

> Hear, Nature, hear dear goddess, hear
> Suspend thy purpose, if thou didst intend
> To make this creature fruitful.
> Into her womb convey sterility,
> Dry up in her the organs of increase,
> And from her derogate body never spring
> A babe to honour her. If she must teem,
> Create her child of spleen, that it may live
> And be a thwart disnatured torment to her.
> Let it stamp wrinkles in her brow of youth,
> With cadent tears fret channels in her cheeks,
> Turn all her mother's pains and benefits
> To laughter and contempt, that she may feel
> How sharper than a serpent's tooth it is
> To have a thankless child. (1.4.258-72)

Lear's words underscore his tempestuous mind and his rashness at arriving at decisions. Although Goneril treats Lear unkindly, as a father, one would have expected him to have spent more time convincing her about the rightness of his need for many followers rather than plunging into cursing her. At this moment, it would seem that she does not yet deserve such a strong reaction on his part. It is only later in the play that Goneril portrays herself, in the words of Lear, as a "marble-hearted fiend" (1.4.241) and the perfect personification of ingratitude.

Meanwhile, Edmund, having deceived Edgar to go into hiding in order to shun Gloucester's wrath, initiates another scheme whereby Edgar is informed that his hiding place has been discovered by Gloucester hence the need for him to flee. Edmund, then, stages a fight with Edgar and later displays to Gloucester a simulated wound that he sustained as evidence of Edgar's treachery. He further corroborates the charge of Edgar's deceitfulness by inventing a story in which Edgar persuaded him to kill Gloucester. Edmund argues that his dread of retribution coupled with his 'love' for Gloucester restrained him from embracing such mischief. According to Edmund, his refusal to follow Edgar's suggestion provoked the latter's anger against him. Edmund continues his tendentious story by stating that his attempt to dissuade Edgar from parricide instead brought forth calumnies against his honour from Edgar: "Thou unpossessing bastard, dost thou think,/ If I would stand against thee, would the resposal/ Of any trust, virtue, or worth in thee/ Make thy words faithed?" (2.1.68-71)

Ultimately, Gloucester is won over by Edmund's deception and proceeds to banish Edgar. Having wormed his way into Gloucester's heart, Edmund now plays the role of a confidant. In this regard, Gloucester tells Edmund about a planned invasion of England by the king's loyalists and France who, Gloucester affirms, are unhappy with the treatment that Lear has received from Goneril and Regan. On her part, Regan is unwilling to further play hostess to Lear and his followers, whom she considers boisterous and burdensome. She questions why Lear should be attended by servants granted that he is no longer king. She instructs Lear to apologize to Goneril for his attitude towards Goneril. Lear is again disgraced by Regan through the trussing up of his emissary—Kent— in the stocks. It should be recalled that the punishment meted on Kent by Regan constitutes an act of rebellion on her part and it symbolizes the dethronement of Lear. Through her action, Regan rejects the age-old belief that the subject is to the king as the child is to the father, and that age itself should be treated with respect. As a result, Lear leaves her home and he is determined to fend for himself. Derek Cohen, in *The Politics of Shakespeare*, makes an interesting reading of this scene by envisioning it as a symbolic affirmation of the spirit of individualism that the play seems to suggest (81).

Assailed by the stormy weather, Lear manifests an agitated mind. He arranges a mock trial of his wicked daughters and appoints the disguised Edgar and the Fool as judges. This particular scene shows the demented state of mind of Lear and he ends up tearing his clothes, which appears as a symbolic renunciation of foolishness in favour of wisdom. Robert Bechtold

Heilman, in *This Great-Stage: Image and Structure in King Lear*, sees in the scene where Lear adorns weeds on his head as reflective of Christ on Calvary with whom Lear shares the redemptive process as preached by Christian teaching (260). This suggests, Heilman avers, that Lear is a microcosm of humankind in his suffering and that he is seen as the scapegoat for human transgression. However, I think that Heilman is rather too positive about the character of Lear in associating him with Christ, who did not manifest Lear's culpability. Pathetic as Lear presents himself, he still retains loyal supporters in Kent and Gloucester. Kent is the self-appointed servant of the king, who berates anyone who confronts Lear. His beating of the obsequious Oswald is quite memorable. On his part, Gloucester informs the king about the threat to the king's life and advises him to go to Dover and seek protection.

However, Edmund intends to reveal to Cornwall the information about a planned invasion of England by France. In this way, he will win Cornwall's friendship while also portraying Gloucester as being sympathetic to Lear's cause. Edmund further incriminates Gloucester by furnishing Cornwall with a letter in which Gloucester professes his loyalty to Lear. In presenting his case before Cornwall, Edmund adopts the posture of an honest and humble servant as evidenced in his reply to Cornwall: "I shall serve you, sir, truly, however else" (2.1.119). Cornwall is gratified and immediately proclaims Edmund Earl of Gloucester, which means that Edmund is the immediate successor of Gloucester.

When Cornwall speaks about Gloucester's collaboration with the French to invade Britain, Regan cries out that Gloucester should be hanged because of his "treason." Oswald later acquaints the gathering of demons composed of Cornwall, Edmund, Goneril, and Regan with the news that the king has escaped to Dover through the complicity of Gloucester. Cornwall immediately dispatches his toadies to arrest Gloucester. In the meantime, Edmund is told by the members of the evil gang to leave the room so as not to witness the molestation of his father. It would seem that the sadistic Edmund would have relished satisfaction out of the torture of his father. When Gloucester is brought in as prisoner, the power-mongers made up of Goneril, Regan, and Cornwall addresses him in derogatory terms: "Ingrateful fox!" "filthy traitor!," and "Villain" (3.7.28-35). The cruel gang begins to molest the helpless Gloucester: he is bound to a chair at the command of Cornwall, and Regan pulls at his beard. The torture of Gloucester symbolizes the consequences of civil strife, or he is depicted as the casualty of the power struggle between Lear and his supporters, on the one hand; Goneril, Regan and others, on the other. When asked by Regan why he sent the king to Dover, Gloucester responds in his characteristic honest and fearless manner: "I would not see thy cruel nails/ Pluck out his poor old eyes, nor thy fierce sister/ In his anointed flesh stick boarish fangs" (3.7.55-57).

According to Sun, Gloucester's gouged eyes "are sign of the collapse of the sovereign order under Lear and of the competing claims to sovereignty in the divided kingdom that has now devolved into a state of civil war" (51). Just before his eyes are gouged out, Gloucester expresses his conviction that "winged vengeance" (3.7.65) would overcome the devilish characters. His belief is an endorsement of the idea that although evil may temporarily prevail, it would eventually be destroyed by goodness. In other words, this is an affirmation of the law of Karma.

In a display of cruelty that is perhaps unparalleled in drama, Shakespeare gives a graphic and disgusting account of the inhuman treatment meted out to Gloucester. Cornwall, in a callous manner, pulls out Gloucester's eye and crushes it while Regan persuades him to do the same with the other eye. She also orders that Gloucester be thrown out of the gates to "smell His way to Dover" (3.7.92). In a change of fortune, Cornwall's servant retaliates on Gloucester's behalf, wounding fatally the sadistic Cornwall before being killed himself by Regan. She informs the tormented Gloucester that Edmund revealed Gloucester's "treachery" to them. It now dawns on Gloucester that he had wrongly cast away Edgar; he is remorseful and prays to the gods to protect Edgar.

In another turn of events, Oswald reports to the astonishment of Goneril and Edmund that Albany is a changed man in that he is sympathetic to the king's cause. Like Lady Macbeth, Goneril considers compassion and morality the signs of meekness. She, then, sees her husband as a moral freak who fails to share in her evil. Albany, in her eyes, "is too full of the milk of human kindness" and is milk-livered, charges which reflect those of Lady Macbeth against Macbeth. Determined to wrest control of events: "I must change arms at home and give the distaff/ Into my husband's hands" (4.2.17-18), Goneril dispatches Edmund to inform Cornwall about Albany's support to Lear.

Albany manifests admirably qualities of honesty and moral courage as he reproaches Goneril for her filial ingratitude to Lear:

> What have you done?
> Tigers, not daughters, what have you performed?
> A father and a gracious, aged man,
> Whose reverence even the head-lugged bear would lick,
> Most barbarous, most degenerate, Have you madded.
> Could my good brother suffer you to do it?
> A man, a prince, by him so benefited?
> If that the heavens do not their visible spirits
> Send quickly down to tame these vile offences,
> It will come.
> Humanity must perforce prey on itself
> Like monsters of the deep. (4.2.39-59)

Goneril is quite upset to hear these reproofs from Albany. According to her, he is "a moral fool" (4.2.58), who will sit back and watch France invade Britain. She considers him the proverbial mad person who will quietly go back to sleep upon seeing his/her roof on fire. Albany is unmoved and calls her a fiend. In a change of fortune, a messenger brings news of the death of Cornwall. In this regard, Albany expresses his joy at what he qualifies the merited fortune of Cornwall: "This shows you are above,/ You justices, that those our nether crimes/ So speedily can venge" (4.2.78-80). Upon hearing about the demise of Cornwall, Goneril's objective now is to abandon her husband in favour of the love of Edmund, now considered Earl of Gloucester: "One way I like this well;/ But being widow, and my Gloucester with her,/ May all the building in my fancy pluck/ Upon my hateful life. Another way/ The news is not so tart" (4.2. 83-87).

Albany's moral fortitude pushes him to the king's camp and Albany is determined to avenge the cruelty inflicted on Gloucester. Similarly, the misjudged Cordelia is deeply affected by the plight of her father. In this regard, she supports the invasion of Britain by France; she argues that her decision is a result of her love for Lear. Cordelia's action is born out of her filial attachment to the king and does not have any political undertone as she affirms: "No blown ambition doth our arms incite,/ But love, dear love, and our aged father's right./ Soon may I hear and see him" (4.4.27-29).

Against the background of an imminent confrontation between the French and British forces, Oswald is commissioned by Goneril to kill Gloucester. The attempt to slay him bungles as Edgar intervenes and kills Oswald. Overcome by despair, Gloucester requests Edgar to take him to the cliff of Dover, where Gloucester intends to commit suicide. Through a ruse by Edgar, Gloucester falls down from a ridge and is persuaded by Edgar into believing that he has been miraculously saved from death. Gloucester sees divine intervention in his abortive suicide and, consequently, resolves to bear his fortune bravely.

In another domain, the contents of Goneril's letter to Edmund, intercepted by Edgar, portray her as politically and romantically expedient as she attempts to seduce him and to goad him into killing her husband—Albany:

> Let our reciprocal vows be remembered. You have many opportunities to cut him off. If your will want not, time and place will be fruitfully offered. There is nothing done, if he returns the conqueror; then am I the prisoner, and his bed my jail from the loathed warmth whereof, deliver me, and supply the place for your labour. (4.6.256-61)

At the same time, Regan suspects Edmund of double dealing, professing love to her while also doing the same to Goneril. This suspicion will create much friction between both ambitious sisters.

Ostensibly, both Albany and Edmund are joint commanders of British forces. However, while Albany is torn between his patriotism for Britain and his loyalty to Lear (for whom the foreign army is fighting), Edmund is preoccupied with assessing his gains in the conflict between Goneril and Regan. In a telling soliloquy, Edmund informs us how he intends to exploit Albany's authority to his advantage and guide Goneril into killing Albany. He also plans to murder Lear and Cordelia immediately after the Franco-British war. In this way, he would optimize his chances of ruling over the British kingdom:

> To both these sisters have I sworn my love,
> Each jealous of the other as the stung
> Are of the adder. Which of them shall I take?
> Both? One? Or neither? Neither can be enjoyed
> If both remain alive. To take the widow
> Exasperates, makes mad her sister Goneril,
> And hardly shall I carry out my side,
> Her husband being alive. Now then, we'll use
> His countenance for the battle, which being done,
> Let her who would be rid of him devise
> His speedy taking off. As for the mercy
> Which he intends to Lear and to Cordelia,
> The battle done, and they within our power,
> Shall never see his pardon; for my state
> Stands on me to defend, not to debate. (5.1.58-71)

In a dispute with Albany, Edmund overrules Albany's decision that Lear and Cordelia be kept in captivity when victory is achieved in the war with France. He gives orders to a captain for the execution of Lear and Cordelia, promising him with advancement if they are killed. In a dramatic twist of events, Albany challenges Edmund's loyalty, and Edgar, disguised, turns up to fight pn behalf of Albany. Edgar is victorious in the duel and then reveals his identity to the dying

Edmund. Commenting about Edmund's fate, Edgar avers that "The gods are just, and of our pleasant vices/ Make instruments to plague us" (5.3.171). On his part, Cornwall dies without any moral redemption. He consistently portrays himself as a diabolical character. Even Lear, a bad judge of people, had preferred Albany to Cornwall to be paramount Duke.

Meanwhile, the jealousy between Goneril and Regan for Edmund's love results in Goneril poisoning Regan before committing suicide. Justice appears subverted when we see Lear bearing the body of Cordelia, who has been killed following Edmund's instruction. Unfortunately, Lear dies from a broken heart. Edgar, then, is thrust into leadership by Albany. While there is relief, on the part of spectators, upon learning about the demise of Edmund, there is tragic loss following the death of Cordelia.

In *King Lear*, the exponents of truth are banished, insulted or tortured while liars generally stay safe, rich, and wield authority. With regard to the villainous characters in the play, Shakespeare presents them with indignation. He gives these characters, as Harriett Hawkins pointedly observes in "Dramatic Judgement in *King Lear*," the "emotional appeal of faceless, soulless automatons" (164). Goneril, Regan, and Edmund, in their love affairs, are vindictive, pusillanimous, and wicked. According to Hawkins, one feels just about the same amount of emotion at their deaths as one might feel while watching the death throes of a swarm of hornets. Like insects, these villains are faceless and stinging (165). However, Lear's appearance bearing the lifeless body of Cordelia is emotionally draining to the audience as we question the death of such a virtuous girl. Interestingly, Lear's endurance of pain, at this particular moment, marks his moment of anagnorisis. He demonstrates the capacity to learn, feel, and grow as he indicts his warped judgement that provoked this tragedy.

The reasons for Lear's downfall are tied with the political expediency of Goneril and Regan. Moreover, Lear's sentimentality wrecks his powers of perception. He is disabused by Goneril and Regan, and he misjudges the sincerity of the blunt Cordelia. His doom stretches as far back as the instance when he decided to share his kingdom among his daughters. Several critics have advanced various reasons for Lear's abdication of the throne, arguing, for instance, that Lear's action constitutes a blatant violation of the Renaissance world picture and the notion of hierarchy. According to Richard L. Levin in his essay "Shakespeare or the Ideas of His Time," Lear's abandonment of the throne, in the words of one critic, is

> an act of betrayal... he divests himself of kingship and gives up the divinely-appointed duties of monarchy. We must here remember precisely what kingship meant to the Elizabethans, if we are to comprehend the magnitude of Lear's ill-doing . . . Here is the Lord's deputy divesting himself, most sinfully and criminally, of his divine duty. (15)

Another critic, Levin observes, states that in order to—

> understand the enormity of Lear's sin, we must recognize the peculiar position of the king in the highly ordered world which Renaissance Christian humanism carried over from the Middle Ages. Lear's resignation of his throne ... would have been regarded by a Jacobean audience with a horror difficult for a modern audience to appreciate, for ... [it was] a violation of the king's responsibility to God, and ... could result in ... chaos on every level of creation... By his resignation of rule Lear disrupts the harmonious order of nature ... [and the] infinite good of God's order which decrees that the king rule for the good of his people until God relieves him of his responsibility by death. (15-16)

These critical contentions are supported by Kent's advice to Lear for him to renounce the controversial decision of splitting the kingdom in line with a love contest involving his daughters. Beyond this objection is the signification that Lear and Gloucester represent the old order in terms of pride and hasty actions against which Goneril, Regan, and Edmund are fighting. In other words, against the brashness and steadfastness of the *ancien regime* are juxtaposed the cunning and expedience of the new order.

Lear could have followed the Biblical example of David, who sought the approval of Nathan, the prophet, and Zodiac, the priest, before handing over power to Solomon. On many occasions, we see Lear acting before reflecting. In this regard, his resolve to forsake Cordelia and banish Kent smacks of uncontrollable wrath which he finds difficult to suppress. This is where his tragedy resides, for had he composed himself, he could have averted his downfall. The Fool is right in pointing out that Lear had gambled with his fortune, and is a complete shadow of himself. Lear's tragedy lies in his bid to enjoy authority that he had wilfully given up. His situation is comparable to that of the proverbial person who wants to have his cake and eat it.

Unlike Duncan in *Macbeth* who announces Malcolm as heir and is prepared to forego royal privileges, this is not the case with Lear. As Germaine Greer observes, Lear is confused, paranoid, arbitrary; he behaves in the manner typical of sufferers from atherosclerosis of the brain, grown old without ever being wise (89). His situation is analogous to that of a person who keeps his or her window open and lets in a storm that blows off the roof of the house. Both Lear and Gloucester console themselves by invoking divine retribution on their antagonists; these two protagonists are convinced that the social order "is naturally ordained and unchanging" (Hughes 264). Thus, Lear and Gloucester are oblivious of the fact that nature is dynamic and capable of turning into socio-political upheavals against their interest.

Nevertheless, the contribution of Goneril and Regan towards Lear's downfall should not be ignored or taken lightly. Commenting on the character of Lear, Regan speaks of his "infirmity of age" (1.2.291) while Goneril holds that the king suffers from "the unruly waywardness that infirm and choleric years bring with them" (1.1.298). These flaws of Lear are exploited by both politically ambitious women. Immediately after Cordelia and France leave, Goneril begins contemplating how Lear can be sent away in order that she exercise full authority that goes with royalty. Both Goneril and Regan are anxious about Lear's exercise of power that they believe he had forsaken. Consequently, they resolve to stop him from enjoying royal privileges such as keeping a large retinue of followers. Put differently, in opposing Lear, Goneril and Regan are questioning the Jacobean belief that placed a premium on age, seniority, or the point, as earlier indicated, that children needed to be always submissive to their parents.

Goneril is the person who takes greater initiative than Regan in torturing Lear. She starts off by proposing to feign illness when Lear requests for her. She orders her servants to treat the king and his train with "weary negligence" (1.3.13). She provokes the blinding of Gloucester. She is talked of as a kite and her ingratitude has a serpent's tooth. Goneril has struck her father most serpent-like upon the heart; her visage is wolfish and she has "Sharp-toothed unkindness like a vulture" (2.4.129) on her father's breast. Albany, her husband, regards her as a gilded serpent and, according to Gloucester, her cruelty appears to have the fangs of a boar. She and Regan are dog-hearted: they are tigers, not daughters and each is an adder to the other (Bradley 218). Both these women, as earlier pointed out, reduce Lear's retinue, molest his friends, and pay little attention to him. By constantly opposing any request from Lear, both Goneril and Regan engage in what I may refer to as *noetics*.

On his part, Edmund justifies his political ambition by questioning why his ambition should be curbed by customs, or issues of age and legitimacy. As remarked earlier in the discussion, Edmund's argument that he is despised because of his illegitimacy is not sufficient to justify his monstrosity. There is no evidence to corroborate Edmund's claim that he is held in contempt because of his bastardy. Nor is his point that he is deprived of inheritance weighty to give cause to complain. By virtue of the Elizabethan and Jacobean concept of inheritance, it is the eldest child, and not the youngest one, that is expected to inherit property. Moreover, this society was "pervasively, visibly hierarchical: men above women, adults above children, the old above the young, the rich above the poor, the wellborn above the vulgar". (Greenblatt 76)

In fact, Edmund's rhetoric shows a strenuous attempt by a greedy and individualistic person to justify his ambition. He is at loss for reasons for his action and, consequently, takes recourse to the issue of illegitimacy in order to draw sympathy for his cause. He conducts himself as a consummate deceiver, activated by his political ambition and lack of filial love. Like "a most toad-spotted traitor" (5.3.138), he is goaded into action by his materialism and love for power. Edmund exploits the credulity of Gloucester and colludes with the vicious Cornwall to attempt to materialize his political ambition.

In *King Lear*, Shakespeare essentially depicts Jacobean attachment to traditional aristocratic values. However, in Edmund, Goneril, and Regan, he portrays a tendency to separate from an old feudal and aristocratic system as these characters chart their destiny in a new era of individualism, scientific inquiry, and industrial revolution. These characters are portrayed as driven by their impulses; they understand the world and manifest a great deal of empiricism. The deaths of Lear and Cordelia would seem to subvert the notion of a powerful aristocratic society as it clashes with the individualism of Edmund, although Edgar's victory over him appears to re-inscribe the principles of aristocracy and feudalism. Whatever conclusions can be drawn about this scene, it is evident that the feudal and aristocratic system would hardly be the same as before. Through this conflicting ideological frame, Shakespeare comments on the major traits of his protagonists such as wrath, credulity, and vaulting ambition in Lear, Gloucester, and Edmund respectively.

WORKS CITED

Bell, Millicent. *Shakespeare's Tragic Skepticism*. New Haven and London: Yale UP, 2002.

Bevington, David. *Shakespeare: The Seven Ages of Human Experience*. Malden: Blackwell Publishing, 2002.

Bradley, A.C. *Shakespearean Tragedy*. London: Macmillan, 1904.

Cohen, Derek. *The Politics of Shakespeare*. New York: St. Martin's Press, 1993.

Danby, John F. "Edmund and the Two Natures." *Twentieth Century Interpretations of King Lear*. Ed. Janet Adelman. Englewood Cliffs: Prentice-Hall, 1978. 50-55.

Greenblatt, Stephen. *Will in the World: How Shakespeare Became Shakespeare*. New York: W.W. Norton & Company, 2004.

Greer, Germaine. *Shakespeare*. Oxford: Oxford UP, 1986.

Hawkins, Harriett. "Dramatic Judgement in *King Lear*." *Shakespeare: The Tragedies*. Ed. Robert B. Heilman. Englewood Cliffs, N.J.: Prentice-Hall, 1984. 163-74.

Heilman, Robert Bechtold. *This Great Stage: Image and Structure in King Lear*. Seattle: U of Washington P, 1963.

Hughes, John. "The Politics of Forgiveness: A Theological Exploration of King Lear. *Modern Theology* 17.3 (July 2001): 261-87.

James I. *The Political Works of James I*. Cambridge: Harvard UP, 1616; 1918. Print.

Levin, Richard. "Shakespeare or the Ideas of His Time." *Shakespeare: The Tragedies*. Ed. Robert B. Heilman. 11-27.

Shakespeare, William. *King Lear*. Ed. Grace Ioppolo. New York: W.W. Norton & Company, 2008.

———. *Macbeth*. Ed. Robert S. Miola. New York: W.W. Norton & Company, 2004.

———. *Othello*. Ed. Michael Neil. Oxford: Oxford UP, 2006.

Sun, Emily. *Succeeding King Lear: Literature, Exposure, and the Possibility of Politics*. New York: Fordham UP, 2010.

10

The Pure Trace: *The Ramayana, The Mahabharata* and Shakespeare*

Manju Dutta Gupta

In recent times there has been a generalized interest in placing works of literature—both Western, and non-Western, within broader cultural context. To consider some characters, their situations and some devices from *The Ramayana, The Mahabharata* and Shakespeare in parallel and contrast, I regard to be a unique experience. At the beginning, I would like to confess, to enlarge on the subject would be an impertinence in which I have no intention to indulge. The subject needs extensive research. *The Ramayana, The Mahabharata* reveal the deeper impulsions of India. They are whole literature in themselves. In 1769 by inviting London to the Stratford festival, Garrick confirmed what the editors and commentators began to tell the world about Shakespeare. Thus the worship of the wonder began, never to halt again. 'Shakespeare across cultures' describes a field of research which Professor Michael Mullin calls the 'Shakespeare Universe'. Shakespeare crosses national and cultural

* First published in *Colonial and Post Colonial Shakespeare* published by Shakespeare Society Eastern India and Avantgarde Press, Kolkata-2001, the Journal of the Department of English Vol. vii, 2000-2001 Rabindra Bharati University.

boundaries with apparent ease and means many things to many different people. Our two epics, again, containing various codes of life has relevance for us even today. "Experience has always designated the relationship with a presence whether that relationship had the form of consciousness or not", said Jacques Derrida in *Of Grammatology*[1]. Derrida argues that the totality of natural experience must discover a field of transcendental experience. Derrida believes that there is a beyond of transcendental criticism. To see to it, that beyond does not return to the within, is to recognize in the contortion the necessity of a pathway. That pathway must have a track in the next. The value of the transcendental arch must make its necessity felt before letting itself be erased. The trace is not only the disappearance of origin; it becomes the origin of the origin. The living present is the Universal absolute form of transcendental experience. Keeping in mind that the pure trace is the condition of plentitude, the structure of the sign is contained in the arch-trace. I would like to make brief comments on certain aspects of our epics which have something in common with certain features of Shakespeare's works.

The story of Rama and Sita recommends ideal human love. In Raghuvamsha XV, Kalidasa describes people who sat and listened to the story of Ramayana. He writes "Enraptured they listened,/Their faces pearled with tears,/ Like dew-dropping trees in a forest/On a windless morning." Nearly all the comedies of Shakespeare have something of a tragic strain about them. Othello is the supreme tragedy of human love. Love being a straining after the impossible has within it the seed of its own death. Nearly at the end of Ramayana, when Rama asked Sita to vindicate her purity in public, Sita prayed to the Earth-Goddess to accept her, if in thought, or word and in deed she dwelt only on Rama. The earth opened and Sita descended into the nether world. Into what element did Sita pass at death? Our imagination cannot help asking this question, however idle it may seem. Air, harmony, heaven are the symbols, which our fancy seems to call for. With the last word of his account Othello stabs himself. For Othello, who loved not wisely but too well, to commit suicide was the only way to earn that profoundly moving dying kiss. In The Ramayana, Rama ruled long, the kingdom became prosperous. Many years passed, Rama then came to the sacred river Sarayu and entered the water. A classical and idealized character from the epic ended his life after completing his duties to his people. On the contrary, the romantic Othello could not keep his promise to the Senate of Venice.

The Ramayana[2] is the adi-Kavya, or the first and ideal poem. Poetry can be a good history or even, more important perhaps, history can be good poetry. Shakespeare's history plays are political writings and there are several ways of taking Shakespeare's treatment of politics. That Shakespeare turned high politics into poetry and drama, and that he freed himself from or transmuted the mainly political motive, seems to be the most illuminating idea. In the context of the battle of Towton, confounded by the cruel Queen Margaret and fierce Clifford, Henry VI contemplates on the grief and woe of the world. In a pathetic soliloquy Henry VI regrets that he was born a king not a shepherd. The celebrated lines worth noting are:

> Ah, what a life were this!how sweet!how lovely!
> Gives not the hawthorn bush a sweeter shade
> To Shepherds looking on their silly sheep,
> Than doth a rich embroder'd canopy,
> To kings that fear their subjects treachery?
>
> Henry VI, Part III (II. V.)

This is not merely a bit of lyrical escapism but Henry's yearning for an ordered life. Henry's speech clearly unfolds his longing for achieving a relative balance between his spiritual aspirations and his material miseries.

A tragedy of major proportions is an accurate way of describing *The Mahabharata*[3]. It ends with the Pandavas leaving Hastinapur with the taste of ashy triumph still in their mouth. Vyasa wrote about his own grandchildren and their conflict.Vyasa portrays the massive moral collapse—he witnesses things falling apart, the centre refusing to hold. In Shakespeare's Royal histories there is hate, lust and violence. Our epics are successful chronicles of our land but are wonderfully laced with myths and legends. At this point I would like to make a brief comment on an important aspect of Shakespeare's history plays. Shakespearean perspective is largely Tudor since Shakespeare wrote during the reign of Queen Elizabeth, the last and the greatest of the Tudor line. Queen Elizabeth, the dominating feminist of Shakespeare's time encouraged and instilled a sense of intense patriotism, bordering on chauvinism in the nation, as well as in the nation's chief Bard. There was the necessity to justify the Tudor acquisition of the throne, hence Richard III is made spectacularly villainous. In King John, Shakespeare does not allude to the Magna Carta, an event of great constitutional significance. The audience was trained to respect Kings rather than to respect the people who tried to limit their power. Shakespeare's Henry VIII includes only two wives and deals scantily with the Reformation. Joan of Arc opposed the English. She is portrayed as a somewhat comic character who wins her victory through witchcraft in Henry VI Part I. Shakespeare's history plays take so many liberties with the chronicle account that Prof. Bulough describes this as a "fantasia on historical themes" rather than a historical drama in Narrative and Dramatic Source of Shakespeare, (Vol III, 1964). In Henry VI, Part I Act IV Sc VII, after the death of the great English General, Talbot, Joan's disparaging remark is given below:

> Him that thou magnifi'st with
> all these titles,
> Stinking and fly – blown lies
> Here at our feet.

It is to be recognized that Joan was burned by the English in May 1431, twenty-two years before Talbot was killed by the French in 1453. Joan certainly had no role to play in the killing of heroic Talbot. Shakespeare's patriotism breathes in all his history plays and binds them together. Mythicized history of India as presented in the two great epics has similarly enhanced the Indian imagination. Shakespeare immersed himself in the Queen's world. The problems for the world, inherent in each gender—principle and in the relation between or amongst them continued to fascinate Shakespeare to the end of his career. Shakespeare was concerned with the issues of power, the consequences of power tortured him. He breathed life into his female characters. As a female reader, Desdemona awakens me to the significance of her sexual codes. In her response to Othello's tales of adventure, she wished 'heaven hath made her such a man'. The line is obviously a determinative point at issue. Desdemona has defied convention by her downright violence. She has identified herself with husband's life-commitment as a soldier. She can no longer be a moth of peace, she is Othello's fair warrior. By 1603 the Turks were dubbed by Richard Knolls in his monumental work.[4] *History of the Turks* 'as the present terror of the world'. It required a man's courage for Desdemona to follow her husband to the wars of Cyprus. Desdemona stands for freedom.

When Rama was exiled for fourteen years to the Dandaka forest, he asked Sita to stay back in the palace and follow the path of dharma. The gentle Sita replied softly : 'I will go with you/ I will eat after you have eaten/ I will live on roots, shoots and fruits/ I do not want heaven/ If that heaven does not have you in it'.[5]

When Ravana desired Sita in Lanka, Sita placed a blade of grass between herself and the rakshasha—a silent medium between a chaste woman and a stranger. Gentle Sita's strength has always been a source of moral encouragement for women. Even in a negative society, change is possible by the creation of images that have the power to inspire, to revolt against exploitation. Women's lib is echoed in Draupadi's challenge to the hoary male members of the assembly. Yudhisthira lost her in the game of dice. The wicked Duhshashana sped with joy on his errand to fetch Draupadi to the assembly, even if he would have to drag her there. Panchali rose trembling, heart-stricken with sorrow and started to fly for refuge to the inner apartments of Dhritrashtra's queen. Duhshashana darted after her, caught her by the hair and dragged her to the assembly. The situation poses a problem, and a grave one undoubtedly. Why didn't Gandhari, ' the sign of woman', the epitome of righteousness save Draupadi's honour? Cast off by the king father, why did Cordelia only experience horror in the jealousy of sisters? From the feminist perspective there is, perhaps no final answer to this question. Simone de Beauvoir has made an important comment in her article Social Life. She says: 'women's fellow feeling rarely rises to genuine friendship, however. Women feel their solidarity more spontaneously than men: but within this solidarity the transcendence of each does not go out towards the others, for they all face together towards the masculine world whose value they wish to monopolize each for herself'. 'In a given patriarchal society women should adopt strategies to counter patriarchal oppressions.'[6] Draupadi prayed to her lord and fresh garments were supplied to Draupadi by the lord of the Universe. This splendid image signifies, in a sense, Helen Cixous's ideology which recreates the image of mythological universe in which she seeks refuge from the contradictions of the material world. Of course, Catherine Clement accuses Cixous of speaking at non-political level. Helen Cixous claims that a strong woman can do anything if the woman wants to do, of course. Unable to bear the strange situations in the assembly, Dhritarashtra ultimately gave the Pandavas their kingdom. Destination of Dhritarashtra's race was forecast: "suddenly, the howling of the jackals could be heard., donkeys and carnivorous birds began to send forth weired dissonant cries from all sides, portending calamities to come."[7] Murder done in Macbeth, it is still night, the interior of the castle is isolated in time and place. Lady Macbeth hears the owl scream and crickets cry (II,II). Building to the climax of the discovery is the unruly night, chimneys blown down, lamentations heard in the air, strange screams of death and prophecy of the woeful time, the obscure bird clamoured the live-long night. Some say the earth was feverous and did shake.

It is difficult for women to achieve anything like 'full feminity' or of the ways in which women can take up a masculine subject position. After Sita was recovered from Lanka, she had to enter the fire to prove her chastity to angry, suspicious Rama. The will to supremacy relates back to government control, and beyond that to despotism. It is a kind of blemish that persists in Rama. With all her five husbands, the hazards in Draupadi's life give her the title of Nathabati Anatha. Hamlet wants nothing to do with any woman. His mother has given herself to a murderer, and everything about the idea of marriage sickens Hamlet. Hamlet gave his love to Ophelia, and she was to be the future Queen of Denmark. Now he lashes out at Ophelia wildly. Ophelia in sorrow tried to hang a wreath on a willow tree near a brook, and when the branch broke with her weight, she made no effort to save herself. Instead she lay in the water, singing her little songs, some flowers were only on the ripples of the brook. Desdemona has the same fate. Hermione suffers too. The wholeness of the woman's self is the essence of all creativity. A fragmented conception of self, would seem the same as a sick or diseased self.

Calpurnia was subdued in *Julius Caesar*, while Portia demands to be treated as an equal in the same play. Portia's role is of supreme importance in the play. She is Brutus's true and honourable wife accustomed to share all his thoughts, his pleasures, his grief. The virtues of Portia are alluded to in The Merchant of Venice where Bassanio describes his Portia as 'nothing undervalued to Cato's daughter, Brutus's Portia.'

Portia says to Bassanio:

> I am half yourself
> And I must freely have the half of anything
> That this same paper brings you.
>
> *The Merchant of Venice* (III,ii)

In Tagore's dance-drama Chitrangada (a character from the Mahabharata) made the same claim to Arjuna. Her speech is revealing when she discloses her identity. She plainly states that she was neither a deity nor even an ordinary woman. She does not expect worship from Arjuna, nor would she tolerate neglect. She would like to share hardships in Arjuna's life. Arjuna would know her better when she would send his son to him as a second Arjuna. Arjuna was gratified. This speech comes close to two strands of feminist arguments like the 'Relational' and the 'Individualist'. The first concern stresses the male-female couple as the basic unit of society. This emphasizes woman's rights in terms of her child-bearing and/or nurturing capacity in relation to man. It insists on women's distinctive contributions to the broader society. The individualist argument, on the other hand, gives weight to the individual, irrespective of sex or gender as the basic unit. Though these two discourses are distinctly different, an interplay of these two strands can be seen in Mary Wollstonecraft's *Vindication of the Rights of Woman* (1792), which showed a clear sense of the woman's role as mother. In this paradigm where should we place Kunti's virginal conception? What could she do? Shakespeare has given us large slices of life but this enigmatic feminine point never came up in his works. As a result, we do not have the chance to attest any possibility of intimation emerging from the contradictions within and between ideologies upheld by Shakespeare. If Kunti's peril does not come within the vision of 'the woman question', we at least have feminist Cleminta Black reviewing *Tess of the d'Urbervilles* who claimed that Hardy had rightly drawn a distinction between 'moral worth' and simple chastity in women. Mary Jacobus's comment on Tess's 'Woman's soul' as co-extensive with the brimfulness of her nature is also revealing.[8]

The split in the feminine principle is associated with darkness, chaos, sexuality. This principle is powerfully embodied in the beautiful feminine figure of Cleopatra. Goneril and Regan, inflict suffering. Lady Macbeth's ambition seems to be prefaced in the evil designs of Kaikeyi in The Ramayana, Kaikeyi's greed is primary, compulsive and fundamental. The fatal vision of seeing Bharata (her son) as the future king of Ayodhya became sensible to Kaikeyi's feeling. As the dagger of the mind marshalled Macbeth the way that he was going, similarly, Manthara was an imaginative projection of Kaikeyi's monstrous thoughts. Duryodhana was determined to burn the Pandavas alive in the lacquer palace. The text is not very communicative on this point. A tribal woman with her five sons came to the palace and slept there. In the middle of the night the Pandavas set fire to the house and escaped. The point is: who fed the six tribals and made them drunk? Not the Pandava brothers. The text says it was Kunti.[9] 'Here is a scene to parallel the gory murder of Duncan, with Kunti playing the role of an eager yet hesitant Lady Macbeth. Vyasa does not say who actually set fire to the palace. Bhima? If so, instigating Bhima was a Kunti.'

Mallarme's deep white of still unopened water-lilies could be a prelude to the innate beauty of Perdita, Miranda, Sita, Shakuntala. It seems that some secondary characters in Shakespeare, like Celia, Emilia did not receive appropriate attention of critics. Valmiki in his passionate concern for Sita and Rama became completely oblivious of Urmila and Mandavi's misery. How could Valmiki become careless to note their sadness? In Sita's distress he merged the affliction of both Urmila and Mandavi's sorrow. Valmiki's purpose was perhaps to heighten the sorrow inherent in the main plot and then to subdue the subplot's desolation only to drown it into the uproar of the larger pattern of the epic. This may be a splendid instance of two parallels meeting at infinity.

We may refer to a critical point made by a woman critic from Maryland in this context. She wrote, "The daub of black upon Othello's portrait is an ebullition of fancy, a freak of imagination.... One of the few erroneous strokes of the great master's brush, the single blemish on a fabulous work". (The Arden Shakespeare Othello: Intoduction).

The art of war was highly developed, and military skill was held in high esteem in the epics. War in Shakespeare has usually a positive, spiritual value. Swords are vivid, spritualised things to Othello. His arms have spent their dearest action in the tented field. But Arjuna's behaviour on the battle field, his refusal to fight and kill his relatives is curious. Why should a Kshatriya hesitate to do his military duty? Hamlet's tragic dilemma could be understood, as murder was not expected of a person who was made for philosophy, love and art. We can certainly imagine Arjuna, the great warrior to be the world's first pacifist. Arjuna's ultimate surrender to the authority of Krishna, and Hamlet's resistance to yield to the father, by killing his uncle are brilliant contrasts in history and literature. Arjuna's submission has given us the celestial Gita, from Hamlet's grief, in a world of sin and evil, we learn the lesson of tragedy.

The pastoral vogue was in the ascendancy when '*As You Like It*' appeared. An ideal landscape tinged with gentle melancholy gave so much to Rosalind, Orlando and others. The exiled Duke bravely makes the best of Arden and this is reminiscent of the tranquil ashramas of the rishis. In the epics we certainly get the 'purge' by contemplating the affliction of characters thrown into the forest. Forest life was not always a delightful one. Iravati Karve, in her brilliant commentary on Mahabharata titled Juganta (The End of the Epoch, 1969) argues that the burning of the forest gives us a glimpse of the larger struggle in which the newly arrived Aryans and the Nagas, the older inhabitants of the land, were in conflict for generations. Krishna and Arjuna encircled the Khandava forest. The forest continued to burn for a week. Perhaps Krishna and Arjuna burnt the forest to provide land for agriculture. It is possible to read the Ramayana as an account of colonial penetration by Aryans of Ayodhya, led by Rama, who with the help of a faithful mercenary army of forest-folk or treemen called Vanaras routed the anti-god Ravana of Lanka. We can cite Prospero in this framework who constrained Caliban, the 'dull-thing' to obedience in the island with threats of physical pain.

The centrality of disguise is significant in the epics and in Shakespeare's plays. In both, politics is the pointer. It also provides entertainment which is transformed into a subtle instrument for exploring the psychology of role-playing and the philosophical problem of appearance and reality. In Shakespeare's theatre a boy actor impersonates a woman who pretends to be a boy and creates his own problems of credibility. In Othello Shakespeare juggles skilfully with two clocks. Shakespeare used contraction of time and heightened tension to disguise the incongruities of the action. As a mongoose, Hanuman searched for Sita in every corner of Lanka. In pretence of an old, good-willed Brahmin he seized the shaft which contained Ravana's spirit from his palace. It is helpful, if we remind ourselves that in Brecht's aesthetic, the question of identity is important. The contrast between mind and face as a moral commonplace has involved writers in problematic situations. In a hopeless state Shen Te becomes Shui Ta, the good woman who safeguards her livelihood but cripples her life.

Again the question of the role-playing cannot be denied in the scheme of things. In Hamlet, the actor playing the role of

Hamlet first appears as the Prince of Denmark, then as the revenger, and in the course of the play, he becomes the director of the "Mousetrap."

During the Kurukshetra battle in Mahabharata sometimes the established conventions went overboard. In chapter XCI, the wheel of the chariot of heroic Karna sank in the bloody mire. He jumped from the chariot to lift the wheel up, appealed to Arjuna's sense of honour not to take unfair advantage of the accident. Krishna intervened and reminded Karna of many incidents when he supported immoral actions of Kauravas. Krishna asked Arjuna to send his shaft and slay his greatest enemy. Arjuna wavered but accepted the command. According to the laws of war, it was an ignoble act. Who could bear the responsibility for breaches of honour except Krishna? Krishna had to play this role for the cause of justice; he participated in the battle to establish Dharma on an earth torn to shreds by the ghastly power of violence. Krishna on earth is the charioteer of Arjuna, his beloved disciple, and at the same time He is Lord of the universe Himself. In *As You Like It*, one of the best loved of Shakespeare's plays, Duke Frederick knew that Rosalind was beloved by the people and decided to banish her in the same way he banished her father. Celia refuses to be left behind and the two cousins plan to disguise themselves and make their way to the Forest of Arden in an idealized make believe pastoral world. Since Rosalind was the taller, she dressed as a boy and swaggered about as effectively as possible, with a boar-spear in her hand, while Celia dressed as the boy's sister. *Twelfth Night*, one of the loveliest of Shakespeare's romantic comedies takes place in Illyria, on the shores of the Adriatic Sea, a land of sunlight and laughter and the most beguiling poetry. The Duke of Illyria is in love. On the seashore of Illyria there has been a violent storm. A lovely lady Viola, comes ashore after a shipwreck to mourn a brother whom she believes to be lost at sea. Viola, the most charming of Shakespeare's heroines, hearing of the love-sick Duke, decides to disguise herself and become his page. Edgar disguised himself in filthy rags as a "Tom of Bedlam" and Kent's disguise was indispensable in *King Lear*.

In Mahabharata, after the death of Pandu, who had endeared himself to the people by the nobility of his character, now began to idolize the Pandavas. The jealousy of Duryodhana began to grow and he sought in various ways to kill Kunti and her sons at Varanavata. A wax palace was built there and the plan was to set fire to it. People began to praise the beauty of Varanavata and spoke of the festival which would be celebrated in honour of Siva with pomp and splendour. The unsuspecting Pandavas proceeded to Varanavata. Vidura pointedly warned Yudhishthira in words intelligible only to the prince. In the meantime Vidura had sent an expert minor to help the Pandavas. One midnight, Bhima set fire to the palace in several places. Pandava brothers hurried out through the subterranean passage, groping their way out in the darkness of the forest. After much pain and agony the Pandavas met Vyasa who advised them to put on the garb of brahmanas and stay in disguise for sometime. Then followed a new story.

The difference between epic and drama is admittedly abysmal, but the affinity is clear, whatsoever. There is no question of these works being swayed by each other. The epics combine momentum and momentousness. The poems simultaneously exhilarate and frighten by catching the moment just before, or just as, a tremendous tension peaks. The supreme poets invented for their poetry new urgency, dramatic moments, adorned the epics consequently. They make up for the lack of dramatic matter. Shakespeare invented supreme poetry that gave epic dimensions to his tragedies.

As the Indian epics abound in supernatural incidents, the reader naturally has the experience of passing from the world of senses into something beyond itself. *A Midsummer Night's Dream* is a miraculous revelation of the fact that man's imagination is often more useful than his reason. The study of dreams was therapeutic centuries before Freud. When Othello speaks of the Cannibals and Anthropophagi, his speech casts a spell on the audience even today. In *The Tempest*, Shakespeare has built the fable of a master magician who with the machinery of spirits and masques, music and miracles brought symbolic dimensions to his actions.

To project ideas produced by writers like Ibsen and Bernard Shaw was not the plan of Shakespeare. The idea, of course, emanates from plot, character and thought, all are taken together, in his plays. In all the plays there is intense realization of the conflict between the forces of Good and Evil. Is there some power to help us in distress? Divinity responded to Sita in her last trial of chastity in Uttarkanda. Madhavi, the Earth Goddess took Sita in her arms, placed her on the celestial throne, and both descended in the nether world. Gods from heaven showered flowers. All suffering Sita's story ends here.

Rosalind leaves the forest merrily with her father, the Senior Duke, but Jacques stays back in the forest in search of that great philosophy that gave the usurped Duke so much of contentment in the forest. Shakespeare is true to his characters, for so many times in life, one is confused as what to choose, what could give one the greatest benefit. Maitreyee, in the Upanishads, of course, chose to have Amrita (God, eternal life, salvation) when interrogated by her husband Jagyabalka.

Along with Shakespeare's aesthetic philosophy as revealed in his plays, a large number of characters fill our imagination with great sense of awe and wonder. Valmiki's Ramayana has been chanted down the centuries in the Indian continent. It is about Dharma,—in its cyclical journey, the profound message of redemption is conveyed.

The problem of right and wrong has been augmented in the epic battle between the Pandavas and the Kauravas. The question of existence has been heightened in the Mahabharata, when we are "at the still point of the turning world." Glorious characters drawn in both the epics claim our dedication and worship.

All the great works, *The Ramayana, The Mahabharata* and Shakespeare leave the impression that life continues resisting shadow, evil, death. Does the author really die? How could we trace the symbols of good and evil, black and white garbed differently? The old story over again! Edward Bond's Lear progresses from a Shakespeare to a modern archetype. Bond's Lear becomes a social phenomenon; he dies attempting to undo what he has made during his life. If one wishes to interpret Shakespeare's world as the real world, I hope Jan Kott's *King*

Lear, or Endgame in *Shakespeare Our Contemporary* (1965) would flash in one's mind. The themes of decay and fall of the world are drawn in broad outline in the article.

A point of interest in Barthes's criticism is the emphasis he puts on the role of the reader in reading texts. The question of the 'death of the author' has to be seen in the light of Barthes's view that the readers are to open and close the text's signifying process without respect for the signified. They are free to take the pleasures of the text.[10] A linguistic notion can give us the key: diathesis designates the way in which the subject of the verb is affected by the action.[11] 'Today to write is to make oneself the centre of the action of speech (Parole),— it is to leave the writer inside the writing, not as a psychological subject, but as the agent of the action'. We could even say that the agent is not interior to the process. The one who writes does not write for himself, but for a person who is exterior and antecedent. Then shall we imagine the poets have written by proxy through ages for a later artist like Van Gogh whose self-portraits leave an impression of haunting death? Or, why should we find in Picasso's vocabulary the tragic, heavy legacy which he carried within himself in thought and mood?

NOTES AND REFERENCES

1. See Jacques Derrida's *Of Grammatology,* Translator's Preface translated by Gayatri Chakravorty Spivak (Maryland 1976).
2. Valmiki's *Ramayana,* one of the greatest stories of all time, is an epic about *Dharma* and has become the very *Sanskara* of the people of the Indian continent.
3. *The Mahabharata* of Vyasa, or Fifth *Veda,* as it has been called, born of several thousand years of oral endeavour, was written by the sage Vyasa to become a vision for all time.
4. T. Mcalindon, *Shakespeare's Tragic Cosmos* (Cambridge University Press, 1996) p. 127. Knolles's 'Major Themes Christian Disunity, the Enemy Within'. Concerning Cyprus in particular, Knolles viewed its 'bloudie tragedies' as a paradigmatic chapter in the unfinished conflict between Christian & Turk, in that the island fell because of dissentious rivalries between the commanders of the fleet sent to defend it and because of inadequate leadership on the island itself.

5. P. Lal, *The Ramayana of Valmiki* (Tarang Paper Backs, 1989), p. 33. The transcreation is dedicated with love to Sita, model of Indian Womanhood, lady of purity and delight, daughter of the fragrant earth, speaker of sweet wisdom.
6. Simone de Beauvoir, *The Second Sex,* translated and edited by H.M. Pashley (Penguin Book, 1972), p. 558. In another article in the same book the author remarks, 'sometimes the feminine world is contrasted with the masculine universe, but we must insist again that women have never constituted a closed and independent society; they form an integral party of the group, which is governed by males.... They are united only in a mechanical solidarity from the mere fact of their similarity, but they lack that organic solidarity on which every unified community is based'. 'Women's Situation and Character' p. 608.
7. C. Rajagopalachari, *Mahabharata* (Bharatiya Vidya Bhavan, 36th edition, Bombay 1999), p. 114.
8. See, Penny Boumelha, *Thomas Hardy and Women: Sexual Ideology and Narrative Form* (The Harvester Press, Sussex, 1982).
9. P. Lal, *the Mahabharata of Vyasa,* condensed from Sanskrit and transcreated into English (Vikas Publishing House Pvt. Ltd. 1980), p. 31.
10. Contemporary Criticism, ed. by V.S. Sethuraman (M 1989), p. 27.
11. *Ibid.*, pp. 240-4.

11

The Australian Shakespeare: The Nation in Evolvement from Bardolatory to Appropriation

Arindam Das

My paper proposes to trace the inception-to-present-day evolvement of Shakespeare in Australia and read how the same echoes Australia's evolvement from a nation with colonial hangover to a present day appropriated postcolonial entity. Indeed, the trajectory of Shakespearean representation in Australia most non-obliquely suggests the nation's gradual ability towards self-determination. Whether in formulation of a Shakespeare Society in Australia and the 'much ado' with Shakespeare Festival to the recent 'about nothing' to do with Shakespeare in Arts Festival; from a quintessential English Shakespeare performance to the White and Aboriginal reconciliatory or resistive tendencies in a postcolonial Shakespeare adaptation; the adopt to adept phase of transition in Australian Shakespearean in its own way propels towards the nation's postcolonial self fashioning.

Australian Nationalism: An Unease Straddling

For the Australian nation the biggest dilemma is to be or not to be with its British ancestry. The nascent phase of Australia's nationalistic zeal had a strong bourgeoisie affinity to prototypical Britishness. Yet a steady urge towards a distinctive Australian consciousness at the frustration over a colonial brunt was not very late to evolve. As early as 1850 an immigrant Scots Presbyterian minister, John Dunmore Lang in a speech to students in Sydney Arts School (later compiled in Lang's book *Freedom and Independence for the Golden Lands of Australia*, 1852) asserted the sense of non-blue print nationalism as a prerequisite for further progression:

> And must the young Australian be debarred from the exercise of that generous and manly feeling, of which every rightly constituted mind is conscious, when he exclaims, with deep emotion 'This is my own, my native land!'...In one word, nationality, or their entire freedom and independence, is absolutely necessary for the social welfare and political advancement of the Australian colonies. Give us *this* and you give us everything to become a great and glorious people. Withhold *this,* and you give us nothing. (as qtd. in Hancock 58)

Although the separate Australian Federation was formed in 1901, the true sense of 'being Australian' remained relatively weak, which posed a problem of legitimacy for the new, Federal Australian State. John Foster Fraser noted in 1912 that whilst there was evidence of the 'green leaf' of Australian national consciousness sprouting in the new Commonwealth the principal allegiances were to the states, but above all to the Empire and a seeming nostalgia for the metropole:

> And that one word, 'home', more than any arguments about the advantages of imperial trade or demonstrations in favour of imperial cohesion, has soaked into the brain of the Australian, and he appreciates—not always by reasoning about it, but with the regard a son has for his father—that 'home' is his country just as much as Australia, and that what affects the Englishman affects him. (11-2)

However, it was the First World War that geared a sense of strong Australian nationalism. The events of the First World War, and particularly the Dardanelles campaign, provided a fund of myths for Australian nationalism. According to the official war historian Charles Bean, service overseas enhanced that 'passionate love of home, marked in Australians' (as qtd. in D. Winter 141). The main straddling factor and unifying element between Australia and Britain has been the monarchy. According to Australian Constitution the British monarch is also the Australian monarch and thereby the Australian head of state. During 1990s the attention did rise to brush off the imperial link. In 1994, the chairman of the Australian Republican Movement (ARM), Malcolm Turnbull wrote that 'A nation defines its self by being different' (4). But the proposal did never materialize and did fall face-flat in 1999. In April 2004 the Australian Parliament again considered ways in which Australia might become a republic and remove the monarch as head of state. The contention still continues regarding the development of Australian nationalism and its association with Britain. But, meanwhile what remains undeniable is the colonialist heritage of Australian nationalism.

It is this colonialist basis that has time and again defined and re-defined the relationship between the Aborigines and White Australians. The White nation's declaration of *terra nullius*, genocide, ethnocide, child-stealing, pseudo-eugenicist assimilationist policies, depriving of human, economic, social and cultural rights had strained their relationship with the Black populace. Thus, the paranoid, exclusionary nationalist policy of White Australia had caste a shadow over its past; and no less threateningly looms over its present. The recent reconciliatory tendency, between the Whites and Aborigines of Australia, as evident in the form of an apology by the erstwhile Prime Minister Kevin Rudd (13 February 2008) is little more than a tokenism. Resistance, not reconciliation is therefore the byword that unsettles the White Australian nationalism. Such Aboriginal resistance is dual in nature: the power movement of aggressive tactics and hardy resistance as fostered by Aboriginal activists like Gray Foley and Paul Coe; and the postmodernist

Bhabhaesque tendencies of cultural appropriation of the White Nation. The later stratagems of 'sly civility' of the Aborigines in making a cultural narration of a 'non-derivative' nation of their own—in differencing out an identity by playing with, and paying back the White national culture—is well brought about by the words of Glender and Jacobs in *Uncanny Australia: Sacredness and Identity in Postmodern Australia*:

> The nation (Australia) becomes unfamiliar to itself precisely because of the post-colonial condition in which an indigenous population is increasingly able not just to "write back" but to produce a range of special effects, which can be unsettling right across the board. (135)

Australia and the Bard: Let's Part(y) with Shakespeare

The Melbourne Shakespeare Society, inaugurated on the playwright's birthday, April 23, 1884, was the first step towards the institutionalized celebration of the Bard. The society hoisted the plays of Shakespeare, various paper readings on Shakespeare, essay competitions, original poems and prose passing an encomium unto the bard. The Society turned into a literary club, filled with enthusiasm and surcharged with gusto. The motto of Shakespearean Society was "Would I Knew His Mind"—an adage that transformed the bard into an unfathomable storehouse of eternal Knowledge, and the society members into thirsty knowledge seekers. James Smith tended to find in Shakespeare even a justification of Aristocracy and a source of culture which might counter the immaturity that produced "a sense of rebellion, a frowardness as well as a forwardness among our youthful 'cornstalks' and 'gumsuckers' which makes young England seem tame, temperate, soft spoken and submissive by comparison with young Australia":

> If the absurd principle that 'all men are equal' has been anywhere established, it is in the colony of Victoria. We have no aristocracy of descent, and my only fear is, lest we should erect in its place [...] an aristocracy of money [...] Art needs for its support what art finds in England—a large class of men with cultivated minds and independent fortunes. (Smith 142)

At its first anniversary celebration, the Society's President, Professor Edward Morris, suggested that the Australian colonies together in their true spirit are but White *Terra Shakespearia*. Morris proclaimed (much like modern nation theorist Benedict Andersons' promulgation of nation as an "imagined community") that global recognition of the Bard by all English speaking peoples would maintain "virtually one nation, so that they could not fall out and fight, but live at peace, in brother-like intercourse, helping one another":

> Here I say is an English King, whom no time or chance, Parliament or combination of parliaments, can dethrone! This King Shakespeare, does not he shine in crowned sovereignty over us all, as the noblest, gentlest, yet strongest of rallying signs; indestructible, really more valuable in that point of view than any other means or appliance whatsoever? We can fancy him as radiant aloft over all the nations of Englishmen, a thousand years hence, from Parramatta, from New York, wheresoever, under what post or parish constable soever, Englishmen and women are, they will say to one another, 'Yes, this Shakespeare is ours, we produced him, we speak and think by him, we are of one blood and kin with him.' (*Shakespeare Society Papers: Argus and Age,* 24 April 1885)

Three months after Morris's unparallel paean, the Society had its first major public controversy. E.E. Dillon, a young man, presented a paper titled *The Hero Shakespeare*, (and was supported by the majority of young men audience) which was designed to show the playwright's moral influence and importance had been "tremendously overrated" (*Shakespeare Society Papers: Argus,* 15 August 1885).[1]

If staging Shakespeare in various festivals was the 'in thing' in Australia during mid-twentieth century then the condition has gone a sea-change of late. The elitist tendencies of colonial nostalgia with its Anglophile predispositions have encountered a perfect volte-face. Arts Festival of Australia has ever been the cultural lynchpin factor of the nation. But today such festivals endorse the Shakespearean dramas as mere sop tokenism without any zealous indulgence in the same.

Australia's first attempt at a major Arts festival was the Festival of Perth, inaugurated in 1953, although drama festivals had been taking place in many regions of Australia for some time before this. Currently the Confederation of Australian International Arts Festivals draws together the Energex Brisbane Festival, the UWA Perth International Arts Festival, the Sydney Festival, the Adelaide Festival of Arts, the Melbourne International Arts Festival, and Tasmania's Ten Days on the Island. But, a National level Shakespeare Festival has never properly geared up in Australia. Although, the local Shakespeare festivals as those promoted by Swan Hill group did catch community frenzy and was crucial in creating a community pride and local identity. Swan Hill became so devoted to Shakespeare that it instigated an annual festival that continued for three decades. Local interest in Shakespeare was engendered by Mrs. Marjorie McLeod. In 1947 McLeod persuaded the Swan Hill National Theatre to perform scenes and highlights from *Romeo and Juliet* in honour of Shakespeare's birthday, and at the same time local businesses were organized to create floats for a Shakespeare procession through the main street. Around thirty Shakespeare productions were mounted in the Swan Hill Memorial Hall over the years and many associated events took place outside in the streets and Local Park. The festival week grew to include street processions, film screenings, fairs in the park, puppet shows, Shakespeare readings, lectures by visiting scholars, and a fancy dress Arts Ball. Local shops carried window displays promoting the festival, and in 1955 a color film of the event was made and screened in the town hall. Feature articles about the festival appeared in *Woman's Day*, *The Women's Weekly*, *The Weekly Times*, and *The Argus*, expressing amazement at the breadth of community involvement. But from a pure elitist attachment to canonical Shakespeare the Swan Hill productions started to appropriate the texts to suit the Aussie demands. Festival directors felt free to play with Shakespearean texts, cutting and pasting according to their needs, writing their own songs, and even pioneering the use of modern dress and Australian settings. *Twelfth Night* was produced in modern dress as early as 1959, and *As You Like It* the following year was promoted as being in modern dress with an Australian setting. The passion with Shakespeare waned away from '70s, and finally in 1976 the festival's last Shakespeare production, *Macbeth*, was poorly attended, whereas *Dimboola* played to capacity audiences at the Oasis Hotel. The Festival of Perth in a dispersed manner included Shakespeare in its programme, whereas the Adelaide festival—the premier Arts festival of Australia—which started six years later did not have Shakespeare in its agenda. Tasmania's ten-day festival has never had any Shakespeare in their list and even the Sydney festival rarely did hold any Shakespeare: apart from the Bell Shakespeare Company's *Troilus and Cressida* at the Olympic Arts Festival in 2000 and Theatre de Complicite's *The Winter's Tale* in 1992, the only recent inclusions have been foreign-language productions, namely Declan Donellan's brilliant all-male Russian *Twelfth Night* in 2006 and the Yohangza Theatre Company's Korean *Midsummer Night's Dream* in 2007. These are accompanied by a handful of interesting productions from the Melbourne Fringe, including an acrobatic *Dream* in 1994 and a puppet theatre *Twelfth Night* in 1996.[2]

This ebb tide in Shakespeare affinity at the cost of an inclination towards recent quintessential Australian drama most palpably suggests Australia's search for its own identity—a shaking off of its Anglophile brunt. Thus Australia in its gradual laying off of Shakespeare aims towards a 'non-deriviative discourse' of modernity that forms a basis of its own national culture. Or to put it in a more direct Partha Chatterjee manner: Australia is in the quest for "modern national culture that is nevertheless not Western" (5).

This modern national Australian culture in a postcolonial realm shares a 'liminal' site where two distinct voices interface, communicate and co-exists with 'unease'. The Australian postcolonial national culture is no less a hybrid zone where the 'White Settler' colonies and the Aboriginal community share the same space thereby interrogating any given hegemonic culture, be it even the canonized Shakespearean drama. Thus, Australia narrates and performs the linear holism of 'Shakespeare Culture' thereby creating the contested site of postcolonial 'interstitial' space. Keeping constraints in mind, I will briefly discuss Queensland Theatre Company's (QTC) version of *The Tempest* directed by Simon Phillips which incorporates the work of 'Jagera Jarjum', an Australian traditional indigenous dance company (performed in September 1999 in Brisbane festival and restaged by Melbourne Theatre Company in Centenary of Federation Festival in 2001).[3] In this version of *The Tempest* the colonial construction of Aborigines is challenged through Philip's direction. Further there have been open political agenda of having a greater control over the construction of Aboriginality by 'Jagera Jarjum' while being involved in the production of the play.

The very fact that the Jagera Jarjum group declined to remain the 'fringedwellers' is evident in the words of Narjic Fogart, a key person of this corroboree group:

> ...got to have a better understanding that in this place here, there are still, young people, old people, that still have traditional links to this land and have an understanding of traditional dance, song, stories—all of that. We wanted to get across that we still understand traditional laws. Still we live by them, even though it's hard sometimes for the living. So that's one thing I know, before we even come to rehearsal, we all sat down and spoke about that and said that's what we want to put across. Let people know that we're still alive. (as qtd. in Campbell, n.pg.)

The dance group who performed a key role in the play especially in the masque scene at the end through a 'Dreamtime' ritual dance using fire, earth and water took the entire event of raising spirit in their earnest traditional sense, and it is here made evident that the entire events for the Aborigines were far from a make belief theatrical world of Shakespeare. Thus, far from being silent purple patches with commercial agenda, the use of Jagera Jarjum in the play and expressing their Aboriginality thoroughly appropriated the Eurocentric 'narrativity' of the Shakespearean text. The Aboriginal depiction of Ariel (played by Margaret Harvey, an Aboriginal actress of Torres Strait Island) added another dimension to the discourse of colonialism. In the context of postcolonial reading, Ariel acts as the Spivakesque subaltern woman lacking the agency over her speech/identity. It is here to be remembered that no Aboriginal songs were ascribed to Ariel and the original English lyrics were retained instead—an explicit example of deracination and linguistic colonization. At the moment of freeing of Ariel she was made to doff with the whale-bone corset and the spirits of the land helped her wash the white marks off her body—a thorough indication of decolonization of body. But the key focus of Aboriginal de-humanization and dispossession lay in Philip's depiction of Caliban. If Caliban's being seduced to alcohol by Stephano insinuates at the health problem of the present Aborigines in Australia due to same; then him being made to wear red ochre coloured military dress with a nameplate equally suggests the poor Aborigines thriving on welfare dependency. On the contrary, the hint might also lay in the red soil of the Aboriginal land, and the forceful seizure and tagging of the same. But in the entire process of renegotiating with Shakespeare the most contentious and problematic aspect for Philips, as Campbell also reinstates, was the end:

> ...the most difficult beat in the whole production was the last moment between Prospero and Caliban. That was difficult because I was playing against the text and because I was negotiating with two people who were kind of the most immensely proud representatives of their individual culture. I was treading on glass to make sure that that moment could be meaningful without making John, who hates to lose power on stage feel he was losing power and not make Glen feel like he was losing power. And it was also the sense to which that was reconciliatory. Because I think I managed to create a sense, visually in which Prospero said to Caliban 'forgive me'. We were exploring the moment of Prospero holding out his hand and Caliban would then be raised up to his level and then there was that question, is it Prospero's right to raise? Where is Caliban making the choice? And Prospero having said, 'please forgive me',

> does Caliban say, 'fuck you' I'm not going to forgive you, you have done too much damage to me, or does he go, OK, I will forgive you. Finally, the decision was that Caliban ran, having been freed, he left, didn't stay and the sense being that he would be wandering for a long time. It wasn't over yet. (Philips as qtd. in Campbell, n.pg.)

If the efforts on the part of Philips were praiseworthy attempts towards reconciliation, then his very last aforesaid words say it all: 'It wasn't over yet'. Thus, any attempt towards 'reconciliation' (as done through the recent appropriations of Shakespeare)—an attempt to create one large Andersonian imaginative community called the Australian nation, is fraught with unease and might instead run to result in a 'wreck', 'con', 'silly', 'nation'.[4]

NOTES

1. In this section while discussing the 'Melbourne Shakespeare Society' I have borrowed all the information and paraphrased the same from Ken Stewart.
2. In this section while discussing the 'Arts/Drama Festival in Australia' I have borrowed all the information and paraphrased the same from Rose Gaby.
3. In drafting this section I am indebted to the brilliant discussions in the article of Angela Campbell.
4. In 1996, Deborah Mailman and Wesley Enoch wrote in their play, *The 7 Stages of Grieving* (1996) that the very term reconciliation if is broken down into syllables what we are left with is "wreck", "con", "silly", "nation".

WORKS CITED

Anderson, Benedict. *Imagined Communities: Reflections on the Origin and Spread of Nationalism.* 1983. Rev. Ed. New York: Verso, 1991. Print.

Campbell, Angela. "The Tempest: Creating Dialogue from the Points of Difference." *The Australian Public Intellectual Network*. Web. 19 June 2012.

Chatterjee, Parta. "Our Modernity." *SEPHIS–CODESRIA Lecture*. No. 1. 1997. 1-20. Web. 25 Aug. 2008.

Enoch, Wesley, Deborah Mailman and Hilary Beaton. *The 7 Stages of Grieving*. Brisbane: Playlab Press, 2002. Print.

Fraser, J. Foster. *Australia: The Making of a Nation*. London: Cassell, 1912. Print.

Gelder, Ken, and Jane Jacobs. *Uncanny Australia: Sacredness and Identity in Postmodern Australia*. Melbourne: Melbourne UP, 1998. Print.

Gaby, Rose. "'An Australian Stratford?' Shakespeare and the Festival." *Journal of Australian Studies*. 90 (2007): 167-76. Print.

Hancock, W. K. *Australia*. London: Ernest Benn, 1930. Print.

Melbourne Shakespeare Society Papers. La Trobe Collection, State Library of Victoria, MS9635 Box 2797/1-2.

Smith, James. "England and Australia Contrasted and Compared." *Victorian Review*. 22 February 1861. Print.

Stewart, Ken. "Ken Stewart: "The Much Ado About Everything: The Melbourne Shakespeare Society 1884-1904." *Australian Literary Studies*. 19.3 (2000): 269-78. Print.

Turnbull, M. *The Reluctant Republic*. Melbourne: Heinemann, 1994.

Winter, D. Ed. *Making the Legend:* The *War Writings of CEW Bean*. St Lucia: U of Queensland P, 1992. Print.

12

Reinventing Shakespeare's Plays: A Cinematographic Approach

Pratik Chowdhury

All art, according to Aristotle, is a type of mimesis, an imitation or a representation of reality which is dependent on a medium, through which it is expressed, and a mode or the manner in which this medium is utilized. Imaginative literature particularly fiction, and films, are two of the most contemporary art forms that share many features and yet diverge in some areas. The commonality is in their primary objective of communicating. Imaginative literature like novel, short-story, non-fiction, poetry and drama are discourses relying on narrative elements; they employ specific figures of speech like simile and metaphor to create verbal images, thereby making the reader see them as they read. The art of cinematography[1] is also a narrative which is essentially pictorial in nature. It narrates by showing the viewers, images projected on a two dimensional screen. In other words there is a fundamental difference in the means and mode of expression; one relies on verbal content and the other offers visual content. The codes employed in literature are intrinsically linguistic relying on a system of signs, signifier and signification; it works by manipulating these into images. Literature must become visual and convey images through words, "to project it on to that inner screen of the brain a moving picture of objects and events, events and objects, moving towards a balance and reconciliation of a more than usual state of emotion with more than usual order" (Read, 210-11). A work of fiction then, conveys emotions, scenes, actions, and sounds through symbols and images which 'can be seen by the reader only through the stimuli of words which project their images on the screen of the mind's eye' and resonates in the 'sound chamber of the mind's ear' (Madsen, 254). Cinematography on the other hand, is a perceptual form of art, having evolved an independent language, grammar, syntax and modes of expression. Its equivalent to literary "words, phrases, sentences, paragraphs, chapters, and punctuations are scenes, sequences, scene sizes, camera and lens movements, editing tempos and concepts, and optical effects." (Madsen 27-28). It communicates by appealing to the audio-visual faculties of its viewers by relying exclusively on certain conventions engendered and reinforced by technology-photography, editing and sound recording[2]—all extraneous forms of art, having their respective unique code and syntax, which collectively function in unison to show its viewers the emotions, feelings, sights and sounds in real time.

There is however, a need to differentiate between the type of ingenuity which engenders visual literary representation and cinematographic vision, with that which creates images in space and time. Literature, as mentioned earlier, is visual by virtue of its verbal content, and cinematography by virtue of its pictorial content, presents a narrative through the medium of a number of disjointed images projected on a screen in sequential order to create the impression of a continuous whole. Cinematographic vision, thus exclusively depends on certain intrinsic elements manipulated and controlled by the ubiquitous camera, which translates the narrative into images, unlike drama or poetry, which relies on language to achieve similar effects; like them, cinematography also depends upon certain extraneous features like sound, both in the form of dialogue and music.

II

After establishing the basic differences between the means and modes of representation—verbal and visual content—it is imperative to understand that cinematography, as an independent form of art, is subjected to its internal dynamics. Like any art form it too is governed by a set of codes and syntax. These terms have altogether a different connotation in cinema. Codes are critical to constructions of cinema; they are systems establishing logical relationship and yet they cannot be accepted as preexisting laws to be consciously followed by the film maker. A number of codes usually combine to create the medium in which films express meaning. Some codes are culturally derived, while some are shared. The former exist outside the film and the film maker has to reproduce them; the latter are generally artistic codes that may be commonly shared by other arts or may be specific to cinema. For instance, gesture is a code common to both cinema and theatre, while montage can be considered unique to cinema. (Monaco. pp.175-76)

Syntax in film is defined as its systematic arrangement ordering its rules and indicating relationship among them. In comparing and contrasting syntax in spoken or written language systems and cinema, James Monaco observes "In written/spoken language systems, syntax deals only with...the linear aspect of construction: that is the way in which words are put together in a chain to form phrases and sentences, what in film we call the syntagmatic category. In film, however, syntax can also include spatial composition,..So film syntax must include both development in time and development in space" (172). I would therefore, like to discuss some of the elementary techniques, along with the associated jargon, that go into creating a cinematographic work of art. The preliminary stage begins with choosing a story, or a novel, which has to be adopted for the *screenplay*.[3] The story is first given a broad outline, which delineates the essence of action. It is then built up into a prose narrative called treatment which is "then broken down into the format of a screenplay. Like its stage counterpart, the screenplay sets out the dialogue, describes the movement and reactions of the performers and at the same time gives the breakdown of individual scenes, with some indication of the role, in each scene, of the camera and the sound." (Lexicon Universal Encyc. p. 89) The screenplay therefore becomes the blueprint or the verbal design of the edifice of the film as conceived by the director. Every scene[4] is thus broken down into *shots*. A particular scene maybe photographed from a number of vantage points, and edited into ten or twenty *shots*. The camera then assumes a significant function, it ceases to be a mere tool for capturing pictorial images, in addition it also becomes a very powerful medium of creating an ambience and imparting a dramatic unity to the narrative. The camera can remain stationary or mobile; it can be moved straight or at an angle, high or low. All movements[5] of the camera are aesthetically directed to impart a dramatic quality to the pictorial images that can be cut, or juxtaposed to reveal the progression of the narrative. The movement of the camera is either in relation to the character in motion or at rest. When the character is in motion, the camera may, either follow from the rear, or dollies ahead, or captures the motion from a higher perspective, always maintaining synchronization. On the other hand, a camera can also move in relation to a character at rest or in repose. For example, it can move forward to capture the expression of the character in a 'close up'[6] for emphasis, or gradually shift away at the end of the scene—'fade-out'[7]—to dramatize a lonely figure. The camera can capture a scene from a distance (long-shot)[8] and gradually move in closer (medium-shot)[9] to very 'close-up' shots. This technique ostensibly serves to shift the focus from the wider to the narrower or from the general to the particular.

Having discussed the elementary techniques, it is essential now to take into account some of the methods employed by the director to convey emotion, drama etc. through images. The problem of the film maker can be understood in the context of his medium. The succession of images that his camera has captured of the sequences when projected, will merely turn out to be an "affidavit-exposition" of moving or static characters, totally de-sanitized of emotion or drama, and such a presentation would lack a unifying principle. One of the modes that a film maker has at his disposition is the 'montage'[10], (Fr. putting together) which essentially involves the juxtaposition of separate images to create a new idea arising of it. (Eisenstein: 1970. p. 14). For example, if three images or shots are juxtaposed and placed in sequential order-man looking at something, a baby, a man smiling, then the inference would be of a kindly person; but if the same sequence is repeated with a girl in a swimsuit substituting a baby, then certainly the meaning would acquire a different dimension. Similarly, if in another example, a shot of a grave were juxtaposed with a woman mourning, the immediate conclusion would be that the woman is a widow. In this context, Eisenstein says, "that two film pieces of any kind, placed together, inevitably combine into a new concept, a new quality, arising out of that juxtaposition" (1970, p. 14). The process of montage also directly involves the audience in that they have to apprehend the inherent meaning of the montage. Montage can further be accentuated by editing i.e. "the splicing together of pieces of film in order to build continuity... or to establish a series of associations by cutting back and forth between images." (*Lexicon Universal Encyclopedia*, p. 434)

To sum up then, the art of cinematography primarily relies on the motion picture camera which presents the reality restricted by the four edges of the frame. According to Paul Madsen, the movie- camera "... is the means of capturing movement. The lens is the eye of the camera, but it differs from the human eye in that it is unselective, rendering everything within its scope and depth of field with equal emphasis...." (Madsen. 32) However, such drawbacks are compensated by recording only those aspects of a subject that needs to be shown to the viewer at a given time. The camera is moved forward or backward, its motion takes the audience into the scene or distances them from it respectively. The camera, thus, becomes the perspective or the point of view of narration. The process of montage and juxtaposition of shots evoke the unifying emotions. It is against this technique of cinematography that this paper examines a few scenes from Shakespeare's *Macbeth* (Act II, sc.i) in detail.

III

On reading some sections of Shakespeare, one is at once arrested by the 'screenplay' quality of their narrative. Some of the passages in Shakespeare are extremely cinematographic; they give the impression of a well orchestrated screenplay, replete with directions not only for the movement of the characters, but also apparently to specify the positioning and movement of the camera. It would be a fallacy to look for any such overt references in the passage, but nevertheless, the instructions are well implicit in the text.

An attempt is now made to examine the first ten lines of Act II sc.i of *Macbeth* against the perspective of cinematographic idiom as discussed above.

Banquo : How goes the night, boy?
Fleance : The moon is down; I have not heard the clock.
Banquo : And she goes down at twelve.
Fleance : I take't, 'tis late, sir.
Banquo : Hold, take my sword.—There's husbandry in heaven;
Their candles are all out;-take thee that too.—
A heavy summons lies like lead upon me,
And yet I would not sleep:—merciful powers,
Restrain me in the cursed thoughts that nature
Gives way to repose! Give me my sword, who's there?

The scene is set in Inverness, a courtyard in the castle. The stage direction provided in the text mentions "Enter Banquo, preceded by Fleance with a torch." This is significant, in the Elizabethan society obsessed with order, a son usually follows the father, but in this scene he leads, and with a flaming torch. The images of the man and the torch, through association, imply night. When Banquo speaks to his son, both are in a state of motion, and as he speaks Banquo's hands are busy taking off his armour, one by one. Banquo's opening words draw the attention of the audience to the night — "How goes the night, boy?" Fleance's reply, "The moon is down; I have not heard the clock." The audio-visual signification of these two lines is obvious. There is a juxtaposition of the signs or the visual syntax[11]—images of Fleance with the torch, the waning moon, the expeditious actions of Banquo's hands — with the auditory syntax of the unheard clock, which together build up and reinforce the image of the night and convey a sense of exigency. In the cinematographic jargon, it is as though Shakespeare has used a succession of separate shots to build up an image and mood. The lines can be considered an ideal montage script, using a series of disparate shots to convey the passage of time. In the further exchange when Banquo says, "Hold, take my sword, there's husbandry..." it is almost a clear instruction for the camera to close in not only on the physical action but also to take in his expression in close-up. The camera or our attention is again drawn to Banquo's physical action of taking off his armor, "Take thee that too... repose." Here is another instance of a 'shooting-script' direction. The camera as though, is asked to move away from Banquo's close-up to his body-movement and again refocused on his expression with the subsequent lines. This deliberate impulsive jerky motion of this sentence establishes Banquo's tired expression and troubled conscience. There is a dramatic pause, Shakespeare allows the action to linger for a few seconds, and then Macbeth enters. Banquo immediately orders Fleance, "Give me my sword — who's there?" There is a violent shift from troubled calm or introspection to alertness. As is evident from this analysis, these ten lines are cinematic in their construction.

A quick analysis of the opening lines of Act I Scvi may serve as another case study. The scene shows Duncan, Banquo and other attendants arriving at Inverness, and the royal entourage awaits the lady of the house at the castle gate.

Duncan : This castle hath a pleasant seat: the air
Nimbly and sweetly recommends itself
Unto our gentle senses.

Banquo : This guest of summer,
The temple- haunting martlet, does approve,
By his lov'dmansionry, that the heaven's breath
Smells wooingly here: no jutty, frieze, buttress,

Nor coigne of vantage, but this bird hath had made
His pendant bed and procreant cradle:
Where they most breed and haunt, I have observ'd
The air is delicate.

Duncan's opening remark, followed by Banquo's observations, present a panoramic view of the castle against the calm light of the evening — Duncan says, "This castle hath a pleasant seat, the air/ Nimbly and sweetly recommends itself/ Unto our gentle senses." This sentence consists of three dominant images — that of the castle, imposing in its majesty, enchanting in the glow of the setting sun; the calm and serene atmosphere of the evening; and its total impact on his senses. The pictorial quality of the images cannot be missed. In the cinematographic sense, this scene is an example of an 'establishing shot'; such scenes establish the time, mood and place of action that is to follow. The visual content in these lines could be divided into three shots establishing the images. If a film maker is to capture the essence of the visual, one can very well imagine the nature of the shots or the perspective that he would employ, from which the camera would capture the images. The first shot would definitely be a panoramic long-shot showing the whole castle standing in its splendor bathed in the evening glow. The second shot would be a long slow sweeping movement of the camera or the pan-shot taking in the evening sky, the fading light and the castle. The third shot would close in on Duncan and his companion's faces, thereby drawing them into the ambience of the scene. These images taken together certainly build up the required mood and emotion.

Banquo's response to Duncan's utterances is equally cinematic; he refers to the "temple-haunting martlet" making its nest at every corner of the castle — "no jutty, frieze/ Buttress, nor coigne of vantage, but this bird/ Hath made its pendant bed and procreant cradle/... I have observed/ The air is delicate."

In these lines, Shakespeare's use of language is suggestive of the movement of Banquo's eyes, as they take in the details. The shifting focus of Banquo's attention is established by his reference to "jutty", frieze, buttress, "coigne" of vantage etc. this is another example of a 'shooting script'. The direction for the camera movement is implicit within the lines. Banquo's eyes function as the camera lens as it moves in an arbitrary manner, capturing every nook and corner in random. In doing so, the observing eye/camera deliberately breaks up the unity of the whole, as earlier presented through Duncan's observation. The general is fragmented into particular, and again, it is presented as a whole, through the last section of Banquo's speech, "I have observed/ The air is delicate." The introduction of the first pronoun brings back the focus on Banquo, thereby completing the structural pattern, from general to particular, and to the personal point of view. Moreover, in the phrase "pendant bed and procreant cradle" there appears to be an ostensible direction for the camera to shoot these objects in motion. Here Shakespeare verbally shifts the focus from the general to the particular; cinematographically, this would be represented by making the camera move from object to object, capturing these images in succession.

One cannot resist the temptation of examining the murder scene in Act II sc.i by adopting this approach. This scene has Lady Macbeth on the stage, keyed up and waiting in anticipation for Macbeth to complete the deed. She confesses that she had to resort to alcohol to make up her resolve. She apparently seems to be eased and but she is in a state of neurosis; tensed up, a picture of anxiety, restlessness, and suppressed energy. Shakespeare's cinematic vision is evidently on display here. Encoded within the text, there are clear instructions provided for any director to shoot the scene. His use of language describing her state of anxiety and restlessness provides the clue to shoot. In terms of cinematography, the camera moves in tandem, sometimes following her or sometimes beside her as she utters her lines. This establishes her anxiety and restlessness, and her sharp utterance, "Hark! Peace", breaks up the rhythm of her movement and quickly shifts attention on her. This mobility and violent interruption make the tension palpable. She continues with her dialogue, "It was the owl that shrieked the fatal bellman/ Which gives the sternest goodnight. He is about it:/ The doors are open and the surfeited grooms/ Do mock their charge with snores; I have drugged their possets..." The images of the shrieking owl and the fatal bellman juxtapose in the mind to create the image of death. The further images of the open door, the drunk and sleeping grooms reinforce the idea of death creeping towards Duncan's chamber. In terms of cinema, Shakespeare seems to have incorporated a number of cinematic codes. First, this sequence can be visualized from the perspective of Lady Macbeth's point of view; the camera assumes her perspective and moves through the open doors, takes in the inebriated guards in a tight shot, and then closes up to show their inebriated sleep. On stage, the same function is achieved through Lady Macbeth's utterances, creating the same images. The attention or focus is riveted back on her as she hears Macbeth's voice from within — "Who's there? What, ho!" the camera as though on cue, gradually zooms in closer to frame her expression reflecting palpable tension. Her utterance again conjures the images of the grooms awakening, the daggers laid ready, and the image of patriarchal Duncan in sleep. The cinematographic representation of this scene would involve the principles of montage and cuts[12]. The images of the grooms, followed by daggers and sleeping Duncan, are rapidly cut and juxtaposed evoking the contrast between the murderous designs of Macbeth and Lady Macbeth and the innocent victim. The entrance of Macbeth into the scene prompts a short exchange of words —

> Macbeth: I have done the deed. Didst thou hear a noise?
>
> Lady Macbeth: I heard the owl scream and the crickets cry. Did not you speak?
>
> Macbeth: When?
>
> Lady Macbeth: Now.
>
> Macbeth: As I descended?
>
> Lady Macbeth: Ay.
>
> Macbeth: Hark! Who lies in the second chamber?
>
> Lady Macbeth: Donalbain.
>
> Macbeth: This is a sorry sight.

This short exchange is essentially cinematic. It is another instance of an 'establishing—shot' or rather an 'establishing two- shot'. James Monaco explains this in terms of the popular "Hollywood dialogue style" which begins with a shot of both the speakers and then proceeds to use montage shots of individual speakers as they speak and respond.

> 'Often these are "over- the- shoulder" shots, an interesting use of the code, since it suggests the speaker's point of view but is also physically separate from it. The shot of the first character from (approximately) the second character's point of view is usually termed a reverse — angle shot. The rhythms of this insistent and intimate shot-counter shot technique are often intoxicating: we surround the conversation.' (Monaco, p. 211)

One can very well visualize this crisp exchange between Macbeth and Lady Macbeth in terms of the cinematic technique discussed above. Here, as it were, Shakespeare seems to be capturing each character in a tight frame as they utter their lines, and splicing or editing them to produce alternative images first of Macbeth and then of Lady Macbeth along with their clipped dialogues — "When? Now as I descended? Ay, Hark" etc. This alternate focus on the characters against the darkness of the room, built up by a series of shots, transforms it into a tightly knit sequence. The visual and auditory images converge to project the tension, it is tangible, vibrating.

The genius of Shakespeare immediately slackens reins and releases the audience from the tension, by drawing their attention to Macbeth's hands — "This is a sorry sight." Shakespeare's cinematographic vision, allows the perspective to retreat a little and enclose both the characters into focus together. This physical proximity consolidates their association in crime and is also reinforced in the following exchange of words. Lady Macbeth tries to allay her fears, while Macbeth in his strung up state keeps referring to the incident, the "hangman's hands", the awoken guards, their horror, their prayer and his inability to pronounce 'Amen'. In this unrelenting sequence one can imagine the camera lingering on the speakers, occasionally shifting focus.

Then with Macbeth's speech — "Still it cried, Sleep no more/ ... Macbeth shall sleep no more!" —the focus or the point of view is shifted. The perspective is gradually pulled back, eventually isolating Macbeth. As his words echo, "Sleep no more", the camera, as it were, retreats, and as the words reverberate, it restlessly moves through the empty corridors of the castle and finally reverts on him. In the process Macbeth is reduced to an isolated pathetic figure.

The next exchange between Lady Macbeth and her husband shifts the mood from pathos to mockery of Macbeth. Her interrogation — "who was it thus cried?" mocks Macbeth's failing resolve. She bids him to wash his hands and remove the filthy witness. This conversation too, is cinematographic, gathering momentum to reach the crescendo-final moments of tension introduced by the sudden knocking at the gates. As Lady Macbeth goes to place the daggers and smear the grooms with Duncan's blood, the sudden knocking intrudes upon the scene violently. It evokes Macbeth's startled reaction — "whence is that knocking? / How is it with me when, every noise appalls me?" The focus is brought back upon Macbeth and his horror of the deed he has just committed. Implicit in this short speech of Macbeth are the cues for its cinematographic representation. His reference to his hands constitutes the shot of his bloody hands. The sound of the knock and his startled expression forms one shot, the mention of his hands cuts the shot from his face to his hands — "What hands are here! Ha! They pluck out mine eyes." The remaining utterance with its image of the hands turning green sea red is unquestionably the most cinematographic visual composition. The scene is immensely graphic; one can visualize the image of the bloody hands juxtaposed with the image of the sea, the former image gradually dissolving into the latter, the green of the sea, slowly "making the green one red". The image derives its force by the deft use of the language, which Shakespeare employs like a powerful tool. Here the verbal and visual elements coalesce to create a powerful impression. This cinematographic merging of one image into another can be understood in terms of enjambment in poetry, which involves the sense of a sentence or a clause to flow into the succeeding line.

Lady Macbeth's return and her sense of bravado — "My hands are of your colour, but I shame/ To wear a heart so white" is merely registered, when the knocking is heard again. Lady Macbeth is held in focus, and her rising terror is studied, as though by the moving camera, which follows every action and emotion of hers. The intensity of the scene is sustained by the knockings at gradually reduced intervals. As the staccato volley of knockings grow louder, her actions acquire urgency, the camera follows them both, as she literally pushes Macbeth ahead of her, giving instructions— "And show us to be watchers. Be not lost/ So poorly in your thoughts." The scene ends with Macbeth, as though held in a close-up shot, his face registering a final vicious effort to overcome and forget his deed — "Wake Duncan with thy knocking! I would thou couldst!"

The close analysis of these scenes compels one to wonder at the extraordinary ability of Shakespeare of rendering a scene cinematographically. In this article there was an attempt to reinvent Shakespeare's plays from the point of view of a contemporary art—cinema. The objective was not to see if his plays are suitable to cinematic productions, but to find how closely they conform to the language of this medium. Through this short analysis, this article has demonstrated that the difference between the pictorial representation of images and scenes (through metaphors and similes, as is common in poetry), and the cinematographic representation, lies fundamentally in the momentum inherent in the images or scenes being conveyed. The cinematographic images or scenes are exclusively dependent on specific cinematic codes that include explicit direction for the camera, in terms of its position, movement and shot division working in unison to build up a scene. Both these representations however, share one common feature—that is to project a succession of images on the mind's screen. Literature achieves this through the medium of words, and the other, through visual and auditory modes; both strive to achieve a totality of experience and create an organic whole, developed out of fragments. Shakespeare's plays achieve this by incorporating elements of both these forms.

NOTES

1. Cinematography— A broad term encompassing art and technology of motion picture photography. It involves the composition of a scene, lighting of the set and actors, choice of cameras, camera angle, and integration of special effects to achieve the photographic images desired by the director. Cinematography focuses on relations between the individual shots and groups of shots that make up a scene to produce a film's effect.
2. Photography, editing and sound recording— These three are employed in unison to communicate sense, emotion, mood etc. of the narrative in films. Photography uses the camera to capture motion on film, called shooting. It is the stage of producing raw material (negative) which has to be fashioned into finished product. Editing is the post-production stage in which every shot recorded on the negative is physically spliced and joined in such a way so as to present a logical sequence of events. It also helps in creating a time and distance relationship to reality.

   Sound recording or sound track, as it is popularly known, presents the auditory component of the narrative with the aid of dialogue, music and sound effects thereby contributing to the exposition of the narrative and adding realism to it. A major part of the emotional quotient in the narrative is added by the sound track.
3. Screen play is the written format of the story which provides the basis for film production. It includes, among other things, dialogue spoken by the characters and a shot-by- shot outline of the film's action. Screen plays are generally revised a number of times by the writer, director, producer and others involved in the film making process. The early drafts of screenplays only contain brief suggestions for planned shots, but by the time actual shooting commences, they evolve into a shooting -script which include detailed instructions on actions and gestures. The shooting-script is therefore, a more elaborate, precise, and overwritten version of the screenplay. The shooting-script is generally written by the director and his cinematographer after mutual discussion on their ideas and desired shot plans.
4. Scene— In the language of cinema shot, scene, sequence and setting have special meanings which differ widely from its use in the theatre. Explaining this Madsen writes that in cinematic conventions a scene is defined as 'that length of film footage exposed in one uninterrupted roll of the camera, unbroken by any change to another visual'. It can be as short as a frame or as long as the roll of film that may be practicably photographed.

   A sequence in cinema corresponds to an act in the theatre, or a chapter in a book, and 'consists of a series of scenes constituting a complete dramatic action within the film, containing a beginning, a middle and an end. Theoretically there is no limit to the number of scenes that a sequence may contain, nor to the maximum number of sequences in a film.'

A setting like its literary counter-part refers to the location of the dramatic event. It also refers to its mood and atmosphere. (Madsen. 33) It has been suggested that shot is the word of the film, scene its sentence and sequence its paragraph. (Monaco. 160)

The shot is the basic unit of film construction; it is defined physically, as a single piece of film, without breaks in the continuity of the action. It may last as long as ten minutes (since most cameras only hold ten minutes of film); it may be as short as 1/24 second (one frame)...but the standard fictional feature is comprised of as many as five hundred or a thousand separate shots. (Monaco. 129)

Another important aspect of arranging shots or sequences is through editing, which is second most important aspect of film production. By physically splicing and joining scenes into logical sequences the totality of meaning is achieved. Film editing is an art by itself requiring knowledge of the 'relationship between the content of two scenes, their internal movements, the screen directions of their subjects, their associated image shapes and the lengths of each scene used to create tempo.' (Madsen. 42)

5. Movement is essential to cinematography. It is of two types—movement of the subject before the camera; and movement by the camera or its lenses over the subject. In the first form, movement is made by the subject within the frame of the scene. In the latter form, the camera or its lens follows the actions of the subject. The camera itself has two basic forms of movements; it can either revolve around one of the three imaginary axes that intersect in the camera (pan, tilt and roll) or it can move itself in space from point to point (in following people or objects in motion as in "trucking shot", "dolly shot", "crane shot" or "hand held-shot") the lens of the camera, by changing focus can also imply movement. (zoom and "shift focus")
6. A close-up usually is a head shot of a person or an object; it frames expression and is used to create a dramatic emphasis or highlight the meaning of a particular moment, expression, or scene.
7. Fade-away or 'fade-out' is a form of transition; one of the methods for changing from one scene to another retaining the continuity and meaning unchanged. This technique involves the gradual disappearance of a scene to darkness. It signals the termination of a scene or a sequence. A prolonged 'fade-out' intensifies the emotional effect of the scene. Its converse is 'fade-in' in which a scene is slowly made to emerge out of a darkened background. It is generally employed at the beginning to introduce the film.

8. Long-shot, also called an establishing shot, is an introductory shot generally used at the beginning of a sequence, scene or a film. It is usually a wide angle view establishing the mood, setting, or revealing what is to follow.
9. Medium-shot is a waist-up view of a character generally focusing upon the actions of his hands.
10. Montage is the sequential assembling of separate pieces of thematically related film by the director, film editor, and visual and sound technicians, who cut and fit each part with the others to produce visual juxtapositions and complex audio patterns. (*Britannica Ready Reference Encyclopedia* Vol. 7. 16) Monaco suggests that montage has the specific usages in terms of 'a dialectical process that creates a third meaning out of the original two meanings of the adjacent shots; and a process in which a number of short shots are woven together to communicate a great deal of information in a short time'. (216)
11. Film theory also relies on semiotics borrowing terms like signs and syntax. A language is a system of sign, signifier and signification; the arbitrary relationship between the last two, form the focus of literature. However in film, the signifier and the signified are identical. An image of a rose is conceptually much closer to the object than its orthographic representation. Thus, in film a sign is a 'short circuit sign'
12. The *cut* is a method of portraying smooth transition and is onc of the primary techniques of editing. It is a rapid shift from one scene to another.

REFERENCES

Britannica Ready Reference Encyclopedia Vol. 7. p. 16, New Delhi: *Encyclopedia Britannica*, 2004.

Eisenstein, Sergei M. *The Film Sense*. Edited and Translated by Jay Leyda. London: Faber and Faber, 1943.

Lexicon Universal Encyclopedia, Vol. 8.

Madsen, Roy Paul. *The Impact of Films*. New York: Macmillan Publishing Co. Inc, 1973.

Monaco, James. *How to Read a Film*. New York: Oxford University Press, 2000.

Read, Herbert. "The Poet and the Film". In *The Art of the Essayist*. Edited by C.H. Lockitt, Delhi: Orient Longman Ltd. 1988.

Shakespeare, William. "Macbeth". In *The Complete Works of William Shakespeare*. 14th Impression, London: Spring Books, 1971.

13

Feminist Perspectives and Post-Feminist Possibilities: A Reading of Selected Texts of Shakespeare

Madhumita Purkayastha

The wonderful paradox of William Shakespeare's canonical status as a transnational author lies ironically in the fact that he is one of literary history's most "deconstructed" canons. Shakespeare's texts have lent themselves to unconventional interpretations down the ages, which reinforces the present contention that these are enduring masterpieces which have survived deconstructions and reconstructions! Contemporary readings of Shakespeare's writings have opened up critical apertures that enable multidimensional approaches to his canonical texts. One such approach has been the post-colonial feminist approach. Post colonial feminist approaches have explored intersections of feminisms and colonization with the latter operating as a metaphor for subjugation and 'othering' of the female and the objectification of the female body under the "male gaze". While feminists have engaged in debates regarding the political positioning of the much celebrated heroines of Shakespeare's tragedies and comedies, which seem to represent distinctly diverse strands of his aesthetic consciousness of the feminine, the sexual colonization of women and the hegemony of the white male has been questioned in terms of his androcentric poetic vision and representation, socialization and historicity. Dramatic representations of Shakespeare's women are further problemmatized by theatrical performances of the Elizabethan age where cross-dressing male actors played cross-dressing women characters. The gendered texture of his texts and the "sexual, textual politics" (a term popularized by Toril Moi) operating thereof has made for fascinating studies. His sonnets on the other hand represent a complex aesthetic vision which subvert traditional concepts of feminine beauty, masculinity and hetero-normative love. The present study posits that Shakespeare possessed a rare unique bi-gender vision/consciousness, which could, by virtue of its double lens and gender fluidity, lend keen insights into human psyche and bring the verve and texture of life to his writings. The present paper attempts a study of selected sonnets of Shakespeare to validate the stated hypothesis. The paper would first examine briefly the key feminist perspectives that have lent perceptive insights into the multilayered complexity and gendered texture of his texts. Subsequently, the post-feminist stand in terms of theoretical/conceptual understanding of discourse in the present context shall be specified and a reading of the selected sonnets within this interpretative framework shall follow.

Feminist Perspectives

Tracing the trajectory of feminist criticism of Shakespeare's works would underscore the diversity of feminist approaches to his text. In the two decades of the 20th century 1970s and 1980s, feminist enquiry was directed at putting issues of gender and sexuality on the critical agenda. Analyses focused on the portrayal of women characters in each genre (drama and its sub genres and non-dramatic poetry). Gender stereotypes and patriarchal norms in his representations were examined along with his ability to create unconventional female characters who defied or challenged gender norms (especially in his comedies). Subsequently, psychoanalytical feminist readings focused on the socialization and formative moments of family life as the key to a character's gendered behaviour and also traced Shakespeare's own psychic development in these works. One such play was *Coriolanus* where the protagonist's demanding mother holds such sway over him that he desperately craves her approval. In her book *Suffocating Mothers* Janet Alderman has read the influence of the dominating mother figure on the protagonist in Shakespeare's plays and argued that in the second half of his career, Shakespeare was working through a deep ambivalence toward the mother figure and while Volumnia of *Coriolanus* is a monster created during that phase, at times he achieved a partial reconciliation with the mother figure.[1]

The 1980s saw feminist enquiry turning towards a historicizing of Shakespeare's texts in terms of an emphasis on and an enquiry of the gender system within which Shakespeare lived. If earlier ahistorical feminist enquiry focused on enduring and timeless stereotypes of women, the latter work looked at the particular way in which male and female behaviour was structured in the culture of the Elizabethan period. Some of the most provocative work of the decade was based upon research suggesting that in the early modern period, that is, during renaissance, scientists and medical writers saw men and women as more perfect and less perfect variations of the same sex and same prototype. The implications of such a view are far-reaching and complicated. While feminists objected to biological determinism which stressed on the biological differences of the male and female bodies in order to justify the gendering of sexes and determination of social roles on the basis of physiological differences; the early modern rationalizing of the "natural" inferiority of women made for volatile masculine-feminine binaries in the early modern culture. In the crossdressing comedies of Shakespeare, boy actors who played the part of women who in turn disguise themselves as men, there is a dizzying play with gender categories, which however is non-threatening and humorous. On the other hand, Shakespeare's plays of other genres cast the mannish woman and the womanish man in a far more problematic and threatening light. A Volumnia destroys all before her, a Lady Macbeth, having bloodied her hands with the blood of Duncan can never ever erase the stain from her hand or her mind, while Henry VI, because of his "feminine" irresolution and weakness, loses his wife, kingdom and son.

It is especially noteworthy here that since in the culture of the early modern period gender difference was not guaranteed by bodily difference, gender divisions would then be enforced by other distinctions, social codes and legal measures and moral repressions. England had sumptuary regulations regarding distinctive dress codes for each class as well as strict religious and moral codes against crossdressing. In this context, the Elizabethan all-male stage was already potentially disruptive of gender norms in terms of daily performance practice (where male actors wore female clothing) as well as aesthetic plot requirement (where women characters crossdressed as men in disguise narratives). This is an interesting pointer to the fact that early modern public theatre and therefore drama (Shakespeare's work and workplace) was a place of experimentation with gender roles and behaviour.[2]

Another strand of feminist enquiry focused on critical examination of both feminity and masculinity, both poles of the male-female binary and their relationship under the larger rubric of gender studies. The most contemporary strand of feminist enquiry termed as "difference feminism" is based on the premise that gender categories cannot be understood in isolation from other categories of difference such as race, class and sexuality as men and women do not form homogenous groups. Postcolonial and subaltern feminisms have examined the intersections gender, race, class and sexuality in Shakespeare's texts and how they have influenced the construction of female characters as well as problematized his notions of feminity and his aesthetic re-visioning of the female and feminine. Kim Hall has argued that Shakespeare shared with many of his contemporaries a 'beauty discourse' or a concept of ideal feminine beauty in which the 'fairness' of the heroine implied virtue/chastity (read moral superiority) and implicitly creates the idea of England as a white nation.[3] By contrast, his dark Cleopatra is exoticized and sexualized or Caliban's mother is demonized, marking their non-European identity and utilizing the trope of the seductive Eastern woman who lures away the white male from his responsibilities and duties and thus perpetuates the negative stereotype of the dark woman. In this context, the controversial figure of the "dark lady" of Shakespeare's sonnets (124-154) poses a challenge to the post colonial feminist critical discourse as, historically and aesthetically, the "dark lady" is an English national and therefore "white" in terms of the racial category and all that it signifies. However, the universal stereotype of woman as an irrational, passionate being of nature that has ever been responsible for depravity and downfall of man, does emerge in his representation of the dark lady.

Post feminism: Historically, what is today understood by the term "Post feminist" is the present/contemporary era of affirmative and confident celebration of feminity in the aftermath of third wave feminism, which has shifted feminist interest from the struggle for the "sisterhoods'" common cause and located it in the achievement and consolidation of the woman as an individual. However, post feminism is also misunderstood as the redundancy of feminism or a rejection of it[4], which, I contend, is an amnesiac discounting of the immense contributions of the latter not only in terms of women's rights and dignity but also in terms of intellectual and critical insights. Contemporary post feminist representations have "flattened out the complex and often disturbing patterns of gender and sexuality in Shakespeare's plays to authorize a "postfeminist" view of society and to suggest that feminism is outdated, irrelevant, and even harmful."[5] The post feminist identity has been seen as focusing on "pampering and pleasuring the self", 'celebrating feminity' by reclaiming and rejoicing in feminine stereotypes and as "girling women" to encourage a youthful disposition in women of all ages.[6] In doing so, creative representations (literary as well as media) and critical discourses in the post feminist trend have reconstructed confining stereotypes in a conservative reclaiming of imposed roles and expectations, albeit as conscious choice rather than imposition.

The present study posits post feminist critical discourse as "looking beyond" the premise of gender polarities and binaries to gender fluidity and gender ambivalence as well as an engagement with the problematic overlappings and intersections of heteronormative love and fixed sexualities with homoerotic friendships/relations in literary and cultural texts. I would look at selected sonnets of Shakespeare from this specified post feminist point of view rather than an occlusion of valuable feminist perspectives.

Shakespeare's Sonnets and the "sexual textual politics": Shakespeare's sonnets were published in 1609 by Thomas Thorpe and the ambiguity in its dedication coupled with the mystery of the identity of the 'I', 'thee' or 'you' kindled and sustained an everlasting interest in his sonnets. Anthony Hecht in his Introduction to *The Sonnets* points out two very pertinent facts about Shakespeare's sonnets—one, that they "regularly outsell everything else he wrote" and another that these poems are read for a variety of reasons including voyeuristic pleasure in prying into his private life and decoding them to reveal a narrative of exciting intimacy.[7] His sonnets have been treated as biographical fiction and since the advent of feminist critical perspectives, the sexual politics in the texts has been closely scrutinized. In this context, it is interesting to note that since it has never been clear whether Shakespeare intended or planned the publication of the sequence, individual sonnets could be read both in isolation or as part of a larger textual narrative. Although it is practically impossible not to bring in biographical connections and assumptions in reading sonnets written by an iconic figure, whose acquaintance with and engagements in courtly traditions of wooing, love-making and intrigues of the Elizabethan court are undeniable, it is possible to construct a story out of the sonnet sequence with four 'characters': the poet speaker, a fair youth/ patron (idealized as adored beloved in sonnets 1-126), a seductive dark mistress with sexual prowess (the denigrated "dark lady" of sonnets 127-154) and a rival poet whose supplications to the fair youth further complicate the peculiar triangle of relationships where hetero-normative love and sexuality are indicted as destructive and immoral while homo-erotic love is elevated and eulogized. Given the circumstances of the age when, in early modern England, sexual identities (homosexual or heterosexual) were not assigned in terms of exclusively erotic commitment to one sex or the other, sexual practices seem to have been fluid. Nor was it unusual to find erotic friendships between men of equal status as well as cutting across power, age and status differentials. However, there are few textual traces of homoerotic friendships among women as marriage figured centrally in their lives. Renaissance England women were defined in terms of their marital status—as maids (women who were peparing to marry), wives (married women), or widows (women whose husbands had died). The only other category was for whores (women who would never marry). While maids and widows were supposed to be sexually chaste and married women faithful to their husbands, whores were, by definition, unchaste and sexually promiscuous, who took money in lieu of their sexual services unlike the wife who rendered it for "love".[8] This makes the "mistress" in Shakespeare's sonnets a volatile figure, combining in its essence the sexual overdrive of a whore, the seductive powers of a temptress, the "dark" exoticism of the eastern enchantress and the irrational, mindless and wild passion of the archetypal Eve who can only lead man to "sin" and "death."

Nowhere are the problematic issues of gender, sexuality, love, loathing, morality, guilt, passion, attraction, revulsion and anguish more problematically enmeshed than in Shakespeare's "dark lady" sonnets. Aesthetically, his bi-gender vision facilitates the gender fluidity of his characters which subvert normative expectations. Hence the key convention of sonnet writing—the tradition of idealizing the beloved as an embodiment of fair beauty, virtue/chastity, aloof disdain, unattainability and immortal youth is constructed in the character of a beloved male friend in a sequence of sonnets replete with puns, subtle and humorous innuendos and oblique homoerotic expressions. In sonnets 1-126, he seeks to immortalize the feminine beauty of his friend and his glorious love for his eulogized "beloved". The cynicism and bitterness of the "dark lady" sonnets are not discernible here as the poet speaker's unwavering faith in his friend never falters despite repeated instances of disillusionment and betrayal. Here, his unquestioning faith on the male friend's fidelity is subsequently juxtaposed against his violent repudiations and denigration of the dark mistress on whom he places the onus and responsibility of breach of trust.

With the commencement of the dark lady sonnets, the conventional beloved of poetics is jettisoned. Sonnets 127-14 present a woman courted by the poet speaker. She is an absolute antithesis of the fair youth and in the poets courtship of her as a suitor, none of the inspiring and magical experience of love, none of the devotion or eternal commitment that characterize many of the love sonnets to the youth are evident. Persistent and recurring images of "blackness", "darkness" in connection with his mistress associate her with "mourning", "sin", "despair" and "death". She is denigratingly referred to as "the bay where all men ride" (Sonnet 137) and an unworthy object of sexual obsession. She has been constructed as the classic "dark foil" to the shining virtue, truth and beauty of the fair youth.

I argue that looking beyond the trope of subvertive surprise could enable us to look at another construct of the dark lady. In Sonnet 127, the argument of the poem seems to be that his beloved mistress is black because it is symbolic of a mourning for the debasement of true beauty. His love having taken on this guise of black mourning, it has now become so fashionable that common opinion has swung round to believing that dark beauties alone are truly beautiful. He therefore feels that his passion for her is justified.[9] The poet speaker may appreciate "fairness" in terms of its moral associations or even praise blonde beauty, but the appreciation of genuinity in his mistress is evident in that she is not guilty of "*Sland'ring creation with a false esteem". In Sonnet 128,* there is a ray of sunshine, and the poet takes pleasure in seeing his mistress playing. But the pleasure is not entirely unalloyed, for it is mixed with unfulfilled longings, and a jealousy that suspects that her favours are being too liberally bestowed on others. Sonnet 130 brings us to the unconventional praise that the poet bestows on his mistress. Although apparently, the praise of his mistress is rendered so negatively that the reader is left with the impression that she is almost unlovable, the sestet contrives to make one believe that the sound of her voice is sweeter than any music, and that she far outdistances any goddess in her merely human beauties and her mortal approachability. She "treads on the ground" unlike any goddess impossible to attain and the poet thinks his "love is rare" and precious. In Sonnets 133-34, the poet agonizes over the dual entanglement of his beloved friend and himself with the dark lover. Here Shakespeare has wrested the tradition of the love sonnet from its sweet ideal of courtly and refined love to show the unpalatable and coarse side of human desire and the darkness and savagery of worldly love. It is noteworthy that initially, the blame of betrayal that was placed on the dark lady was gradually turned inwards to portray the landscape of a tortured soul caught in the grips of fierce lust, anger, jealousy, shame and moral guilt. In subsequent sonnets, the dark lady becomes the alter ego of the poet as much of his self-loathing and self-blame of the poet can be vented upon her. Here, Shakespeare uses the trope of the aggressive, sexually active, hunter/pursuer deviant woman stereotype in order to shoulder the burden of the poet speaker's inability to break free from the vicious circle of desire, sexual passion and obsessive attraction. The excessive sexual appetite of the dark lady that is harped upon in sonnet after sonnet is deliberately deployed to justify the poet's ambiguous attractions towards both the male friend and the female/ *femme fatale*.

A case in point is Sonnet 142 which lends insights into Shakespeare's attitude to love. It plays out the old battle between spiritual and physical love, a subject which had been the jousting field of argument for centuries. The poet seems to ally himself with the traditionalists who believed that the nature of woman was such as to corrupt pure love. In Platonic terms she was the material dross of which bodies were made, but the spiritual ideal love was independent of her, and true love could really only subsist between males. In terms of Christian theology, woman was the devil and was responsible for the fall since she had tempted man to eat forbidden fruit. Any form of congress with a woman was corrupting, and the ideal life would always be one of chastity and abstention from sex. The doctrine was alleviated slightly by devotion to Mary, the Mother of God, but despite giving birth she was a virgin, and worshipped as the Blessed Virgin Mary. A mitigation to this view was the reality of life itself, which always returned to insist that the majority of men would continue to desire women.[10]

Sonnet 150 is thematically reminiscent of Sonnet 116 where the poet speaker makes a series of positive and oratorical declarations, which however cannot be substantiated in the final analysis. The poet declares in Sonnet 116:

> Let me not to the marriage of true minds
> Admit impediments. Love is not love
> Which alters when it alteration finds,
> Or bends with the remover to remove:

Sonnet 150 is framed instead as a series of questions, to which there appear to be no answers. From an idealized and abstract love which can find expression in philosophical ruminations and declarations here, idealized love has metamorphosed into earthly love for a beloved who embodies the grosser aspects of physical love and does not measure up to the expectations that ideal love demands. The series of interrogations seek to define the limits/limitlessness of love. The questions raised in this sonnet, What power?, Whence? and Who? seem to implicate a terrifying choice between succumbing either to the blind and irrational power/force of love and/or to the satanic powers of darkness.[11] In either event, there is no escape for the soul as the darkness of desire of the human heart draws the lover into a vortex of passion and an inferno of inescapable desire—a love that is fuelled by a sexual motive force and is driven by an irrational and mysterious regenerative force. Here, all expectations of mutual and everlasting love that is found in the optimistic earlier sonnets is replaced by a dawning of the bitter realization that his love and fidelity are unreciprocated. Shakespeare has here delved into the deepest core of some of humanity's most baffling and most overwhelming concerns (as also aesthetic preoccupation)— the complex web of man-woman relationships, entanglements of love, hate, desire, power and the plethora of psycho-sexual, emotional and moral implications of gendered relations.

Sonnet 152, the final sonnet of the dark lady series, underscores the supreme irony that an eternal commitment of love to the dark mistress involves the breaking of marriage vows. It is as if the poet is appealing to a higher court, the court of a deity, a divine power that recognizes the eternal commitment which transcends all limited human values. The fact that the appeal is made to this court on behalf of a love for a woman whom the poet considers at times to be little better than a whore, adds a dimension to the sonnets which in the end diverts attention away from the immediate words and forces us to look back into ourselves, to consider the deeply perplexing question of what is love and why does it bring us to the edge of the abyss?[12] The biblical ring of Job's despairing cry against injustice and sorrow could be the renaissance spirit's anguished grappling with religion and God on the one hand and faith in humanity on the other. The concluding sonnet in the sequence to the dark lady leaves the reader with the uncertainty of not knowing and a denial of resolution, which is again unexpected in love sonnets.

Shakespeare's sonnets are evocative of inner experience. In scaling the nadir and zenith of both hetero-normative and homo-normative love, Shakespeare's vision, paradoxically, albeit bi-gender, appears to be andro-centric. His sonnets especially lend themselves to a feminist deconstruction perhaps because, unlike his drama or his narrative poems, the dark lady has not been given a voice/speech. She is what the poet speaker makes of her. Her "blackness" of appearance and heart are constructed for repeated repudiation. The poet interprets, agonizes over, anticipates and accuses her of infidelity. She is the "betrayer" and both he and the fair youth are "betrayed". The play of love and the politics of sex engage opposite sexes in an encounter of adversaries, where, one must point out, the battle of sexes is made out to be an entrapment for the male who is the "hunted" and the "victim", subject to feminine wiles and helplessly drawn in a libidinous game, which is controlled by the sorceress. The liberal humanist renaissance world was the world of man. The faith in immense human potential was faith in *man's* abilities and *man's* aspirations (italics mine, read exclusion of women in all aspects of public life). The strife between intellect and spirit, between divine agency and human will, love and sex, was played out on a terrain of masculine interpretations. The "feminine principle" was amoral, "natural" and irrational, an uncontrolled sexual and regenerative drive that could be brought under control if circumscribed by the human institution of marriage and the "divine" vows of fidelity in marriage. Within the protestant Christian Church, the "husband" was the owner and possessor of the wife and entered marriage with expectations of lifelong fidelity and obedience. The "dark lady", being the mistress, obviously could not be "controlled" by sacred vows. While a number of Shakespeare's women protagonists are represented as independent, intelligent, strong-willed, eloquent or capable, such women were operative within the make-believe world of theatre. If a Venus predominates and directs a passionate love relationship, acting as the pursuer and initiator of erotic love, she is a recreated goddess of myth and fantasy. If Cleopatra has supreme sway over the men she captivates, she is an eastern enchantress. If Portia is more eloquent and intelligent than Bassanio, her proficiency in argument can find recognition in a public space only in the guise of a man. If Lady Macbeth, Margaret (wife of Henry VI) or Volumnia are strong, aggressive and powerful women, they are made out to be monsters and deviants. A Kate has to be "tamed" in marriage and turned into a docile, obedient wife to bring her into the patriarchal fold and Hamlet's mother Gertrude must stand humiliated in the shame that her son feels at her sexuality and "crime" of fornicating with her husband's murderer, albeit unknowingly. There is always the comforting pre-supposition that errant women would be chastised and women with qualities of head and heart would eventually take up their "real"/expected role after a temporary stint in the topsy-turvy world of drama.

The sonnet sequence however treads the fine line between art and life and the slippery area of autobiographical association must be grappled with as the politics of personal relationships are fore-grounded. A post feminist reading, while reconstructing the sonnets as abiding documents of human love and its complex landscape of emotions, as capturing the essence of life in its dizzying multiplicities, also takes cognizance of the fact that "sonneteering" in the Elizabethan age was often an intensely personal exercise, sonnets being read only among a coterie or close group of people, thus bringing this aesthetic exercise so close to real life as to colour it with the spectrum of felt emotions. Perhaps, that is why the sonnets are fraught with such keen self criticism and also so much turmoil and struggle to come to terms with unresolved emotions. Unlike most sonnet writers of the age, Shakespeare subverts poetic conventions to infuse his sonnets with the pulsating throb of life. Expecting him to transcend totally the fundamental social, cultural and ethical beliefs and practices of the age would be a historical impossibility.

NOTES AND REFERENCES

1. Janet Adelman. *Suffocating Mothers: Fantasies of Maternal Origin in Shakespeare's Plays.* London: Routledge, 1992
2. Jean E. Howard. "Feminist Criticism", *Shakespeare: An Oxford Guide.* Eds. Stanley Wells and Lena Cowen Orlin, New York: Oxford University Press,© 2003, Indian Edition, New Delhi: DeUnique, 2007. pp. 418-421
3. Kim Hall. *Things of Darkness: Economies of Race and Gender*, Ithaca: Cornell University Press, 1995, pp. 62-122.
4. McRobbie, Angela. 2004. "Post-Feminism and Popular Culture." *Feminist Media Studies* 4.3: 255-64.

   As Angela McRobbie puts it, postfeminism describes the conservative backlash that "positively draws on and invokes feminism ... to suggest that equality is achieved, in order to install a whole repertoire of new meanings which emphasize that it is no longer needed, it is a spent force" (2004, 255). Here, McRobbie highlights the postfeminist gesture as a kind of cultural shorthand that enables the death of feminism to be taken for granted.
5. "The Postfeminist Mystique: Feminism and Shakespearean Adaptation in *10 Things I Hate About You* and *She's the Man*" Jennifer Clement, University of Canterbury. © Borrowers and Lenders, *The Journal of Shakespeare and Appropriation*, 2005-2012. ISSN 1554-6985
6. Michelle M. Lazar. "Entitled to consume: postfeminist feminity and a culture of post-critique", *Discourse & Communication* Copyright © 2009 SAGE Publications. Vol 3(4): 371–400
7. Anthony Hecht. "Introduction", *The Sonnets*, The New Cambridge Shakespeare. Ed. G. Blackmore Evans. Cambridge University Press, 2003. p.1.
8. *Shakespeare's Sonnets*, Oxquarry Books Ltd., UK.© 2001[www.oxquarry.co.uk]
9. *Ibid.*
10. *Ibid.*
11. *Ibid.*
12. *Ibid.*

14

Shakespeare in the Light of Rasavada

Ratri Ray

My first effort in this inter disciplinary direction had been an essay on Romeo and Juliet published in 1983. On looking it over, it seems to have been a somewhat amateurish affair, woefully in need of revision. So, that is what this present essay sets out to do all over again: interpreting Romeo and Juliet in the light of Rasavada.

Sanskrit poetics gives us ten kinds of plays. Acarya Dhananjaya enumerates them in his Dasarupaka. According to his classification RJ will be a natika and not a nataka; one of the reasons for this is that the story has not been taken from the scriptures or the epics. Shakespeare based his play on the narrative poem *Romeo and Juliet* by Arthur Brooks. This play is particularly well suited for analysis from the Rasavada view point. As Dhananjaya Says:

> Prakhyato dhiralalitah Srngaroangi salaksana[1]
> (The hero is a well known dhirala
> lita figure and the angi rasa is Srngara)

Romeo is definitely a dhiralalita hero, and the main rasa is Sringara. As a matter of fact there are three tragedies with this as their angirasa: *Romeo and Juliet, Othello* and *Antony and Cleopatra*. Romeo and Antony approach the dhiralalita and Othello the dhirodatta hero.

Sringara is definitely the main rasa. The three characteristics of the angi, vathuvyapti, patroddyama and phatagama, can be easily found in Sringara as used here. It is present from the beginning to the very end of the play, there being but few scenes with no Sringara in it. Secondly, the hero's personality and actions are stepped in this rasa. Thirdly, the overall impact of the play is that of the misfortunes of a pair of star crossed lovers. The reader realizes that it is their love that has brought about the tragic end of the play. Karuna rasa reigns at the end, but it rises out of Srngara. The influence of it is so strong that the figures of Romeo and Juliet are remembered as synonymous with lovers. It may be said that his first love does not create Srngara rasa as powerfully as his love for Juliet. But we shall see different gradations of love here as evidence of the dramatist's wonderful powers.

Raudra rasa is created in the first scene. Members of the two families fight and the Prince intervenes to bring about an uneasy peace. The beginning thus prepares the reader for the future evocation of vera and raudra rasa. It is with the dialogue between Benvolio and Romeo that Srngara makes its first appearance. Romeo's love for Rosaline is expressed in elaborately rhetorical language:

> Why then, O brawling love! O loving hate!
> O anything! of nothing first create.
> O heavy lightness! serious vanity![2]

This highly rhetorical language, and there are fairly long passages of it, expresses bhava, but one hesitates to declare that rasa is created. The diction is too rhetorical to express depth of emotion. Shakespeare knows that this love of his hero is only infatuation, the real thing is going to come later. So he gives us some entertaining fireworks. If one likes to call it rasa then it can be called kusumbha Srngara.Such love is richly expressed but not enduring love. This is how Visvanatha Kaviraja expresses it:

Kusumbharagan tatprahuryadapaiti ca sobhate.[3]

They call that the safflower love which should but depart, like the dye of safflower, which fades in the washing.

The next scene is barren of rasas. Many bhavas rise and fall and intermingle. Vatsalya bhava, for example, can be seen in the dialogue between Capulet and Paris, and later humour and merriment but these bhavas do not attain the elevation of rasahood. A gentle hasya rasa is found in the next scene, with the reminiscences of the nurse. The reader can easily imagine Lady Capulet and Juliet similing. We have hasya rasa of the vihasita variety where, which is accompanied by gentle voice: madhura svara vihasitan.[4] As mother, daughter and the nurses, all are present, Vatsala rasa could easily have been created, but this does not happen. We have vihasita hasya with mother and daughter as asraya and the nurse as alambana. Her words are the uddipana. This is because of repetition. Nurse describes the same incident so many times and at such length that all depth is lost and hasya, instead of vatsala is created. Acarya Anandavardhana has said: "pariposari gatasyapi paunah punyena dipanam" which means repetition spoils the effect. This is one of the causes of rasabighna. Here however, instead of rasabighna we have another rasa hasyarasa.

The fourth scene shows Romeo, Mercutio and Benvolio preparing to gatecrash into capulet's party. The dialogue sparkles with wit and rasa is created in the Queen Mab passage:

> Her wagon -spokes made of long spinner's legs.
> The covers of the wings of grasshopper.
> The traces of the smallest spider's web[5]

Here indeed we have adbhuta rasa. Romeo and Benudio are the asraya of the rasa and Mercutio's speech the alambana. It could have been said that Mercutio is the asraya with Queen Mab as the atambana, but that would not be quite correct since he is merely describing queen Mab, not being awestruck by her presence. One of the elements accompanying this rasa is that of camatkara which has been divided into ten categories by Acarya Ksemendra. Without going into its complexities I would like to say that here we have camatkara of the avicarite ramaniya variety which does not involve the intellect.

The next scene is the one in which Romeo and Juliet meet Love at once invades Romeo's heart "O she doth teach the torches to burn bright." The emotion deepens.

> My lips, two blushing pilgrims, ready stand
> To smooth that rough touch with a tender kiss.[6]

As the scene proceeds the emotion (bhava) deepens into rasa. But they express their love in a few short phrases. Shakespeare does not give them long speeches here. Yet rasa has been created, for we come across a wealth of religious images in Romeo's dialogue. He uses five such words in three lines: profane, holy, shrine, sin and pilgrimage. The next 14 lines have a generous sprinkling of more such words and images. This gives a fervour and depth to their emotions which turns ninto Srngara rasa. This can be called manjistha Srngara which is characterized by highly attractive expression as well as depth and performance:

> Manjistha ragamahustada yannapaityati sobhate.[7]

Both of them are equally deeply in love so it can be said that both are the asrayas of this love as well as the alambana. The jubilant mood of a masquerade, the youthful beauty of both, their wit, all act as uddipana. It can be objected that the repeated use of religious terms act as deterrents, as Santa and Srngara are mutually exclusive and therefore there is rasa virodha here. But this is not the case. The religious images lend depth and purity here.

The second scene of the next Act is the famous balcony scene. The two lovers tell each other of their love and manjistha Srngara glows incandescent. The reader establishes identity (tadatmya) almost automatically Romeo and Juliet get universalized (Sadharanikarana)as eternal lovers and the reader experiences the indescribable bliss of pure Srngara rasa:

> Vedyantara sparsasunyo brahmasvada – sahodarah
> Lokottara camatkarapranah kescit pramatrbhih[8]

Free from the contact of ought else perceived, akin as a uterine brother to the ecstatic contemplation of God, the life whereof is hyperphysical wonder, is enjoyed by those competent.[8]

The passages are such as have reverberated in countless memories down the ages:

But soft, what light through yonder widow breaks?
It is the east and Juliet is the sun....
See how she leans her cheek upon her hand
O! that I were a glove upon that hand.[9]

Just as the Sanskrit scholar will automatically think of the Janak Vatika scene in connection with Srngara rasa so the student of English literature will automatically think of this scene as the archetype of love scenes. The frequent interruption serves to introduce variations in a scene which is long enough to have become monotonous without these interruptions.

After such empyrean heights any scene would be an anticlimax. So the next scene begins at a low pitch, and continues in the same manner. Vatsatya bhava is there is Fr. Lawrence's love for Romeo and Surprise or vismaya is felt when the properties of the herbs is described but these do not deepen into rasas.

In the 5th scene Juliet is waiting, like an utkanthita nayika for her duty (Nurse) Hasya rasa is enjoyed for a brief spell as Nurse teases her a bit, with Nurse as the asraya and Juliet as the alambana, her eagerness is the uddipana:

Nurse : Jesu ! what haste ? can you not stay awhile ?
Do you not see that I am out of breath?[10]

There is gentle evocation of Srngara in the next scene when the lovers meet:

They are but beggars that can court their worth
But my true love has grown to such excess
I cannot sum up half my sum of wealth[11]

From the 3rd Act the possibilities of a tragic end become more and more prominent. The very first scene gives another brawl between the two families. Raudra rasa is introduced with Tybalt's arrival, who hates Romeo:

Romeo, the hate I bear thee can afford
No better term than this – thou'rt a villain[12]

Tybalt is the asraya of this raudra rasa and Romeo the atambana. Tybatt's anger is the bhava which generates the rasa. But we do not experience Karuna at Mercutio's death as Tybalt and Romeo start fighting at once / Tchaikovsky, when filming the play, was not restricted by dialogue and his Mercutio takes quite a few minutes in dancing to his death.

Romeo wants to avenge Mercutio's death. This nobility of motive is one of the requirements of vira rasa. He hills Tybalt not out of anger, but as a matter of duty. Acarya Dhananjaya has said:

> Virah Pratapa vinayadhyabasaya sattvam[13]
> —The vira rasa demands might, courtesy, perseverance and nobility.

Each of these vibhavas manifest themselves in Romeo. He reveals himself as a warrior hero or yuddha vira. He is the asraya and Tybolt the alambana with Mercutio's death as Uddipana. Both raudra and Vira are created and this does not give rise to rasa virodha since these can and often do, go together. The scene ends with Romeo's banishment.

Juliet's yearnings and hopes create Srngara in the next scene. The scene veers towards karuna rasa when Juliet comes to know of Tybalt's death and Romeo's punishment. Juliet's emotions change from moment to moment. She grieves for her cousin and rails at Romeo for killing him. At the same time she is struck to the quick at Romeo's misfortunes. This tension is depicted in moving details. Karuna, Raudra and Sringara, all three rasas are created. Visvanatha Kaviraja has declared Karuna and vira to be rasas that are inimical to the latter. It might be said therefore that we have a case of rasa virodha here. It is with just such possibilities in mid that Ananda varadhana had said that, if after the main rasa is fully established, an opposing rasa is evoked in such a way that it does not challenge, the supremacy of the former, then there is no rasa virodha[14]. Madhura rasa reigns at first,

> And Romeo
> Leap to these arms, untalk'd of and unseen!

Lovers can see to do their amorous duties
By their own beauty.[15]

Juliet is the asraya of this rasa, the absent Romeo is the alambana and Juliet's eagerness, her impending marriage, the coming of nightfall—these are the uddipana. But when she starts lamenting then too srigara and karuna well up again and again with her as the asraya and dead Tybalt the alambana. Two mutually conflicting rasas sway the reader, by there is no difficulty in establishing tadatmya—such is the situation.

The fifth scene (III.V) shows the last meeting of the lovers we get the famous passage:

Wilt thou be gone? It is not yet near day
It was the nightingale and no the lark
That pierced the fearful hollow of thin ear.[16]

The current of Srngara runs deep and quiet here and karuna becomes more perceptible. It is a perfect scene from our view point. The two lovers are both the alambana and asraya and Romeo banishment is the uddipana of both Karuna and Sririga rasa. Both are universalized most successfully.

Raudra rasa is created for a brief spell when Capulet tells Juliet of her impending marriage:

Hang thee, young baggage! Disobedient wreatch!
I tell thee what, get thee to church O' Thursday
Or never again look me in the face
Speak not, reply not do not answer me.[17]

This raudra rasa has Capulet for its asraya. Julet is the alam bana and her disobedience is the uddipana. Then in her lament Karuna rasa wells up again.

There was a possibility of the creation of sriraga rasa is IV is as Paris is deeply in love with Juliet. But that does not happen. Then when Fr. Lawrence reveals his plan adhuta rasa is generated. Juliet is the asraya of the rasa with Fr. Lawrence as the alambana and the wonderful drug the uddipana. Surprise (Vismaya) is the bhava that ripens into rasa. Joy and relief are the sancari bhavas. Much will depend on the actress's skill here as the dramatist has given Juliet very few lines.

In the long soliloquy in Sc.3 there is the play of many emotions like fear, suspicion, uncertainty etc. Bibhatsa rasa is created for a short time:

> Where Tybatt, yet but green in earth
> Lies festering in his shroud ....
> And madly play with my forefather's joints
> And pluck the managed Tybolt from his shroud.[18]

There is no room for Srngara in this soliloguy—only bhayanaka and bibhatsa are there. Why is she afraid, why does she not think that this deathlike sleep will take her to her beloved? A decade later Shakespeare will show us his mature heroine Cleopatra welcoming certain death, for it will unite her with Antony. But then that which suits Cleopatra will not suit Juliet, who is only fourteen. It is natural for her to be afraid.

When the Capulets discover and lament her supposed death there is a very curious case of the generation of karuna rasa, for it is experienced by the characters only. The reader's foreknowledge prevents a true experience of the rasa. At most one can say that there is the abhasa of Karuna rasa here. But this is a rather complex thing and a discussion will take up undue time.

Romeo reaches the graveyard in V.iii. The fight between him and Paris is entirely against his will so neither vira nor raudra is created. Romeo's last speech evokes both karuna and srirara. He is the asraya of both and Juliet is the alambana. The surroundings of a graveyard, her supposed, death, the recent duel, all are uddipana. The spectator knows that Juliet will awaken in a few minutes and so his death becomes doubly pathetic. This is a case where the reader's foreknowledge enhances the rasa experience unlike as happens in the former scene. Srngara and Karuna are inextricably mingled.

> O here
> Shall I set up my everlasting rest,
> And shake the yoke of inauspicious stars
> From this world wearied flesh Eyes look your last
> Arms, take your last embrace.[19]

Karuna rasa reached its climax when Juliet stabs herself.

There is no Taasa virodha at any time. It is as if the two complement each other. Tadatmya is easily established and gives rise to the wonderful rasa—experience that goes beyond individualities, beyond time:

Parasya na parasyeti mametina mametica
Tadasvada vibhabade paricchedo na vidyati.[20]

The rest of the play after this evokes only karuna rasa. Tragic equilibrium overwhelms us with its peculiar effect. Phalagama is achieved most successfully.

Romeo can be said to be a dhiralalita hero. Dhananjaya says:
Niscinto dhiralalitah kalasaktah Sukhi mrduh.

The dhiralalita hero is free of care, appreciates the fine arts, ease loving and gentle by nature.[21]

The same epithets are repeated by Visvanatha Kaviraja. Romeo fulfills almost all of these requirements. He is a carefree young man. There is no indication as to whether he is *Kalasakta* or not. Dhanikacarya comments on the verse in *Dasarupaka* and says that the sringara rasa dominates such a hero and yet he is a brave fighter. It is sringara rasa that dominates Romeo and since he kills two men in two duels there can be no doubt that he is a good fighter as well. He is soft and gentle by nature (mrduh) For example, after buying the poison he bids the apothecary a courteous and sympathetic farewell.

Farewell, buy food and get thyself in flesh.[22]

This inborn courtesy and gentleness manifests itself again and again, notably in his dialogue with Tybalt and with Paris.

Juliet can be classified as a mugdha nayika. There are detailed descriptions of this kind of heroine but only one line can suffice:

Mugadha nava-vayah-kama-ratauvanama-mrdu-krudhi[23]
She answers admirably to this description. She is an adolescent, not having yet crossed, fourteen. Acarya Dhananjaya has also said "sitarjabadiyukta." Modesty and discipline are notable features of her character. Though impelled by intense love she yet expressed herself with artless modesty:

If thou thinks I am too easily won.
I'll frown and be perverse and say thee nay
I am too fond[24]

A few lines later we come to know of her sense of discipline:

I have no joy of this contract tonight
It is too rash, too unadvised, too sudden.[25]

Such sentiments befit her well brought up gentle nature. However young she might be, she is a true lady.

The play is a most successful natika, running straight towards its tragic end. The curtain comes down upon the double experience of karuna and Sringara rasa. Visvanatha Kaviraja has said that the same events that produce ordinary sorrow among ordinary men become endowed with extraordinary value when depicted in poetry:

Alaukika vibhavatnan praptebhya Kavya Sansiayat
Sukhari sanjayate tebhya.[26]

This is exactly what happens. The spectator experiences an extraordinary joy at the end, a joy that comes out of the experience of rasa—be it srngara, be it karuna—anandaghanam —asvadyate. Tatra ka dukhasarika?[27]

REFERENCES

1. Dwivedi, Hazari Pd. & Dwivedi, Prithvinath, Natya Sastra Ki Parampara aur Dasarupak, Rajkamal Prakashan, Delhi , 1971, 3:43.
2. Craig, W. J., ed., The complete works of William Shakespeare, OUP, London, 1957 rpt, romeo and julietI,I, 181-83.
3. Mittra, Babu P. and Ballantyne J.R. transl, The Sahitya Darpana or Mirror of composition, Bibliotheca Indica, Calcutta, 1861, p. 115.
4. Op. cit., 4775-77
5. RJ, I.III, 59-62
6. I. Av, 103-4
7. Op. cit., p. 115
8. Op. cit., 3:3

9. II.ii 2-25
10. I.v 29-30
11. II.vi 32-4
12. III.i. 65-66
13. Op. cit., 4:72
14. Op. cit., 3-20
15. III.ii 6-9
16. III.v. 1-3
17. III.v.161-5
18. IV.iii. 43-55
19. V.iii 109-13
20. Op. cit. 3-12
21. Op. cit. 2-3
22. V.i. 84
23. Op. cit., 2:16
24. II.ii. 95-101
25. II.ii. 117-18
26. Op. cit., 3-7
27. Abhinava–Bharati, Gaekwad, Oriental Series, Baroda, n.d. 1-292 .

15

Shakespeare through Sri Aurobindo's Lens

Goutam Ghosal

A large part of Sri Aurobindo's prose is devoted to the basic Shakespearean substance: the human vital, the Lear and the Timon, the Hamlet and the Othello, and all its other varieties dramatically imaged by the great vital creator. Sri Aurobindo brings in Shakespeare directly in *The Future Poetry*, in his letters and in his notes on Kalidasa. In his letters and *The Future Poetry,* he shows the evolution of poetry and the point reached in Shakespeare. In doing so, he also indicates how Shakespeare's creations or characters may be studied by examining the history of their consciousness. There are hidden forces behind the great figures and these subtle forces are clear to Sri Aurobindo, the yogi, who has an extra pair of eyes. This is consciousness approach, an effective way to tell all by a single synthetic glance. How do we know about the real forces working behind a Hamlet or a Timon unless we make a research into his consciousness? The recluse of Pondicherry has left enough clues for the posterity, for those who wish to go beyond the surface being to examine the various levels of consciousness, to detect the chaotic zones inside a Malvolio or a Timon, to discover the whole truth about them.

Sri Aurobindo has characterized the sources of Shakespeare's poetic inspiration. He has made new discoveries in the human consciousness showing the existence of numerous planes inside us, working either separately or in collaboration, fused together at times, often a deeper plane overlapping from behind to be mixed up with a crude surface layer. He makes outlines for serious investigations into Shakespeare's characters, offers clues within a single clause, which light up the inner structure of a play or the hidden worlds of its hero.

Who wrote Shakespeare? Nobody knows for certain, even after Joseph Sobaran's laborious linking him with Edward de Vere, the 17th Earl of Oxford (*Alias Shakespeare*, 1997). But, we know for certain with the help of consciousness research that there was just one man behind the plays, the poems and the sonnets and that he was an exceptional portraitist of the human vital. The rhetoric evolves with a poet blooming late, but it was the same creator's rhetoric throughout. The rise and fall of his poetry cannot hide the man veiling himself behind his creatures. It is he whom we know today as Shakespeare. Does the phrase 'negative capability' really apply to him? In a way his true identity comes out even through his objectivised mode. The mask falls before Sri Aurobindo, the ultimate detective of consciousness.

One of the commonest demands of the human vital is the craving for praise. Lear's elocutionary speech act in Act-I is an extreme case. Flattery affects culture, democracy and decent living. Lear recovers, Richard-II fails to reconstruct himself. Hamlet is permanently trapped by the zone because of his marriage with depression and melancholy. Timon hardly knows that his nobility is leading him to a dangerous arena. If we give a swift glance over the wide range of Shakespeare's characters, we catch "him" in various moods: the sensational man with varying faces. The filthy rhetoric of Othello and the abusive words of Lear directed to his daughters speak of that problematic area, which lies between the heart and the physical centre. Timon is caught in that zone which lies between the heart and the sex centre, the most dangerous province in man, a place where joy is curiously mixed up with pain, depression with excitement, despair with optimism. Most human catastrophes have been caused by this plane. Sri Aurobindo has named it "MR Dramatic" and "MR Melancholy". A careful examination of our vital self will reveal that it always sways our being from one extreme to the other. Apemantus' speech in Act IV, Sc III, lines 301-2, shows what exactly happens in Timon:

> The middle of humanity thou never knewest,
> but the extremity of both ends.

The consciousness investigator sees easily the essential crisis of consciousness in Timon and the amount of ruin it may cause to a human being. In *Shakespeare's Life and Art*, Peter Alexander uses the phrase "passionate power" (P. 183) to characterize the temperament of Timon. This comes close to the discovery of the force that guides Timon from within. For the vital is both a great strength and a great weakness. In the great catholicity of Timon, which we see in the first two Acts of the play, it is the vital that works secretly behind his proud aristocratic nobility ("I am wealthy in my friends"). The plus point of this nature is that Timon is devoid of any meanness. But then the vital does not spare the noble, rather it exploits quite often the Rajasic nature of the protagonist.

> ... We'll share a bounteous time
> In different pleasures.

When in Act II, Sc ii (188). Timon claims, "I am wealthy in my friends", he does not know how his cheerfulness is going to be turned into bitterness a little later. By Act III, Sc iv. Timon is totally gripped by that consciousness. Then come abuses followed by animal images:

> Most smiling smooth detested parasites,
> Courteous destroyers, affable wolves, meek bears ...

> The rejection of humanity comes after this haughty reaction.

> Burn house! Sink, Athens!
> Henceforth hated be of Timon, man and all humanity!

Act IV, Sc I, begins with Timon's rage, which is contained in a series of directive verbs. Our "MR. Dramatic" has now become extremely unbalanced having lost every contact with that being which had once given a refined glory to his nobility. The speech ends with Timon's resolution to go to the woods. In the whole range of Shakespearean drama, where we have also seen cases of madness, there is no other instance of such a devastating play of the human vital. Timon's "everlasting mansion" is like an everlasting marriage with the vital. Shakespeare, the "seer of life" was aware, in a way, of this psychological drive in certain aristocrats.

Ewan Fernie (*Shame in Shakespeare*, 2002) writes remarkably well on the shame-affected figures, but fails to identify the plane of its birth. He speaks of Othello's 'bestial degeneration' (163), but is unable to characterize the history of his consciousness. Phillip Armstrong's *Shakespeare in Psychoanalysis* (2001) is certainly more penetrating, although it does not refer to that particular centre, which Sri Aurobindo has dissected with supreme authenticity. The great Indian Yogi had no time to speak in detail of every Shakespearean hero or heroine. But, for a consciousness researcher it is not difficult to see that Prospero operates from the "mental vital", that the happy and the semi-happy heroines centre round the "central vital", and that Falstaff and certain figures from the dark comedies are distinctly motivated by the "lower vital".

Some of the sonnets image the downward vital, the consciousness moving from the central down towards the lower. Richard Danson Brown rightly equates the 'paranoiac poet-speaker of Shakespeare's sonnets with the jealous husbands and fathers of plays like *King Lear, Othello, The Tempest* and *The Winter's Tale* (82). Stanley Wells becomes a consciousness researcher when he links the narrator's 'self-destroying lust' for the dark lady with Angelo in *Measure for Measure*, 'wrestling with emotions that he cannot control' (17). And yet the strangest thing about his characters is that at times some of them listen to the tunes from their true being standing quietly behind the boundaries of the physical, the vital and the mind.

Shakespeare was a seer of this Life, not just the seer of the surface life, but its subconscient zones, which may be called the inner of the outer. Even in this life, there is in a Hamlet or in a Macbeth a much vaster and more potent subconscious mind, which loses nothing of what the senses bring to it. It keeps all its wealth in an inexhaustible store of memory. Shakespeare wished to explore that "computer" by deliberately rejecting the Cosmos of Dante. It was a choice that helped humanity to a degree and keeps him still relevant to this day. Life thinks itself out in him through many mouths, exemplifying various problems created by the human vital, which stands as a stumbling block against the transformation of our nature. As this world is not outside the Cosmos, Shakespeare slipped quite often in the territories of Dante's *Inferno* without of course any motive to explore that continent in the Dantesque manner.

> How heavy do I journey on the way ...
>
> (Sonnet : 50)
>
> What freezings have I felt, what dark days seen!
>
> (Sonnet : 97)

Sri Aurobindo wishes to put a hyphen between Dante and Shakespeare, between Matter and Spirit, and to draw a new map for tomorrow's pilgrims, the map that moves inward, upward and downward. Apart from the Shakespearean sweetnesses and sensualities in Sri Aurobindo's *Rodogune* and *The Viziers of Bassora*, there are very obvious images of the Shakespearean world in his representative works like *Savitri* and *The Life Divine*, the world he wishes to explore before extending the limits of Dante's realizations. In Book-II, Canto IV of *Savitri*, he reminds us of the subconscient zones of a Shakespearean hero when he says, "... in memory's crowded sleep/The past lived on as in a bottomless sea". (1993: 145) The whole of the Canto (entitled *The Kingdoms of the Little Life*) is replete with the memory of Shakespearean soliloquies: sensations, stabs, edges of desire, passion's leaps, the casual colloquy of flesh with flesh, the ill-lighted mansions of our thought etc.

Sri Aurobindo chooses eleven poets for the utter first class. Shakespeare, who has very little to do with the mystic and the spiritual stuff, appears in the first row along with Valmiki, Vyasa and Homer. He characterizes Shakespeare as a vital poet indicating his mastery of life where the vital operates very actively, and shows how the higher and the highest poetic styles (Overmind) have coloured the vital substance of his poetry. The highest or the Overmind inspiration gives birth to the poetry of incantation or *mantra*. When K.D. Sethna culled two lines from sonnet 107 and brought it to Sri Aurobindo's notice, he was surprised and wondered what such an expression was doing in that very vital context. From Sri Aurobindo's remarks Sethna gathered that it had an Overmind movement as well as substance coming strongly coloured by the vital consciousness in which Shakespeare was centered. Let us listen to the lines:

> The prophetic soul
> of the wide world, dreaming on things to come (1-2)

We have here an unexpected and unusual bringing together of words and phrases, giving us a suggestion of the Infinite. There are more subtle observations on Shakespeare's style and I would like to refer to a few of them. Sri Aurobindo sees in Shakespeare a late blooming poet and remarks that great poets with varied gifts usually take time to mature. "A narrow though a high faculty works best on a single line and may show perfection at an early stage; but powerful and complex minds like Shakespeare and Kalidasa seldom find themselves before a more advanced period". He also detects in Shakespeare two different types of style. Quite often Shakespeare uses a highly imaged style, but his images are neither decorative nor expressive of the mere intellectual sense. They are immediately revelatory, intimate to the thing he speaks and rather the proper stuff of the fact itself than images. He has too a clearer, less crowded still swifter fashion of speech in which they are absent. Sometimes the two manners may become one as in the last speeches of Antony:

> I am dying, Egypt, dying; only
> I here importune death awhile, until
> Of many thousand kisses the poor last
> I lay upon thy lips.

Sometimes a mere clause from Sri Aurobindo's observations on Shakespeare may sum up the whole meaning of play. For instance, the remark "an evolution of speech leading to an evolution of action" (FP: 63-71) sums up the characters of Antony and Cleopatra.

Why is Shakespeare still relevant today? The mask has fallen permanently and man is unable to hide himself. The lower vital is now in the open, and more prominent in the life of an intellectual giant. The only way to change the world is to change the consciousness which Shakespeare had projected in the plays and the sonnets. That particular zone troubles the present humanity more acutely than it did four hundred years ago.

Shakespeare lives, more intensely in the mass-society. His Majesty Ego is stronger today and refuses to abdicate with a more violent "no"; the lure of the lower zones more real; the inconscient a common experience. A mysterious force coming down from above on the weak nervous system has made madness a common postmodern disease. If Shakespeare images the real scenario, the inner of the outer as a seer of life, Sri Aurobindo shows us how to rise above that reality in future.

WORKS CITED

Joseph Sobran, 1997. *Alias Shakespeare: Solving the Greatest Literary Mystery of All Time*, New York: The Free Press.

Peter Alexander, 1961. *Shakespeare's Life and Art,* New York: New York University Press.

Ewan Fernie, 2002. *Shame in Shakespeare,* London: Routledge.

Phillip Armstrong, 2001. *Shakespeare in Psychoanalysis*, London: Routledge.

Richard Danson Brown and David Johnson, 2000. *Shakespeare 1609: Cymbeline and the Sonnets,* New York: St. Martin's Press.

Stanley Wells, 1994. *Shakespeare: The Poet and His Plays*, London: Methuen.

Sri Aurobindo, 1953. *The Future Poetry,* Pondicherry: Sri Aurobindo Ashram. First serialized in The Arya (1917-20) pp. 63-71.

K.D. Sethna, 1965. *Sri Aurobindo on Shakespeare*, Pondicherry: Sri Aurobindo Ashram.

Sri Aurobindo, 1950-51. *Savitri: A Legend and a Symbol*, Pondicherry: Sri Aurobindo Ashram.

Sri Aurobindo, 1993. *Savitri: A Legend and a Symbol*, Pondicherry: Sri Aurobindo Ashram, Revised Edition.

16

The Supernatural as a Major Determinant of Structural Form in Shakespeare's *Hamlet* and *Macbeth*

Reena Mitra

The enormous intractable mass of material available on William Shakespeare and his numerous works threatens all critical or organizational attempts at reasoned research with failure, and rigorous exercises in explication and interpretation, too, often confound one to a point of non-performance. And yet, after more than four hundred years of his having written, his works, whether in the original or in translation—or even in adaptation—are approached with reverence and with academic curiosity, which in its persistence to explore space in the plays of Shakespeare is becoming more and more beguiling and provocative.

Critical awareness down the years has become inconceivably diverse with regard to Shakespeare's "art". In his plays it is not characterization alone that is making a bid for attention now but also the language, the poetry, the plot-construction, the vision, the symbolic overtones and other extra-terrestrial features like the elemental and supernatural forces that are brought to bear upon the work. F.R. Leavis cautions us against any ill-considered approach to Shakespeare's texts:

> ...Shakespeare's methods are so subtle, flexible and varied that we must be on our guard against approaching any play with inappropriate misconception as to what we have in front of us.[1]

Sceptical of the new Shakespeare criticism John F. Danby, too, despairingly foregrounds the fact that in his plays—

> Shakespeare's story has been broken down, into separate and jarring bits : 'themes', 'world-views', 'ideas', even 'images'. The coordinating principle of story (the most primitively obvious one) has been overlooked.[2]

Also, absorption in matters of "pattern" or "structure" has often led scholars to overlook the essential life and energy of action in any particular play of Shakespeare under study. Besides, preoccupation with figurative and allegorical features of the text have, at times waylaid the elemental aspects of the major characters, who would otherwise have overwhelmed us with their physical immediacy in terms of their human longings and deprivations. What is important is the integral and total experience of the story and the action in the play. K.R.S. Iyengar has aptly summed up the unqualified encounter with a Shakespearean play:

> The Ground: creative Energy : Bliss of achieved identity—'sat-chit-ananda'—these together constitute the one incandescent reality of Shakespeare's dramatic art and our dynamic response to it".[3]

Nothing in any play of Shakespeare can be considered as being of negligible import. There is often an underlying significance to the most plebeian and undistinguished of characters and the most obscure of events that transpire in the course of the action of the play. In his book on *Hamlet* (1961), Weston Babcock says in the context of the supposed nonsensical lines uttered by the gravediggers,

> ...It is never safe to take Shakespeare's nonsense for what it may, at first hearing or reading, seem to be. By

> force of his supremely associative mind, Shakespeare was incapable of writing what did not have connection somehow with the implications of the play.[4]

Lascelles Abercrombie rightly talks of the "endlessness"[5] of the bulk of Shakespeare criticism one encounters when attempting to investigate the mind of the genius and his sensibilities that reach out to record perceptions and imprints of the multifarious realm of man, nature and the divine. In exploring great drama like Shakespeare's, one should not be led by what G. Wilson Knight calls "the surface crust of plot and character"[6] but move from overt action and discernible speech to something deeper. Shakespeare's inveterate compassion for all humanity and Nature precludes preference for any one particular view of life and his creative power imbues everyone with vitality and catholicity.

Shakespeare is alive and relevant to us even today and there has been an unbelievable spurt in Shakespeare criticism in the recent years. Some of the scholars whose works dominate this area of analytical studies are Edward Dowden, Richard, Moulton, A.C. Bradley, Edward G., L.C. Knights, Walter Raleigh, Robert Bridges, Edward G. McCurdy, Caroline F.E. Spurgeon and many others.

Edward Dowden's *Shakespeare: A Critical Study of His Mind and Art* (1875) was the culminating analytical work of the Victorian era and contained the first exhaustive critical biography of Shakespeare. For Moulton in his *Shakespeare as a Dramatic Artist* (1885) the story in a play by Shakespeare becomes an encapsulation of an idea and symbolizes certain basic concepts of the playwright. A.C. Bradley's *Shakespearean Tragedy* (1904), like Dowden's work, has given direction to modern Shakespeare criticism.

L. C. Knights' essay, "How Many Children Had Lady Macbeth?" (1933) published in *Explorations* (1946), brought to the fore some misconceptions inherent in Bradley's critical method of character analysis. Walter Raleigh and Robert Bridges are important essentially not for what they wrote but for the fact that in *Shakespeare* (1907), and in "The Influence of the Audience on Shakespeare's Drama" (1907), respectively, they set the trend for the kind of historical criticism that has dominated the study of Shakespeare in the recent times.

McCurdy in *The Personality of Shakespeare* (1953) has attempted to depict Shakespeare's disposition and psyche by applying the Freudian theory to the various elements of fantasy in his plays. Caroline Spurgeon's analysis of imagery in the plays to determine the nature of Shakespeare, the man, was a novel critical method.

Literary commentary on Shakespeare's works down the last four centuries clearly offers us an understanding of the changing intellectual drifts in the various literary epochs but what is really relevant and "most alive and meaningful to us today"[7] is the direction taken by Shakespeare studies in the twentieth century interpretations of his various texts and perhaps, in some of the twenty first century critiques. A survey of the various facets of Shakespeare's literary art that have been taken up for academic investigation reveals to us that few have thought of the supernatural as an integral part of the dramatic virtuosity of the writer. Referring to *Hamlet* which clearly has a supernatural component, Edward Dowden, way back in the late nineteenth century had stated that "no play of Shakespeare's has had a higher power of interesting spectators and readers"[8] though he had not categorically attributed this power of attracting viewers and perusers to the incorporation of the supernatural in the play; but, it is the Ghost that undoubtedly arouses Hamlet to action despite his characteristic inertia and quiescence and thus follow the stormy events in the play leading to the ultimate death of the protagonist, the tragedy significantly ensuing from the unfortunate fact that "Revenge is demanded from one who has only discussed revenge".[9] As in *Hamlet*, in *Macbeth* too, the supernatural determines the structural framework of the play and the direction that the course of action takes in the development of the plot, *A Midsummer Night's Dream* and *The Tempest*, too, may also perhaps qualify as plays incorporating the supernatural but we shall concentrate here on the supernatural in *Hamlet* and *Macbeth* with stray reference to the other plays.

The supernatural element in literature can generally be made to operate in two ways, namely,

> ...(1) in speculation about the influences on human existence of forces that are above or beyond what is natural; (2) in description of a strange, eerie or uncanny event or atmosphere that cannot be explained by logical analysis.[10]

Shakespeare ingeniously draws on both these applications and manoeuvres and designs his material in a manner that makes the other worldly and spectral appear as intrinsic integrants in his plays. Thus, as K.R.S. Iyengar elaborates on the complexion and essence of Shakespeare's world, we endorse the view that it is—

> ...a world where everyman can feel at home, for this world too is rich with its flora and fauna, here too the sky is alternately ominous and benign; there are occasional supernatural visitants and there are spurts of super nature as well; and above all, here is Nature's plenty.[11]

The "supernatural visitants" occasionally encountered in Shakespeare's plays are, as already mentioned earlier, generally introduced by him for purposes none other than the dramatic. The world of Oberon and Puck in *A Midsummer Night's Dream* is made to come alive with a highly imaginative projection of the playwright's creative power. Elizabethan folklore which was steeped in such fantasies was tapped to the full by Shakespeare:

> Shakespeare and his contemporaries bountifully illustrate the superstitious credulity which guided their contemporaries' conduct, moulded many of their social customs, and governed their habitual interpretation of natural phenomena. Superstitions which crystallized into folklore absorbed much that passed for scientific observation even among the educated.[12]

Next came the transition from folklore to what Iyengar calls "ghostlore"[13]. The comedies of Shakespeare are inhabited by fairies and sprites and his tragedies by witches and ghosts. Apart from the unforgettable Ghost in *Hamlet* ghosts are seen in some other plays of his as well. We view Banquo's ghost in *Macbeth,* that of Caesar in *Julius Caesar* and those of all the various victims of Gloucester in *Richard III*. We sometimes wonder whether the appearance of ghosts in Shakespeare's plays are meant to represent hallucination on the part of the characters on the stage. But, in *Hamlet* for example, why should the soldiers on duty and later Horatio have visions and illusions at all? Also, while Hamlet sees the ghost of his father Gertrude is unable to do so for she is not meant to see him just as Banquo at the banquet in *Macbeth* is not meant to be seen by anybody other than Macbeth himself. It is obviously the ghost's prerogative to appear to anyone it chooses to. Hamlet, after meeting his father's ghost, and Macbeth after his first confrontation with the three witches, both conceded the existence of the Supernatural.

Hamlet says to Horatio:

> There are more things in heaven and earth, Horatio,
> Than are dreamt of in your philosophy. (Act I, Sc. v, lls. 174-75)

Macbeth, too, after meeting the witches utters in an aside:

> This supernatural soliciting
> Cannot be ill; cannot be good. (Act I, Sc iii, lls. 130-31)

The 'supernatural' defies logic and has no established motive. Hamlet himself has misgivings about the spirit that speaks to him—is it his father's ghost, he wonders or just a visitant from Hell (Act II, Sc. ii, l. 594) Also, neither in *Hamlet* nor in *Macbeth* is the supernatural the cause for tragedy. The Ghost instigates Hamlet to take revenge, never allowing the latter to forget his goal and leaving him with every nerve strained by confrontation with the supernatural, but the ultimate choice between action and inaction still lies with him. Similarly, the subtle piece of advice given to Macbeth by the witches in the play does spur him to action but the former could always have ignored the promptings of the latter and chosen to disregard their urgings. In *The Tempest* too, the ultimate decisions lie with Prospero though the supernatural in the play is given form in terms of Ariel and his magical powers and perhaps Caliban, too, as he is the son of the witch, Sycorax. Leaving aside the fantasy in *A Midsummer Night's Dream*, in the major plays of Shakespeare—*Hamlet*, *Macbeth* and *The Tempest*—the supernatural is only an initiation or a means to an end but the significant decisions are always those made by men themselves. However, Shakespeare's creative imagination is best witnessed in the devising of three great supernatural environment prototypes in his plays, namely, the worlds of Oberon-Titania-Puck, of Hecate and the Witches and of Ariel and his band of fairies. Referring to Shakespeare's fertile mind, M.C. Bradbrook writes,

> ...In all his supernatural creations, he seems to have created completely new species of creatures, and these of all his characters were most easily copied by his contemporaries and immediate successors. The Witches in *Macbeth* set a fashion for witch plays; the spirits of *The Tempest* again set a fashion; Caliban is a prototype of the Witch's son, a popular figure in Caroline drama[14]

Supernatural emissaries characterize the emotional trajectory of plays like *Hamlet* and *Macbeth* moulding the psyche of the protagonist and affecting his sensibility and probity. The ghost in *Hamlet* is a superhuman agent who demands motivated operation from Hamlet but the latter is disqualified for action by virtue of his proclivity for indulgence in excessive thought. *Macbeth*, as a play, too, is largely shaped by the presence of the supernatural in the form of the Witches and the ghost of Banquo. Shakespeare studies have already established the fact that the factual and historical material of the playwright's work were drawn from Holinshed's *Chronicle* but the appearance of Banquo's ghost and the somnambulism of Lady Macbeth are aspects developed by the dramatist himself to reinforce the consciousness of the power of the Supernatural.

Shakespeare endows his play, *The Tempest*, too, with rare imaginative enchantment, with Prospero "the great enchanter" displaying full command over the elemental powers and over himself. In *A Midsummer Night's Dream*, one of Shakespeare's early plays dealing with the supernatural agencies, the "human mortals" are subjected to embarrassments and predicaments by the fun-loving elves but in *The Tempest*, Prospero, the central character, is shown as being in full control of the enveloping elements rather than at their mercy.

Evidently, then, in Shakespeare's time there was a firm belief in the existence of the supernatural and hence it is present as an integral part of the structure of the plot in many of the dramatist's works. This element of the supernatural provides to these plays a catalytic factor promoting action, a deeper insight into character and a manifold increase in the effect of the pivotal scenes. The supernatural may appear to the audience in varied forms. In *Hamlet,*[15] however, it appears in the most notable form of the ghost—the—ghost of Hamlet's father—and makes several appearances in the course of the play but it speaks only to Hamlet, "to whet thy almost blunted purpose" (Act III, Sc iv, l. III), as he is told, though initially, the latter, himself, like Horatio, is apprehensive of the sincerity of the ghost and its motives. "What if it tempt you towards the flood, my lord, or to the dreadful summit of the cliff?" (Act I, Sc iv, lls 69-70) asks Horatio and Hamlet, in not rebuking him, gives evidence of the doubt in his own mind.

The conversation between the ghost and Hamlet actuates a fermentation of musings and ruminations in the latter's mind determining the subsequent series of actions on the part of Hamlet and providing an insight into his character. The information regarding the untimely death of the protagonist's father divulged by the ghost pushes Hamlet into action against a situation he was already distrustful of, and now, even more so. However, Hamlet does not accept the ghost's version of happenings unquestioningly. Wary of things around, he mulls over the supposed facts and is skeptical of the ghost's identity : "The spirit that I have seen may be a devil... and perhaps out of my weakness and my melancholy... abuses me to damn me" (Act II, Sc ii, lls 594-99). Hamlet's confirmation of the ghost's account of past events comes only after the play within the play has been staged by the actors and after he meets the ghost in his mother's room. "Speak to her, Hamlet" (Act III, Sc, iv, l 115), says the ghost asking Hamlet to seek revenge for his father's death. Hamlet, now convinced of the identity of the ghost, promptly listens to it and allocates himself the task of avenging the grievous wrong perpetrated against his father by setting in motion a concatenation of events that unfortunately ends in the death of Hamlet himself. The supernatural thus gives direction to the course of events in the play.

In *Macbeth*, too as in *Hamlet*, the supernatural assumes the role of a catalyst for action but in the former it appears to the audience in varied forms. In addition to the ghost, we see a floating dagger, witches and apparitions which predict and forecast the future. The supernatural actually may be witnessed four times in the course of the play : in all the appearances of the witches, in the visitation of Banquo's ghost, in the rendition of prophecies by the apparitions and in the "air-drawn" (Act III, Sc iv, l. 62) dagger that leads Macbeth towards his victim.

The most significant of the supernatural elements incorporated in the text of 'Macbeth'[16] are the witches who are embodiments of Macbeth's excessive ambition and his evil endeavours. Macbeth, credulous as he is, falls prey to the witches' predictions and in his unappeasable curiosity to know more about the future seeks the witches in their cave. With little regard for the nature of the consequence that may ensue, he is relentless in his insistence on soliciting the answers to his questions. The witches do undertake compliance and at Macbeth's behest add more unnatural constituents to the cauldron and communicate with their masters. It is at this juncture in the play that the prophetic apparitions appear. The first in order is Macbeth's own head (later to be severed by Macduff) substantiating his apprehension about Macduff. The second apparition conveys to Macbeth that he cannot be harmed by anyone born of a woman. This statement gives him an undue sense of invulnerability and yet, Macduff, we learn, was not born of a woman but of a corpse for his mother was dead when he was born. These prefigurations and deceptive proclamations coming from the apparitions mislead Macbeth and bring about his downfall. A child with a crown on his head, the third apparition, symbolises Duncan's son, Malcolm. Here too, the Birnam Wood prophecy deludes Macbeth into believing that he is invincible and secure from deceit. It is impossible that the great Birnam wood "shall come against him" (Act IV, Sc i, l. 94) for that prediction of the Apparition "will never be" (Act IV, Sc i, l.94) says Macbeth.

Again, the appearance of the supernatural in *Macbeth*, as in *Hamlet*, assists a penetration into and an understanding of the central character. We witness a definite downturn in Macbeth's mind which has lost its former stability and sense of security. At the sight of Banquo's ghost he shrinks with horror and his reactions perturb the guests. Macbeth wonders why the dead are now coming back though murders had taken place even in the past before they were categorically proscribed by law.

> Blood hath been shed ere now, i' th' olden time,
> Ere humane statute purged the gentle weal;
> Ay, and since too, murders have been performed
> Too terrible for the ear; the time has been
> That, when the brains were out, the man would die,
> And there an end; but now they rise again....
>
> (Act III, Sc iv, ll. 75-80)

The endmost form of the supernatural in the play is the "air-drawn" dagger which, covered in blood, guides Macbeth to the room of his victim and makes him perpetrate the crime. The dagger undoubtedly enhances the horror of the scene of Duncan's murder.

The supernatural, thus, is a recurrent feature in many of Shakespeare's plays and as already stated, it is, in these particular plays like *Hamlet* and *Macbeth*, an intrinsic part of the plot-structure providing an understanding of the major characters and playing the role of a catalyst promoting action and leading this sequence of events to its logical conclusion. This supernatural constituent appeases the curiosity of the audience with regard to the mysterious and the inexplicable and draws the latter further into the developments of the play.

Shakespeare's dramatic works and their effect on the world of literature have been instrumental in widening one's cognizance of life around and opening up new vistas of perception within one's ambit. The playwright's fascination for all that is mystical and mythical explains his depiction of fanciful and irrational characters in his works. Incredible popularity came his way because he registered cognizantly and tried to relate to the mode in which people thought and endeavoured to reach out to the supernatural during his time.

The Elizabethan period was characterized by magic, wonder and sometimes, terror. Witch-trials were often held and the pagan influence was evident in the way the common folk approached life. Many of the superstitions prevalent in those times have filtered down the generations and exist even today. Shakespeare discreetly and deftly made capital out of this belief in paranormal and spectral existences but also cleverly veered away from the existent matrix of the supernatural in creating a diverse range of characters in worlds that the viewers could visualize and identify with.

REFERENCES

1. Leavis, F.R., *The Common Pursuit* (U.K.: Hogarth Press, Peregrine Edition, 1984), p. 174.
2. Danby, John F., *Shakespeare's Doctrine of Nature*, (London: Faber and Faber, 1949), pp. 202-3.
3. Iyengar, K.R.S., *Shakespeare: His World and His Art* (New Delhi: Sterling, 1964, rpt. 1984), p. 621.
4. Babcock, Weston *Hamlet: A Tragedy of Errors* (Purdue: Purdue University, 1961).
5. Abercrombie, Lascelles *Aspects of Shakespeare* (Lectures) (British Academy: Clarendon Press, 1933), p. 253.
6. Knight, G. Wilson, *Shakespearian Production, with Especial Reference to the Tragedies* (London: Methuen, 1964).
7. Ribner, Irving, *William Shakespeare: An Introduction to His Life, Times and Theatre* (New Delhi: Wiley Eastern Ltd. 1969 U.S. Edition, pt. 1978), p. 194.
8. Dowden, Edward, *Shakespeare*, ed. John Richard Green (London: Macmillan, 1914), p. 121.
9. Brooke, Stopford, A, *Ten More Plays of Shakespeare* (Ludhiana: Lyall Book Depot, 1969), p. 106.
10. Coles Editorial Board, *Dictionary of Literary Terms* (New Delhi: Rama Brothers, 1991 Indian edition), p. 195.
11. Iyengar, K.R.S., *Shakespeare: His World and His Art*, p. 640.
12. Littledale, H., "Folklore and Superstitions", *Shakespeare's England*, ed. Walter Raleigh et al., Vol. I (Great Britain: Oxford, 1916), p. 529.

13. Iyengar, K.R.S., *Shakespeare: His World and His Art*, p. 642.
14. Bradbrook, M.C. essay in *Shakespeare Criticism*, 1935-60, ed. Anne Ridler (London: Oxford University Press, 1965), pp. 381-82. Ms. Bradbrook points out that the fairies in Shakespeare's *A Midsummer Night's Dream* became the originals for similar spirits in the works of Drayton, Herrick and Jonson.
15. Shakespeare, William *Hamlet* ed. Harold Jenkins, Arden edition (London, Methuen, 1982, rpt. 1984), p. 213.
16. Shakespeare, William *Macbeth*, ed. Bernard Lott (Moscow: Progress Publishers, 1977).

Contributors

Anthony Kubiak is Professor of Drama at the University of California, Irvine. He is the author of *Agitated States: Performance in the American Theater of Cruelty,* and *Stages of Terror: Terrorism, Ideology, and Coercion as Theatre History*. His more recent work appears in *MLQ, Performance Research,* and *PA J.*

Bryan Reynolds is Chancellor's Professor of Drama at UC Irvine. His books include, as author, *Transversal Subjects: From Montaigne to Deleuze after Derrida, Transversal Enterprises in the Drama of Shakespeare and his Contemporaries: Fugitive Explorations, Performing Transversally: Reimagining Shakespeare and the Critical Future,* and *Becoming Criminal: Transversal Performance and Cultural Dissidence in Early Modern England;* and, as coeditor, *The Return of Theory in Early Modern English Studies: Volumes I & II, Critical Responses to Kiran Desai, Rematerializing Shakespeare: Authority and Representation on the Early Modern English Stage,* and *Shakespeare Without Class: Misappropriations of Cultural Capital.* He is also an internationally produced playwright, performer, and director of theater.

Mohit Ray is a Former Professor of English, Burdwan University with about 42 years' experience of teaching English in Undergraduate and Postgraduate classes. He has authored eight books and around seventy-two of research papers published in scholarly journals and anthologies in India and abroad. He has also edited 22 scholarly anthologies on literature in English, criticism, translation studies and comparative literature, etc. He is a member of various recognized and reputed associations like, Association Internationale de Littérature Comparée, an Ex-Member of Association Internationale des Critiques Littéraires, a life member of Indian Association of English Studies, Indian Association of American Studies and Indian Association for Canadian Studies. He has attended various national and international conferences held in India and abroad: England, France, Portugal, Austria, Finland, America, Canada, Japan, Hong Kong, Turkey etc.

His academic achievements are as under:

(i) Received the C.V. Kapoor Education Foundation Distinguished Teacher Award in 2000, (ii) Associated with UGC and UPSC in various capacities, (iii) Felicitated at Burdwan as Distinguished Professor of English on 5 September (Teachers' Day) 2003, (iv) Chief Editor (Honorary) M/S Atlantic Publishers and Distributors (P) Ltd., New Delhi, (v) Editor, *The Atlantic Critical Review*, a peer reviewed journal indexed in the *MLA Directory of Periodicals,* (vi) Member of the Scientific Board for *The Grove: Working Papers in English Studies.* University of Jaen, Spain, (vii) Felicitated at Durg (Chhatisgharh) on 22 October 2005, on the occasion of the official release of the festschrift *Widening Horizons: Essays in Honour of Professor Mohit K. Ray* (eds. Rama Kundu, *et al.*, New Delhi: Sarup & Sons, 2005). Jayanta Mahapatra, an eminent Indian English poet released the book, (viii) Many eminent scholars have acknowledged their debts, (ix) Was awarded the title *Vachaspati* and the degree of D.Litt. (*honoris causa*) by Rashtriya Sanskrit University, Tirupati in 2010. Contributed, on invitation, four entries to the fourth edition of *Princeton Encyclopedia of Poetry and Poetics* (2012).

Maria Kladaki is a Lecturer at the Faculty of Humanities of the University of the Aegean (Rhodes-Greece). She has a post graduate degree M.A. in Education specializing in Theatre and Dramatic Play from the Hellenic Open

University and a Ph.D in Theatre Studies (Panteion University of Athens, Greece). She teaches Drama in Education and theatre history. Her field of research includes theory and history of theatre, gender issues in theatrical works for children and theatre and education.

George Papantonakis is an Associate Professor and teaches Greek Literature and Greek Children's Literature at the Aegean University, Rhodes, Greece, in the Department of Primary Education.

Chiara Biscella graduated from the University of Milan, Italy, with a thesis on the intersections between figurative arts and contemporary Anglo-American drama. In 2013 she received her PhD in English Literature from the same university, with a thesis entitled "*Shakespeare Amongst Women. An Investigation in Contemporary Novel Writing*". Her main research interests centre on contemporary drama and literature and on visual arts, with a special focus on interdisciplinary relations. She has recently published two interviews in the volume Caryl Churchill. Un teatro necessario, edited by Mariacristina Cavecchi and Margaret Rose (Pisa: Ed.It, 2012), and the essay "*The Museum as Playwright: A New Stage for Contemporary Drama*" in the volume *The Museal Turn* edited by Sabine Coelsch-Foisner and Douglas Brown (Heidelberg: Winter Verlag, 2013).

Isabella Bruschi is a teacher of English Language and Literature at High School (Liceo Classico "V. Alfieri", Turin) and a teacher-trainer at the post-graduation School for Foreign Language Teachers (University of Turin and East Piedmont). She was temporarily posted at the University of Turin—Department of English Studies—where she researched in the field of Indo-Anglian Literature; in particular she has dealt with Partition Literature. Her publications relate both to her teaching and academic activities. She has co-authored five school books—*Primo Manuale della Lingua Italiana per Alunni Stranieri, Worldwise. Attività per la Revisione della Lingua Inglese, Mind the Gap. Mastering English at Intermediate Level,*

Speaking Better. Strategies for Life, Strategies for Certification. She has also written abridged versions for students like—*Great Ghost Stories,—Tales of the Supernatural* and *King Arthur and the Knights of the Round Table.* She has also written many articles and essays which have been published in various books and journals.

Her other achievements are as under:

Translations (from English to Italian)

—Lamb, C. M., *Dieci Racconti da Shakespeare,* Edisco, Torino, 1994

—Twain, M., *Wilson lo Zuccone,* Edisco, Torino, 1995 (The volume contains introduction, notes and reading guides by Bruschi, I.)

Amitava Roy was former Shakespeare Professor of English at Rabindra Bharati University, Kolkata. Currently, he is Director, Shakespeare Centre for Advanced Research, RBU; Co-founder and President, Shakespeare Society of Eastern India. Has authored and co-edited over 20 books on Shakespeare, Brecht, Beckett, John Osborne, Ray Lawler; written over 250 articles and papers on drama and academic subjects and has co-directed plats with Gunter Grass, Hans Heyme and other international theater directors.

Suchandra Ghosh is currently engaged in PhD research work at Rabindra Bharati University on adaptations from Shakespeare in Bengal and India. She has co-translated Bratya Basu's *Hemlat* into English; is a noted translator and has published academic papers in national and international journals.

Carole Rozzonelli, Associate Professor of English, ITC, and Communications Law (Law of the New Information Technologies, Media and Communications Law) at the Institute for Information & Communication, University of Lyon 2, France. Former Vice-Chancellor in Communication of the University (2008-2012). Associated with the Research Centre PASSAGES XX-XXI and Le Grimh in Lyon. After specializing in the area of English language and ITC literacy, English literature and cinema, now, she specializes in Media Law, covering both traditional mass media as well as the law of the New Information Technologies. She currently lectures on English, ITC and Media Law. Speaker in conferences in France and also in international conferences on English and ITC (Bergamo, Torino, Antwerp). She collaborates with Professor Alessandro Monti and has participated in the research international series *DOST* on Oriental Studies with the Department of Oriental Studies, Torino, Italy. Also, she edited the series *DOST Educational.* She published in Italy, India and France with Loescher Editore, L'Harmattan Italia, Edizioni dell'Orso, Atlantic Publishers, CercleS Editions, EADTU, Le Grimh Editions. On the advisory editorial board of *The Atlantic Review of Feminist Studies.*

Alessandro Monti, Retired Full Professor of English and Contemporary Indian Studies, University of Palermo then University of Torino, Italy. Formerly Head (for six years) of the Department of Oriental Studies (Turin). Member of the National Committee for the evaluation of University Research. Visiting Professor with the Kakatya University (Warangal). Joined the Committee for Commonwealth Studies (Delhi) replacing Mulk Raj Anand after his demise. ICCR Fellow with the Banares Hindu University. Associated with the Research Centre CESMEO for Advanced Studies in Oriental Studies, Turin. Chief Guest in Tirupathi at an International Conference on Indian Contemporary Literature. Speaker in analogous conferences in Edinburgh, Delhi, Trivandrum, Singapore, also speaker in international conferences on Indian and Sanskrit Culture (Milan, Rome, Turin). He founded and directed for six years the research international series *DOST* on Oriental Studies with the Department of Oriental Studies, Torino, editing or taking charge of more than 20 books. Previously, he edited the series

Paradoxa with L'Harmattan, Italy. He published in India with Atlantic Press, Prestige, Women Unlimited and others. Internationally with Greenwood, Hong Kong University Press, University Press of America, Rodopi, Le Grimh Editions. On the editorial board of *The Journal of Aesthetics* (no more published, Kerala) and on the advisory editorial board of *The Atlantic Review of Feminist Studies*.

Niranjan Goswami is Associate Professor in the Department of English, Chandernagore College, Hooghly. Previously he taught at Presidency College, Kolkata, India. His areas of interest include the European Renaissance, Ramist rhetoric, Ciceronian and Senecan styles, Reformation thought and early American Puritan sermons. He has published on early modern literature, philosophy and rhetoric and translated Terry Eagleton and Arthur Rimbaud. He was awarded the Charles Wallace Trust Fellowship to the United Kingdom and was Fulbright-Nehru Senior Research Fellow (2010-2011) at Harvard University.

Kenneth Usongo holds a PhD in Comparative literature from the University of Denver, as well as a doctorate in English literary studies from the University of Yaoundé 1. Besides his book, *Ruminations of Ipome,* he has also published two dozen refereed essays in English, Postcolonial, and American literatures as book chapters and journal articles in *Transnational Literature, Matatu, Alizés,* and *Journal of African Literature and Culture.*

Manju Dutta Gupta is the Former Head of the Department and Shakespeare Professor of English at Rabindra Bharati University. She has attended quite a number of National and International Conferences like Conference of University Teachers of English at Southampton (1978), the St. Giles Conference in the University of Edinburgh (1978), International Conference on "Teaching and Research Related to Woman" at Concordia University, Montreal Canada (1982), conference celebrating Bi-centenary of Mary Wollstonecraft's Vindication at Dhaka University,

Bangladesh, (1992). She has worked with Professor John Halker, University of London, for post-Doctoral Studies on "Strindberg and Modern Tragedy" (1977-1978) and received distinction at Oxford University for correcting an error in Sir Paul Harvey's, The Oxford Companion to English Literature. Translation of Shakespeare's Sonnets, Chekhov, Pirandello, Oscar Wilde, Black Poetry, Australian poetry etc. are her areas of interest. Her major publications are—*One Act Play: A Critical Approach, Critical Essays,* released by Nobel Laureate Gunter Grass *(2005) Passage of Time,* Transcreation of Tagore's Kaler Jatra on Tagore's 150th Birth Anniversary (11).

Arindam Das is currently employed as Assistant Professor in the Department of Humanities, Heritage Institute of Technology, Kolkata. He has more than 20 published papers in national and international journals, books and anthologies. He has presented papers and has been a resource person at various national and international level seminars and conferences. He has co-edited three books: *Colonial Spectre and Beyond: Studies in Indian Writings in English; Culture and Identity: Re-reading Raja Rao and Mulk Raj Anand*; and *Intertextuality: Poetics and Practice: A Collection of Critical Essays*. He was a recipient of "Australian Studies Australia India Council Fellowship (Junior)" in 2010-11. He was nominated and fully funded to deliver a paper in the 1st world conference in Australian Studies at Monash University, Prato Centre, Italy.

Pratik Chowdhury is an Associate Professor in English, at the Dibrugarh Hanuman Bux Surajmall Kanoi (DHSK) College, Dibrugarh. He likes teaching poetry, drama, literary criticism and theory. He is also engaged in teaching Spoken English and written communication Course to undergraduate non-major students. His other interests are Media and Film Studies; reading up on science related theories like Chaos, Anthropocene, Quantum Entanglement, Symmetries etc. He has published *Post Musings,* an Annotated Anthology, a *Text Book of Written Communication,* and developed Self Learning Materials (SLM) for postgraduate and undergraduate courses for The Department of Distance Education, Dibrugarh University. He has twice edited *Vak-The Word,* a journal published by the Assam College Teachers Association unit of DHSK College. As a member of the Board of Studies, Dibrugarh University, he has been involved in shaping the syllabus of English, both major and core under the semester system; and for introducing a Course on Creative Writing, under Dibrugarh University's Skill Based Courses.

Madhumita Purkayastha is an Associate Professor and Head of the Department of English at D.H.S.K. College, Dibrugarh, Assam. She holds a PhD in African American literature. Her research interest includes feminist epistemology, literary theory and criticism and gender studies. She has published research papers on areas stated above in national and international journals. She is a reviewer of the Asian Journal of Humanities and Social Sciences and the Editor of a national peer reviewed multidisciplinary annual journal *Perspectives*. Her book on African-American women writers titled "Representation of African American Women as Labor in the Novels of Toni Morrison, Alice Walker and Gloria Naylor" is slated to release in 2014.

Ratri Ray is a Former Professor and Head of the Department of English, Patna University. She obtained her Ph.D. and D. Litt. degrees in 1981 and 2002 respectively. She has attended many seminars and conferences. Her articles have been published in many reputed books and journals. Her studies of six Shakespearean plays, according to the Rasavada, had been serialized in the cultural periodical Mother India during the 80s and the 90s. A series of articles on the element of myth in Sri Aurobindo's poetry, serialized during the late 90s in Srnvantu, has been recently published in book form. At present two of her serialised studies are being published from Kolkata:

Sri Aurobindo's Poetry and the Pastoral Tradition in Rtam and Re-reading Perseus the Deliverer in Rbhu. Besides these, her recently published books, William Shakespeare's *The Merchant of Venice, Twelfth Night, The Tempest, A Midsummer Night's Dream* and *King Lear* (The Atlantic Critical Studies) have received overwhelming response from the readers.

Goutam Ghosal, Professor of English, Visva-Bharati and former Editor-in-Chief of *The Visva-Bharati Quarterly,* is a leading interpreter of Sri Aurobindo's philosophy and literature. He is also a specialist on Tagore's poetry and songs. His major books include *The Rainbow Bridge: A Comparative Study of Tagore and Sri Aurobindo, Sri Aurobindo and World Literature, Sri Aurobindo's Prose Style and Notes on the Renaissance.* He has published two anthologies of poems: *Magic Mirror and Other Poems* and *No High Romance.*

Reena Mitra, M.Phil., Ph.D. (English), a gold medalist from Lucknow University, has taught for over four decades in Lucknow University itself and in Christ Church Post Graduate College, Kanpur. She has to her credit five internationally acclaimed books as author/editor and more than fifty research papers read and published. Eight scholars have already been awarded their Ph.D. degrees under her supervision. She is currently Professor of English in Amity School of Languages, Amity University, Uttar Pradesh (Lucknow Campus).